# AGING, HEALTH, AND FAMILY

# SOME OTHER VOLUMES IN THE
# SAGE FOCUS EDITIONS

# AGING, HEALTH, AND FAMILY

## Long-Term Care

Edited by
Timothy H. Brubaker

**SAGE** PUBLICATIONS
The Publishers of Professional Social Science
Newbury Park   Beverly Hills   London   New Delhi

Copyright © 1987 by Sage Publications, Inc.

*For information address:*

SAGE Publications, Inc.
2111 West Hillcrest Drive
Newbury Park, California 91320

SAGE Publications Inc.          SAGE Publications Ltd.
275 South Beverly Drive         28 Banner Street
Beverly Hills                   London EC1Y 8QE
California 90212                England

SAGE PUBLICATIONS India Pvt. Ltd.
M-32 Market
Greater Kailash I
New Delhi 110 048 India

Printed in the United States of America

Library of Congress Cataloging-in-Publication Data


Main entry under title:

Aging, Health, and family.

   (Sage focus editions ; v. 85)
   Bibliography: p.
   1. Aged—Long Term care—United States.   2. Aged—United
States—Family relationships.   3. Aged—Services for—
United States.   4. Aged—Institutional care—
United States.   I. Brubaker, Timothy H.
HV1465.A346   1987        361.6'042        86-17749
ISBN 0-8039-2591-3
ISBN 0-8039-2592-1 (pbk.)

# Contents

# Acknowledgments

Any book is the result of the cooperative efforts of a number of crew members. Each of the contributors to this book is congratulated for religiously meeting deadlines. Gratitude is extended to Robin Pendery for expertly completing the laborious task of combining reference lists. She worked beyond the call of duty. Carol Webb and Crystal Davis are thanked for typing numerous documents associated with this project. The tedious task of proofreading was expertly completed by Mary Tharp, Samantha Inskeep, and Robin Heltzel. The Department of Home Economics and Consumer Sciences and the Family and Child Studies Center of Miami University are recognized for their support. Without this illustrious crew, this ship would not have made port.

# Preface

Issues related to the long-term care of the elderly have been receiving more attention by gerontology and family-life specialists. As the segment of the population over 75 years of age increases, long-term care will receive even more attention. Researchers and practitioners recognize that the family is extraordinarily involved in the long-term care of older persons. For example, numerous studies over the past 20 years have provided evidence that the family is a vital participant in the long-term care process. Often, family members become the primary caregivers for dependent elderly. At the same time, there are a number of bureaucracies that have been established to provide assistance to the elderly and their families. These bureaucracies include the Social Security Administration, Administration on Aging, and other governmental and private agencies that seek to assist the elderly and their families.

A long-term care triad has developed that includes the older person, family, and bureaucracy. Several years ago, Sussman (1977) discussed the differences between the family and bureaucracy and the need for coordination between these two groups. The long-term care triad refers to the relationships among the dependent older person, the family, and bureaucracy. Each of these components influences the delivery of long-term care services to older people.

The need to examine the interfaces among the older person, family, and bureaucracy was underscored by Streib and Beck (1980) in their decade review article published in the *Journal Of Marriage And The Family*. They write that "There is a need to examine the way in which health and economic factors shape the structure and function of older families and the way in which older families relate to their kin, particularly their children. Family researchers have not investigated how the variegated health and welfare system intertwines with the many forms of families" (p. 951). This book seeks to address the relationships among the older person, family, and bureaucracy in various situations in long-term care, drawing on the research of specialists in the areas of gerontology and family studies.

The primary objectives of this book are to examine further the involvement of family members in the long-term care of older persons, to provide results from research focusing on family and long-term care of older persons, and to explore the interface among the component parts (for example, older person, family, and bureaucracy) of the long-term care process. I hope this information will assist family and gerontology researchers and practitioners as they focus their attention on the long-term care of the older person.

The book is divided into several parts. The first part provides a theoretical overview. Timothy H. Brubaker discusses the structural and social psychological aspects of the long-term care triad. The older person, family, and bureaucracy interactions are influenced by these factors and, consequently, the meshing of needs and services is affected. Jaber F. Gubrium examines the variant organizational definitions within the long-term care setting. These different definitions influence the family's view of its older members. Sheldon S. Tobin's chapter focuses on structural changes within an institution and its implications for families. This chapter provides a discussion of family dynamics and institutionalization.

The second part considers families as caregivers. Research has clearly documented that family members are caregivers of dependent elderly. The two chapters by Linda S. Noelker and Aloen L. Townsend focus on the factors related to the effectiveness of caregiving within the community setting. The older person, family, and community resources are central to their analyses.

Community-based services are examined in the third part. Chapters are included on the following topics: home health care (Ellie Brubaker), a Medicare waiver program titled Home and Community Based-Services Program (Jill Quadagno, Cebra Sims, D. Ann Squier, and Georgia Walker), adult day care (Peggye Dilworth-Anderson), a volunteer program (Rhonda J.V. Montgomery and Laurie Russell Hatch), and rural-urban differences in service use (Rosemary Blieszner, William J. McAuley, Janette K. Newhouse, and Jay A. Mancini).

The fourth part includes two chapters focusing on long-term care within an institutional setting. Kathleen Coen Buckwalter and Geri Richards Hall examine the placement process in a nursing home. The bureaucratic structure of the nursing home is discussed and families are seen as resources that enhance the services of the institution. Clara Pratt, Vicki Schmall, Scott Wright, and Jan Hare examine family caregivers of dementia patients. They are particularly interested in the coping strategies of the caregivers.

Attention is directed toward the hospice and family in Part V. Jane Marie Kirschling discusses the interrelationships among the terminally ill older person, their families, and the hospice organization. The hospice represents a bureaucratic organization that seeks to involve the family in the care of the older person.

The final part includes two chapters related to long-term care planning. Mary Anne Hilker discusses supportive residential settings as long-term care options. This chapter encourages a broad view of the housing situation for the long-term care of the elderly. Donald E. Stull and Edgar F. Borgatta examine the structure and proximity of families and their implications for the long-term care of older persons. Gender differences are examined using census data. This chapter provides information for long-term care planning and policy.

—*Timothy H. Brubaker*
Oxford, Ohio

# PART I

# *Theoretical Overview*

# 1

# The Long-Term Care Triad

## The Elderly, Their Families, and Bureaucracies

### TIMOTHY H. BRUBAKER

As the portion of our population aged 75 years and older increases, families will more frequently deal with the issues of providing assistance to a dependent older person. This assistance may involve providing consultation about the myriad regulations related to Medicare reimbursements. Or, it may involve the provision of transportation to the store, doctor, and other necessary locations. Some of these families commit themselves to provide this assistance for a continued time period. Others, after providing intensive assistance for a period of time, seek the assistance provided by institutions designed to care for older people. In any case, families with older members are faced with the issue of how to provide assistance to their dependent elderly on a long-term basis.

Long-term care seeks to provide assistance to meet the physical, emotional, and social needs of dependent older people and their families. It includes the provision of services within the older person's home as well as within the institutional setting. Individuals involved in the provision of long-term care services include the older person's family members (for example, spouse, children, siblings, and other relatives) and a variety of professionals (for example, doctors, nurses, social workers, physical therapists, and other health care personnel). The services these persons provide are designed to assist the dependent older person in meeting the daily needs he or she may have.

The primary component parts of the long-term care system include the dependent older person and his or her needs, the older person's family, and friends and the professionals who provide specialized assistance. Professionals such as doctors, nurses, social workers, and other health care personnel are members of public and private organizations that are designed to provide efficient and highly specialized care. The bureaucratic structures of these organizations define the type, cost, and clientele of services provided. Thus the long-term care system consists of the older person, family, and bureaucratic service organizations.

The linkage between the family and governmental bureaucracy is well established in the United States. The social security system as amended in 1939 sought to provide older Americans *and* their families with financial support (Achenbaum, 1978). Today, most Americans are familiar with the Social Security Administration and, for many, it is the bureaucracy with which they have frequent contact in their later years. As Kreps (1977) notes, the family and bureaucracy are closely linked through the economic transfers created by the social security system.

It is difficult, within our complex society, for an older person to avoid contact with bureaucracies.

As the family seeks care for a dependent member outside the family unit, contact with bureaucratic organizations is inevitable. Nursing homes, hospitals, home care, and social security benefits are managed by a bureaucracy; private and public organizations are designed around the standardization of a bureaucracy. Presently, later life families cannot avoid contact with these organizations, and in the future, contact is likely to increase. (T. Brubaker, 1985: 125)

The interfaces among the older person, family, and bureaucracies are the primary focus of this chapter.

### The Dependent Older Person

The needs of the older dependent person can be categorized into at least three categories. One category relates to the *financial needs* of the elderly. After retirement, the older person is dependent on social security benefits and/or other retirement programs. Living on a "fixed income" graphically describes the economic situation of many older persons. In addition, some receive support from government programs that subsidize their retirement income. In any case, the older person is financially dependent on various governmental and private systems.

Another category is related to the *physical needs* of the elderly. Older people, especially those over age 75 years, are likely to experience some physical problems. Many of these problems are chronic and require attention over a long period of time. Persons in this age category are more likely to be hospitalized. Many of the physical problems necessitate frequent medication, physical therapy, or other specialized treatment. The increase in health problems may decrease the mobility of the older person. Thus one consequence of physical difficulties is the hindrance in getting around to complete daily activities. The need for assistance in transportation becomes evident.

A third category includes the *social-emotional needs* of the elderly. Older people need the interaction and social contact that characterized earlier stages of their lives. Those who were gregarious need more social contacts. Some desire fewer social contacts. Whatever the interaction patterns of the older person, it is clear that social contacts are important to older people. Contacts from family and friends are valued by older people. However, decreases in mobility may inhibit social interaction. For some elderly, social contacts are dependent on who decides to visit them rather than who they decide to visit. For those elderly who are hospitalized or institutionalized, social contacts may be limited to a close group of family and friends *and* the professionals who provide assistance to them.

For the elderly, one need may confound another. As physical problems arise, the financial burdens may increase and the ability to get around may decrease. Assistance primarily focusing on one need may concurrently address another need. As noted above, professionals who provide specialized assistance, such as doctors, may also become the primary social contacts of the older person. They may be the older person's friend, advisor, and confidant. Meeting of multiple needs can enhance the provision of services for dependent elderly.

## The Family

Results from a number of studies indicate that the family provides support to dependent elderly (Cicirelli, 1983; Seelbach, 1978). Families provide support with transportation, preparing meals, and a wide variety of activities related to daily living. In fact, family caregivers play a significant part in the determination of whether an older dependent person lives in the community or in an institution (Brody et al., 1978; Palmore, 1976). Many family caregivers provide assistance to the older person and only when the caregiving task becomes so extraordinary that they can no longer provide adequate care, do they reluctantly allow their older family member admittance into an institution (E. Brubaker, 1986). Within the United States, the family is a vital ingredient in the caregiving process.

Families are particularly adept at providing care for an older person that does not require a high degree of specialization. Helping an older person get dressed in the morning or providing transportation is an example of the type of assistance families can and do provide. Their assistance enables an older person to live independently even though he or she has difficulty with some daily tasks.

Many times, the social needs of older persons are met by families. Children, grandchildren, and sibling relationships are important to dependent older persons who live in a community or institutional setting. Feeling a part of a family network is important to the older person and the rewards of having relatives who are in frequent contact are significant. There is little doubt that there is a vital and supportive network provided by the family. Numerous dependent older persons live within a community setting because they have family members who are willing to provide assistance on a daily basis. Indeed, if the family did not provide this support, it is likely that our institutional care system would be overwhelmed.

As Sussman (1977) notes, the structure of families lends to three types of issues relating to the caregiving situation. First, families are equipped to provide general knowledge and instruct their members and others about this general knowledge. In the caregiving situation, families have extensive knowledge about the preferences, dislikes, and legacy of the older person that may have an influence on the care that is provided. The information held by families can be particularly useful to the representatives of a bureaucracy in dealing with a care-giving program. In many cases, only families have this general knowledge of the older person's situation.

The second category relates to areas in which bureaucratic specialists do not have the unique set of information that provides the solution to a specific problem. Sussman (1977: 5) states:

> Tasks in the second category beg for expert advice. They remain in the family because specialists do not have the knowledge or skill to deal with them. Consequently, the resolution of issues and problems central to the vital interest of individuals must be self-resolutions. . . . The specialist's contribution is obviously limited because few can command the knowledge required to make an intelligent decision and the variety of options in such problem areas is so staggering that training the expert is impossible.

For the dependent older person, the selection of the type of living situation (for example, community, institutional) may not be adequately solved without the family-specific information held by other family members. For example, although social workers or discharge planners have technical knowledge about services, they may need the family-specific information that only families can provide if they are to match the needs of the dependent older person and the services provided by the bureaucracy.

Events that are unpredicted, infrequent, and/or idiosyncratic are categorized in the third category of tasks that families are equipped to handle. The family can quickly respond to unique situations for the older person. For example, if an older person is hospitalized and needs some assistance during a relatively short recuperation, the family is generally equipped to provide care. The family can prepare meals on a short-term basis until the older person is able to prepare his or her own meals. Families can provide assistance in these idiosyncratic situations because they are equipped to respond in a short period of time. They have the knowledge and the family structure is small enough that it can be activated quickly.

Family support is supplemented by a variety of other bureaucratic systems of support for dependent older persons. For example, some older people receive in-home meals from a community- or government-sponsored program and family members provide transportation. Or, family members receive assistance with the care of their older member during the day because the community has an adult day care program. Government programs such as Medicare and private medical insurance programs provide the dependent older person with financial support with medical expenses. In some ways, there is a team effort between the family and bureaucratic organizations to provide care for dependent older persons.

## The Bureaucracy

Bureaucratic organizations are established to deal with specific tasks related to similar situations. "The bureaucratic structure is organized to handle uniform tasks using an ever-developing technology, vast resources, and extensive lines of communication, buttressed by the ideology of merit and the model of rationality" (Sussman, 1977: 6). Technical knowledge is the area in which bureaucratic organizations operate. They seek to dispense the technical information in a rational manner. Consequently, they are particularly well equipped to deal with similar or uniform situations. The idiosyncracies of families can create havoc within a bureaucratic organization.

One vivid illustration of the uniform nature of bureaucracies can be seen in the forms presented to families at the initial contact. These forms are standardized so that the bureaucracy receives the same information from all families. However, each family may have some unique piece of information that may be crucial to the situation but it is not received because the form fails to request family-specific information. If families are not aware of the need to inform the bureaucracies of this family-specific information, it may not become a part of the planning process.

There is little doubt that bureaucracies are needed to provide long-term care to older persons and their families. Older persons' long-term care needs may require technical knowledge and sophisticated equipment that is beyond the scope of the family. Although the bureaucracy is necessary, it is clear that the family is also an important part of the long-term care process.

## The Triadic Relationship

The interface among the dependent older person, family, and bureaucracy requires different skills from each part. The older person needs to recognize and communicate his or her needs to the family and bureaucratic representatives. As the older person experiences financial, physical, and/or social difficulties, communication of what specific problems need to be addressed is necessary. At the same time, the older person should, as much as possible, carefully examine the resources provided by the family and/or bureaucratic organizations. If the older person does not have the skills to assess the resources, then the primary caregiver, who is usually a family member, may explore the available resources within the family and community (Springer & Brubaker, 1984).

The family needs to be sensitive to the older person's difficulties and, at the same time, explore their own resources as well as those from outside the family. Many times, the family becomes a mediator between the older person and bureaucratic organizations. Sussman (1977: 15) states that "one principle function of the kin network is to assist its member families to adapt to as well as to influence organizational policy and practices." Thus the "family as mediator" between the older person and bureaucracies has two primary tasks. One is to help the older person negotiate the bureaucracy so that the older person's needs can be met. This assistance includes learning about the resources provided by the bureaucracy and how to activate the bureaucracy to assure that the resources are tapped. In some cases, it may involve the education of the older person about how to deal with the bureaucracy. The other tasks relate to advocating for the older person to the bureaucracy. On an individual level, the family has family-specific knowledge that might be helpful in the long-term care of an older person and the family may need to ascertain that this information is conveyed to the bureaucratic personnel. The "family as mediator" requires negotiation and advocacy skills to enhance the interface between the older person and bureaucratic organization.

Although providing for the needs of the older person in a standardized, uniformed fashion, the bureaucracy needs to be responsive to the idiosyncratic features of the older person. Meshing needs and services may require the modification of routine ways of providing care. Families as mediators can provide bureaucracies with the information necessary to modify the delivery systems. However, the bureaucracies need to be responsive to the family-specific information (Litwak, 1985).

The triadic relationships among the dependent older person, family, and bureaucracy is illustrated in Figure 1.1. The dependent

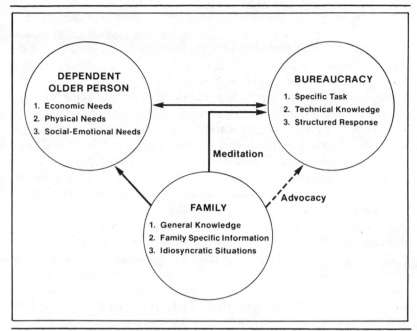

Figure 1.1   Triadic Relationship Among Dependent Older Person, Family, and Bureaucracy

older person has several types of needs and these needs can be met by the family and/or bureaucracy. The family can influence the bureaucratic caregiving relationship directly through mediation or indirectly through advocacy. In any case, partnerships and various team efforts are needed to coordinate the needs with the resources. Also, it is important to emphasize that the older person, even though dependent, may have resources that may be activated to address a need. To mediate or advocate for the older person, the family cannot be passive in its relationship with bureaucracies. At the same time, the older person is a resource and can actively be involved in the mediation and/or advocacy process.

## Social Psychological Aspects of the Triad

Our discussion of the relationships among the dependent older person, family, and bureaucracy has focused primarily on structural characteristics. However, there are social psychological factors within these relationships. These social psychological factors influence the definitions held by the individuals who represent the three component parts of the interaction. For example, when a family member contacts a hospital concerning services, the representative of the hospital provides the family member with information about the "type" of bureaucracy the hospital represents and the "type" of environment within which the service is provided. After the interaction, the family member defines the hospital as a caring, supportive institution or may define the hospital as a highly efficient institution that gives little attention to individual needs.

At the same time, the interaction provides the representative of the bureaucracy with a definition of the "type" of family or older person being served. The family member or older person may indicate that they have a knowledge about the bureaucracy or they may be neophytes in dealing with bureaucracies. The bureaucratic representative develops a definition about the family and may record that definition on a bureaucratic record that is reviewed by others within the bureaucracy. Thus bureaucratic perceptions can become routinized within an organization and these perceptions may be difficult to alter even though the bureaucratic representatives may change.

For all three members of the caregiving triad, several factors are influential in creating definitions of one another (see Figure 1.2). These include attitude or knowledge about older people, technical knowledge about service and bureaucratic structures, and assessment of legitimacy of providing assistance. The first factor relates to the attitudes toward, and accuracy of knowledge about, older people. Several studies (Brubaker & Barresi, 1979; Coe, 1976) indicate that some representatives of the bureaucracy may not be knowledgeable about the lives of older people. They may base their interactions on stereotypic views of older people and, consequently, the older person may define the bureaucracy as insensitive and uninformed. Indeed, the older person and/or family member may not understand the typical aging process and misinterpret the service provider's instructions. All three participants tend to interpret the interaction on the basis of their own attitudes toward, or knowledge about, older people.

Technical or bureaucratic knowledge, the second factor, influences the older person's and/or family member's definition of the

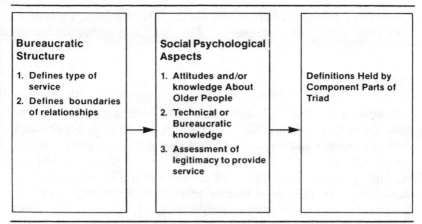

| Bureaucratic Structure | Social Psychological Aspects | |
|---|---|---|
| 1. Defines type of service<br>2. Defines boundaries of relationships | 1. Attitudes and/or knowledge About Older People<br>2. Technical or Bureaucratic knowledge<br>3. Assessment of legitimacy to provide service | Definitions Held by Component Parts of Triad |

Figure 1.2  Bureaucratic and Social Psychological Factors Influencing Definition Within Triad

bureaucratic organization. Knowing what can be done and what should be done to solve a problem enables the older person and/or family member to evaluate the information given by the bureaucratic representative. Also, they may be aware of the restrictions under which the bureaucratic representative is operating. Likewise, a knowledgeable bureaucratic representative can activate the system in an efficient manner and present an impression of being responsive.

The third factor relates to the participants' assessment of legitimacy to provide assistance. Some older people and/or family members do not think that they should receive a specific service. Others consider the service "rightfully" theirs and the bureaucracy should provide the service. At the same time, the representative of the bureaucracy may respond from a contractual agreement and only provide the services prescribed therein. To provide an extraordinary service may be beyond the bureaucracy's legitimately prescribed domain.

The bureaucratic structure sets the environment in which the three participants in the long-term care process interact. It demarcates the boundaries of the relationship and specifies the exchange. The social psychological factors define the way in which the participants interact in this environment. These factors influence the amount of penetration into the predefined boundaries and create the vitality of the exchange. The caregiving triad cannot be understood solely from the structural perspective. Nor can it be adequately comprehended from the social psychological approach. Both perspectives are necessary.

## Conclusion

Long-term care of the elderly involves a complex of interactions between individuals and social structures. The dependent older person's needs can be met by bureaucratic organizations. However, a sensitivity to the resources of the older person and his or her family will enhance the coordination and provision of services. Families can be mediators and/or advocates for the older person. Bureaucracies can enhance their delivery of services if they are open to family input.

Research on the complexity of the long-term care triadic relationship is needed. Because it is a triadic relationship, coalitions can develop within the interactions. These coalitions may have different members depending on the situation. For example, the older person *and* a family member may approach the bureaucracy as a team. Or, a nursing home administrator *and* a family member may encourage an older person to accept a particular facility policy. The dynamics of this triadic relationship are a fruitful topic for future research.

# 2

# *Organizational Embeddedness and Family Life*

## JABER F. GUBRIUM

It is increasingly evident that the vision of the family as a discrete social form is outworn, if indeed the form ever existed. The notion of "The Family" (Thorne & Yalom, 1982; Bernardas, 1985) has undergone widespread social contextualization from quarters as diverse as feminist critique (Barrett, 1980; Nava, 1983; Thorne, 1982), historical (Quadagno, 1982; Demos, 1970; Hareven, 1971), socioeconomic (Zaretsky, 1976), and intra- and interorganizational studies (Gubrium, 1983; Dingwall et al., 1983; Fischer & Hoffman, 1984). One conclusion of the challenges is that the family experience is as varied as its practical articulations. In line with this and following earlier work (Gubrium & Buckholdt, 1977, 1982b; Gubrium & Lynott, 1985b), this chapter considers the discursive formations of family life that arise out of its embeddedness in and about long-term care organizations.

The argument is that the social order of the family is not discerned from careful attention to its component structures and dynamics, as diverse service providers and seriously concerned others are wont to do, but is interpreted against the varied contexts in which considerations of order are undertaken. It makes a difference whether those concerned, say, attend to family order as members of a support group or didactically in a staff review of patient progress for family members. The former may produce considerable disarray in perceived familial responses to chronic illness; the latter tends to present distinct order (Gubrium, 1986a). As such, a family is not so much a self-contained entity as it is a way to frame and represent social relations, gaining meaning from usage and application—as in the related assessment and planning activities of service practitioners, who make use of familial accounts and familial constructions to organize the care and custody of those "in need." Family is also a way of claiming rights and forming obligations, as one might imply in the admonition, "They're surely not acting like family!" Thus family is both expository and rhetorical (Gubrium & Lynott, 1985b).

The approach is not a plea for broadening the concept of the familial to include existing, alternative forms, though it does not preclude the aim. Its focus, rather, is on the shifting experiential status of order perceived in any familial form or component, articulated against the diverse agendas bearing on the concern, especially those in long-term care. To the extent family usage enters into the related activities of diverse care institutions, it is a general means of accounting for treatment and custody.

The organizations considered have been the sites of extensive participant observation—the nursing home (Gubrium, 1975; 1980a; 1980b), the rehabilitation hospital (Gubrium & Buckholdt, 1982a), the day hospital, and caregiver support groups (Gubrium, 1986a, 1986b, forthcoming; Gubrium & Lynott, 1985a; Lynott, 1983). (The names of places and persons throughout have been fictionalized.) Each is a setting in which family life is regularly referenced and scrutinized in connection with matters of long-term care. Moreover, each setting provides manifold institutional contexts and conditions for interpretation, as varied as the roles, established beliefs, interests, and customary familial topics that enter into and crisscross social practice.

The chapter is organized around three interrelated domestic matters commonly taken for granted in family studies. It is regularly assumed that membership is linked with biological or legal ties (blood linkages and in-laws), the ties being final arbiters. Field data, in contrast, show that membership is a matter of social practice, of assignment and reclamation. Accordingly, the organizational embeddedness of the question "Who is family?" is examined. It is also commonly assumed that what it means to be or act like family is evident. Field data indicate that the question "What is

family?" considered next, is also socially and culturally prescribed. Finally, the question "Where is family?" brings us to relationship between households and family life, of how coincident
they are taken to be.

## Who Is Family?

A perennial issue in long-term care is the question of who the
family is in such matters as custody, support, and discharge.
Although family membership is routinely discerned on biological
and legal grounds, they are not the only conditions of assignment.
A hospital social worker who formulates a stroke patient's discharge plan considers not only a proverbial "house" for a possible
discharge destination but whether or not the house is also a "home."
Although a family may reliably lodge a debilitated elder, will that
same family be familial in home care? The question presents those
concerned with the practical reality of family life, suggesting that
the investigation of who is family be emphasized as much as formal
kindred as a criterion of membership.

Consider the definitional complications entering into the deliberation in discharge planning for elderly stroke patients at Wilshire, a physical rehabilitation hospital where the average length of
stay is four to six weeks (Gubrium & Buckholdt, 1982a). Although
Wilshire successfully guides recovery, most patients are discharged
when it is decided they have acquired maximum benefit from hospitalization. Postpatients are rarely fully recovered, usually mani-
festing some symptoms of their ailment, such as slurred speech
and localized paralysis. As such, discharge planning raises the
issue of the advisability of home or extended care, typically including the need to define who the family might be for related practical
purposes.

It is not at all a question of discerning "The Family." Under consideration is who is to be defined as familial, to be assigned family
status for purposes of continuing care. Biological or legal ties are
only candidates for the familial entity. Grammatically, then, were
it not so awkward, we might best write the family form as, say, the-
family-for-discharge-purposes, suggesting how difficult it would
be to discern empirically what "The Family" is, a concrete entity
with no practical function.

Still, it is evident that those concerned—human service providers, family members, relatives, significant others—enter into deliberation with concrete understandings of what they believe to be familial. It is not as if families and family life were merely convenient social fictions. Rather, the task is to pinpoint who can be taken to be "really" familial and distinguish them from those who may only appear to be. In the process, those concerned mingle what they believe to be both fact and fiction as evidence for and against what family really is.

Following one Wilshire family conference, two members of an elderly stroke patient's rehabilitation team—a physical therapist and social worker—met to consider a patient's discharge destination. It had been decided earlier that the patient would not return to her own home, a Victorian house in a once stable ethnic neighborhood, because she could no longer get about the house on her own nor deal with the locale's changing social character. The house had been offered for sale by the patient's son. There were two other destinations to which the patient might be discharged: a younger, widowed sister's apartment and the son's large house. Both had offered to provide a home, seemingly a surfeit of domestic riches.

Yet it was evident in the two team members' considerations that the decision was not an even choice between the two destinations, but took into account what each claimed to know about the sister's and son's family status. Both staffers repeatedly reminded each other that their real concern was, after all, who the patient's "real family" was. The physical therapist indicated that she had done an environmental assessment of both households and, although she had found the son's premises more wheelchair accessible, it was evident to her that the son "certainly didn't act like one." The therapist explained that all she had seen and heard led her to believe that, to the so-called son, the mother was just so much human baggage, soon to be tucked away into a bleak back bedroom and not allowed to interfere with "his" family's daily life. The therapist noted further that the son kept referring to what "his" family needed as opposed to what his mother required, which the therapist interpreted to mean that the son did not really include his mother in the family. What is more, the therapist went on to explain, the eagerness with which the son put his mother's house up for sale confirmed the therapist's feeling that the son was no son at all. The therapist believed that, in this case, it would be in everyone's best interest in the long run to plan for discharge to the patient's ostensibly capable sister, if the son made no real fuss about it. The social worker's opinion in the matter centered on two other considerations. The social worker believed that she knew better about both the son and sister, whom she had dealt with frequently by telephone and in office visits during the patient's hospitalization. The social worker stated that, in her opinion, both the son and sister were very concerned for the patient, each keeping in touch for information about the patient's progress and offering to do what they could to facilitate recovery. The social worker noted further that both sister and son took active part in the hospital's support group for the families of stroke victims. She concluded that, as far as she could tell, either the son's or sister's residence would be an adequate home for continued care. Another consideration was what the social worker believed to be a "subtle prejudice" against the son held by other team members, stemming from the son's alleged cold manner. The social worker argued that team members should take care not to let their prejudice affect their judgment, lest it lead the son justifiably to "make a federal case of it" and thereby divide the family against itself.

The therapist's and social worker's opinions were not the only ones in the case; other team members assigned familial status to the son and sister in their own ways, some overlapping and some distinct, entertaining and offering evidence for their beliefs in accordance with both their separate and common experiences with the son, sister, and others. As noted, the physical therapist tended to read signs of family membership in the different household plans intimated by the son and sister. The social worker heard signs of membership in the similar ways that the son and sister "kept in touch" and "touched base" with her about the patient's progress and welfare. To the social worker, the son's presumed eagerness to sell his mother's house was a sign of efficient good will, not selfishness. The physician uncovered signs of membership in the medical family history and comparable "typical" families she had known in related experiences. Other team members, likewise, assembled and assigned their own family bonds. What kept them all going was their common assumption that, despite their different interpretations, some set of persons was, after all, this patient's real family or, in any event, should be. As are others, this patient's eventual discharge destination, as it hinged on family life, would be articulated from the varied organized concerns in which consideration of membership was embedded.

The family is not always on the sidelines in matters of membership. Although staff, at times, may virtually take family assignment away from a family member, at other times members may disclaim or reclaim it in varied coalition with or against staff and others. Consider how both informal and formal organizational interests, ties, and senses of competence eclipse conventional biological and legal definitions of who is family.

It is not uncommon in nursing homes for both staff members and patients to assess patient conduct in terms of its degree of confusion. Although patients may be afflicted by diverse physical ailments, their mental life and daily activity are homogenized along a so-called orientation continuum. At one extreme are those attuned to reality, said to be reality-oriented. Their polar opposites are triply disoriented "as to person, place, and time," respectively, confused about their very own names, their place of residence, and the date and time of day (Gubrium, 1975; Gubrium & Ksander, 1975; Buckholdt & Gubrium, 1983). It is a prevalent means of framing patient conduct in other institutions that similarly treat and house adults.

Maida Wood had been a patient at Lakeview, one of the nursing homes studied, for about two years. Gossip had it that she became a resident one day when, unbeknown to her, she was placed in a medical courier van on the alleged pretext of being taken to the doctor for a checkup and trucked to the nursing home. Her daughter and son explained to the staff and to Maida later, "after things had quieted down," that that was the only way they could get Maida admitted because, as the daughter put it, "Mother just wouldn't hear of it."

At first, Maida was admittedly totally confused. She reported that she did not know where she was, even though, she said, she was repeatedly reminded that Lakeview was her place of residence. She had no idea why she had been left in the facility and not taken home after the "medical people" had finished with her. Confused, she tried to compose herself, locate her whereabouts, and find a reasonable explanation for what had happened. Accordingly, her conduct was considered to be disoriented, a common postadmission status.

As time passed, Maida grew resentful of the abrupt, unforeseen placement. Upon learning that her children had planned it, she resigned herself to being bereft of filial loyalty. The children's visits were decidedly uncomfortable, even though both son and daughter apologized for having felt they had no choice in the matter. They were nonetheless considerate and never relented in being concerned for Maida's welfare, visiting her often and taking her out on numerous occasions.

At the same time, Maida was drawn to a small circle of other patients at the home, two women and a man. They became fast friends, so close and visible that they were known throughout Lakeview by staff members and many other patients as "Maida's group," in recognition of Maida's leadership role. When a member of the group became ill, the others, commonly at Maida's behest, would be highly solicitous and wary for staff inattention. When any of them was temporarily absent from the home, the others became fidgety and worried lest things were not going well for the missing member of the group. There was even a recognizable division of coconcern among them: Maida the organizer and advocate; Freda the warm and affectionate mother; Sara the group's baby; and Harold the purveyor of needed resources and said to be a "very, very handy man."

Various staff members, especially the nurses' aides on the floor, spoke of the group as a family. In fact, the division of concern in the group was frequently referenced by both the aides and the group in kinship terms; for example, Freda was said to be the mother or simply "grandma Freda." In casual conversation, group members themselves routinely spoke of Sara, who was 68 years old and at least 10 years the others' junior, as "the baby," a reference that Sara relished and used herself to describe her role in the group.

Yet Maida's group was not simply one big happy family, as it were. Maida's children bristled at the quasi-kinship, being increasingly deluged by the group's presence and reports of members' genuine familial concern for each other. Maida did not hesitate to remind the children that she now had a "genuine" family, that Sara, Freda, and Harold were her family now. She claimed that no "real" children would have done what the son and daughter had in placing a mother in "a final resting place" against her wishes.

The children saw Maida's quasi-familial conduct as a sign of growing confusion in filial sensibility. They complained to the social worker and frequently sought the support of sympathetic nurses, at one point even trying to have members of Maida's group transferred to different floors. When Maida's group (family) infringed on what staff took to be the customary order of the floor, staff members, too, grew resentful. When the children's and staff members' irritations coincided, they entertained the need, "for all concerned," to put an end to the clique's existence because, among other explanations, all its members were said to have totally forgotten that they were patients and had caring families of their own to think about. Maida was especially singled out, whose separation from the group was considered by some to be both a feasible way to restore proper filial relationships and dissolve what seemed to be a virtual fifth column working against complete and equitable care on the floor. When irritations did not coincide, the quasi-familial source of troubles was less convincing and not commonly invoked.

It was clear that who Maida's family was in practice was not simply a matter of kinship. As far as Maida and sympathetic others were concerned, Maida's son and daughter were not even at best what a real family should be; rather, Sara, Freda, and Harold were. The son and daughter, on the other hand, pitted their actual family status against their mother's ostensibly confused counterclaims. At worst, Maida and her friends touted their sense of kind, flatly asserting that the son and daughter were no family at all. Indeed, the practical familial structure of Maida's group rose and fell with challenges to its self-assigned integrity, now held to be a model of real familism by its members and sympathizers, and now taken to be yet further evidence of Maida's growing disorientation by those negatively affected by it. Membership could not be disentangled from differential claims and claimants embedded in the organization, who respectively presented their perceptions and expressed their desires and resentments by means of an available culture of patient rationality.

### What Is Family?

Not only is the family assigned membership in accordance with practical considerations in and about the organized contexts in which matters of membership become topical, but what the family functionally is, is likewise embedded. The related "what" question references the family project as a whole, answers functionally distinguishing preferred and undesirable forms. In long-term care, families are subjects of considerable attention as means for understanding patients' current conditions and responses to treatment. A common concern is to discern what any family "should be like" and whether or not kindred are being adequately familial; respectively, "What is familial?" and "What kind of family is this?" The two considerations are contingent, of course, being theme and variation in deciphering how families in general and specific kindred in particular affect residential care and chronic illness.

The "what" question was often raised in the proceedings of support groups for the caregivers of Alzheimer's disease (senile dementia) patients, observed as part of a larger study of the descriptive organization of senility (Gubrium, 1986a). The groups were usually comprised of family members, sometimes separated into groups of caregiving spouses and adult children. Some groups were facilitated by service providers, others by experienced caregivers themselves. By and large, the Alzheimer's disease experience for support group participants entailed the daily burdens, personal travails, and looming problems of caring for the patient at home, even though a few continued to participate after they had institutionalized their patient, out of enduring concern for others in their former straits or as facilitators. For all, institutionalization was a pervasive contingency of care and custody.

Although diverse care-related matters were discussed in the support groups, a good share was linked with the question of proper familial concern. The family was considered to be, as Lasch (1977) might have put it, the patient's final "haven in a heartless world." Despite the well-intentioned interest in Alzheimer's disease found in many quarters—medical, psychosocial, legal, custodial—it was believed to be the patient's family who would, in the final analysis, offer the kind of love and continued attention needed for what was otherwise an incurable, progressive dementia, a disease that "steals bright minds" and is "like a funeral that never ends." It was felt there was a limit to what service providers could offer toward the preservation of mind and spirit; institutional custody was likely to become a matter of bed-and-body work as the so-called "brain failure" took its personal toll of the patient.

Because of the extensive burden of care, the caregiver is commonly described as the disease's "second victim." As a support group participant once bluntly informed someone who was believed to be an overcommitted caregiver: "Dear, you're not an old man's lover; you're an old man's slave." Although not all talk and counsel are this terse and accusatory, the issue of home care continually confronts participants. What it means to be family in respect to the mental demise of a loved one underpins many questions: What should a family do for the victim? How much is enough? What is too much? What should be expected from any family member? Each question, as it is deliberated and answered in connection with particular caregivers, raises the possibility that one's concern will be judged unfamilial, the unconcerned risking not "being family" in regard to the patient's welfare.

The overall concern and specific questions, of course, are not unique to the Alzheimer's disease experience, being challenges to anyone dealing with familial responsibilities, from childhood to old age. What the organizational embeddedness of those concerned does is to provide an increasingly formularized stock of options and solutions. For example, although any family might agonize over the distribution and extent of care available to a stricken, disturbed, or abused member, formally organized concern offers standardized means for understanding and coming to terms with the agony. In connection with matters of Alzheimer's disease, it is the Alzheimer's Disease and Related Disorders Association (ADRDA) that increasingly provides a formal interpretive context for assigning meaning to the disease experience in general and, in particular, to what it means to be family in conjunction with it. In this regard, ADRDA support groups can be understood as institutionalized forums for the assignment of familism to the activities of those concerned. What makes the support group different from individual family forums in the household is that a distinct public culture of definitions and interpretations for the disease experience avails all support group participants of a common means of representing their familism, for better or worse (Gubrium, 1986a).

Perhaps the most poignant matter hinging on the question of what is family is the decision to institutionalize the patient (Lynott, 1983). As familiar columns of the many ADRDA chapter newsletters put it, "When is it time?" Support group participants repeatedly raise the question, toward different ends, as their patients now seem to decline rapidly and present an enormous care burden, or now plateau or have so-called lucid moments, suggesting that perhaps continued home care is warranted.

What is an ostensible family to be in the decision to institutionalize a loved one—no "real" family at all, or a realistic one? The public culture of the Alzheimer's disease movement offers a tense stock of options, presented to those concerned by way of local and national newsletters, popular self-help books, government pamphlets, widely shown films, public service announcements, the print and broadcast media, and community awareness efforts. On the one hand, all concerned are repeatedly reminded that, in the final analysis, for a disease such as Alzheimer's it is the family that matters most as a source of care. Indeed, the disease's public culture even has a distinct vein of antiprofessionalism as its self-help theme comes to the fore. There are occasions in support groups when all the facts, information, and formal understanding of the onset and course of progress of the disease and burdens of care are cast aside as just so much professional propaganda in painful favor of the conclusion that there is no rhyme or reason to any of it. The sentiment supports the principle that only the family can sort it all out for what it is worth and negotiate the irrational with its own final arbiter: love. Thus the family is a source and network of unlimited devotion and care, or, properly, what a family should be (see Gubrium & Buckholdt, 1982b).

On the other hand, the concerned also encounter widespread portraits of realistic families, said to have realized that, again in the final analysis, the decision to institutionalize is the most humane course of action and, in any case, inevitable. Although, a true family puts it off as long as possible, offering whatever care it can, as loving and concerned kindred to its stricken member, a true family is also a realistic one, knowing what is finally in the best interest of all concerned. At the risk of caregivers themselves becoming totally incapacitated—second victims—it is believed that being family eventually means optimizing self-help by displacing the burden of care and offering up an ostensibly empty mind to those more suited to harboring its vestige. Ironically, it is sometimes suggested that, if the demented patient were aware of it, he or she would recognize that the disease eventually prevails on a family to act in the most familial way possible, to decide in favor of what all members would desire and deserve in the end. As such, being family means "undeniably" being realistic and ending the familial burden of care.

Consider how the options enter into Alzheimer's disease support group proceedings, confronting members with alternate senses of what an allegedly real family is. On one occasion, at the gathering of victims' spouses, a rather lively discussion centered on a distraught and overburdened wife. It was Kitty's second marriage, her first husband having died in an automobile accident. Kitty married her second husband, John, the victim, ten years afterward. It had been John's second marriage as well. They had had no children of their own, John having brought two daughters from his first marriage to his second one. Presenting this background, Kitty added that she and John had become totally devoted to each other over the years, "like a marriage made in heaven," she remarked. She loved John's daughters as her own, having been a mother to them for over thirty years.

As Kitty described in devoted detail the ways in which she and John expressed their love, she wept when she intermittently lamented the gradual dementia that was "stealing him" from her. She spoke touchingly of his occasional inquiries to her about such matters as whether or not he was John, and whether the house was his own or someone else's. The questions, seemingly innocent, devastated her. She reported, too, that John was at the point where she had to see to virtually all his cares—eating, toileting, dressing, grooming, ambulation—reminding her listeners of what all had heard and expressed many times before, that daily care entailed putting in a "36-hour day." It was a familiar story, of a spouse's and family's total devotion to one of its members.

When Kitty compared her own experience with those less devoted and vented her apprehension about an institution's ability to "handle him right and feel for him as I can," the others sympathized. Kitty's devotion was taken to be the type that exemplified what true concern and care are, evidently "very loving." Other participants presented similar instances of devoted concern, offering evidence of the wide range of concrete particulars that signaled what a family should be. In turn, what was said to be *that* kind of family gained shape and form.

Also sympathizing with Kitty, one of the facilitators, Rhoda (an experienced caregiver in her own right who had already placed her patient in a nursing home), asked Kitty if she had given any thought to the possibility that she was overburdening herself. Rhoda explained that, although she recognized and understood Kitty's devotion, as she did in many others, perhaps Kitty was ignoring herself and the rest of the family. Was it not possible, Rhoda asked, that what was happening was that Kitty's family was actually breaking down and John, as Rhoda bluntly put it, "is really in never-never land," completely oblivious of himself, what was being done for him, or even who was involved? Kitty listened intently, agreed that she had occasionally asked herself the same things, but concluded that she just could not admit that John was totally unaware, that deep down inside, he was not really there, adding, "maybe cold and lonely and really trying to reach out." She rhetorically asked those gathered whether any of them could "really" admit that their spouses, even though evidently demented, were totally gone. Rhoda's response was pointed, asserting that it sounded very much like Kitty was "denying," not being willing to admit that she was destroying herself and the rest of her family by refusing to see that John was gone. At the same time, Rhoda, too, referenced a kind of family, one that never fully realizes what it is to be family in these matters, not facing up to the fact that "it's time," that caring enough means to give up what now is really "just the shell of a former self," a common sentiment.

As that session unfolded, it was evident that Kitty, Rhoda, and the others were articulating, each in his or her own fashion, the caring family by means of themes collectively representative of what they believed a caring family should be, themes more or less formally embedded in an organization engaging family living. The disease's related public culture was ramified as each of those concerned assigned meaning to familial involvement, countervailing understandings presenting Kitty's devotion as denial, on the one hand, and real family, on the other. Whatever Kitty's eventual decision and familism would be, their organizational embeddedness would serve to frame them in terms of increasingly familiar options.

## Where Is Family?

There are some who claim that a critical examination of the surface "fictions" of domestic affairs can reveal the family for what it really is (Jackson, 1957, 1965; Ferreira, 1963). Conventional wisdom has it that to locate the true family of kindred, the actual private goings-on of the household be considered.

The organizational embeddedness of family life shows, however, that the relationship between households and domestic affairs, on the one hand, and family life, on the other, is more complicated.

Practical solutions to the question of where the family is suggest that it is revealed in and about the diverse contexts in which the question is entertained, not the least of which are the many residential facilities that increasingly house, care for, and treat members. One of the facilities studied, an acute care, general hospital, offered an outpatient geriatric clinic and day hospital for Alzheimer's disease patients (Gubrium, 1986a). Clinic and day hospital staff regularly met in conferences, called "staffings," to consider the source, symptoms, diagnosis, and treatment of patients' complaints. Staff members included a geriatrician, general practitioners, a psychiatrist, a psychologist, home-care nurses, geriatric nurse specialists, a social worker, and recreation therapists. Proceedings routinely centered on patients' family lives as they revealed the need for various cares and custody decisions, for example, what a patient's family life suggested about the possible need for institutionalization. Staff members were alert, too, for possible day hospital candidates among outpatients of the geriatric clinic, for signs of those at a stage of Alzheimer's disease that might benefit from long-term participation in the day hospital's "structured, therapeutic environment."

Consider the staffing of Peter Hinman, a 77-year-old man whose daughter had taken him to the geriatric clinic for evaluation because, as she allegedly had put it, "He's doing very careless things lately that really worry me that he's going to have an accident and be seriously hurt." Although Peter continued to drive an automobile, family members felt it was no longer safe because, according to them, Peter had become very confused. The family wondered, too, whether they could continue to keep Peter at home because he "wandered so." Perhaps the day hospital or a nursing home would be appropriate.

The staffing began as usual, with one of the physicians, a geriatrician, summarizing the case from the patient's chart.

> He's an interesting patient. So we'll talk about him. Apparently, his daughter came in here and complained of his memory loss and confusion. But he gave me a history himself and he really gets around. He's really very independent and has everything very well organized. Occasionally he gets car trouble but he calls his nephew, not his daughter. His daughter says that he's more demented than he appears. [describes daughter's concern] He's a 100% salesman,

including selling himself. [relays anecdotes describing Peter's sales prowess] And he's not aware of his Alzheimer's.

Several staffers added information of their own. One of the nurses, who had had the initial contact with the daughter, confirmed that the family was quite distressed with Peter, that the daughter wanted Peter's driver's license revoked. The geriatrician, although sympathetic with the daughter's plight, was not as convinced that Peter was dangerous, certainly alert enough to give the staff pause in supporting a case against continued licensing. Peter's performance on a routine mental status examination was noted, on which he scored only 3.5 correct answers out of 10. His physical exam revealed nothing remarkable for a man his age. The geriatrician concluded:

> In essence, the thing comes down to what should you do with this man. He functions extremely well. I'm concerned with his driving. Is he dangerous to other people? It's a very difficult decision as to how much we should intervene in the man's life. If we restrict his driving, his golfing, his saleswork, everything would go. His daughter wants us to intervene drastically.

Much of the following discussion concerned the family side of the decision. Was Peter really a dangerous driver or was the daughter's distress an overreaction, perhaps reflecting a family's muddled filial priorities? What kind of family was it? Would that shed any light on the situation? Since Peter lived with the daughter, how did domestic affairs figure in the case?

Each staffer, in his or her own way, knew the family under consideration. One of the geriatric nurses, who had made the initial acquaintance, held to a picture grounded in the daughter's testimony. Although the nurse had become as familiar with Peter as other staff members, she felt the daughter was more attuned to the family side of the situation. However, another staffer, one of the home-care nurses, had visited the daughter's home and found what she took to be obvious evidence of agitation on the daughter's part, not the father's. As the home-care nurse reported, the more the daughter literally pointed out to the nurse, in the father's presence, instances of the father's confusion, the more it was evident to the nurse that the household's family life in general left much to be

desired. The social worker, who had interviewed the daughter separately, was not convinced that the daughter was overreacting, that
Peter did not pose a danger and was not a family burden, reminding
the others of Peter's poor performance on the mental status exam.
The geriatrician unsuccessfully tried to limit the deliberations to
what he felt were, after all, the real facts in the case, stating:

> Well I don't know if his driving is dangerous. I haven't driven with
> him. All we know is what's been reported to us by the daughter,
> who, apparently, some of you feel doesn't realize herself what's
> going on in her own home. All we know is that he [Peter] has prob-
> lems finding his car, but a lot of us have trouble finding our cars.
> [laughter all around] We can throw it to the Driver's Bureau and
> he'll not be able to drive. That gets us off the hook. But I don't know
> if we want to do that.

Throughout the staffing, it was evident that what was known
about Peter's family life was considered to be a determining factor
in how staff would intervene in the case. At the same time, that
knowledge was linked to the question of where the family's real
domestic affairs were to be found. According to some, it was
revealed by a direct inspection of actual goings-on in the household. According to others, household affairs could not credibly
stand on their own, for what actually was happening "there" could
only be seen when discerned by outsiders who knew from experience how to distinguish what was apparent from what was actual,
staff's own professional assessment being exemplary. In practice,
the staffing was just as focal a location of family life as the Hinman's domestic affairs were the formal site of its family truths.
Indeed, family membership, itself, was no guarantor of accessi-
bility to family living, for, as several staffers implied, what goes on
in the household is not necessarily understood by its own occupants.

It was clear, too, in deliberations about the family sources and
sides of organizational concern, that concrete family affairs were
not as much the realities of the cases under consideration as they
were signs of realities. Such concrete evidence as the actual testimony of family members, household conduct, domestic atmosphere, material environs, professional household evaluations, the
results of physical and mental status examination of members, and
family histories, in practice, were merely denotable anchors to

which respective familial actualities were tethered. Answers to the question of where the actual family was to be found belied the household, the latter being a mere collection of physical markers for the meaning of its domestic affairs (Gubrium & Lynott, 1985b).

Just as Peter Hinman's staffing intermittently centered on staff deliberations over households as locaters of family life, family members also found themselves in the same circumstance. The day hospital's support group for family caregivers of Alzheimer's disease patients was, for some participants, of greater service in discerning domestic affairs than the individual recollections of actual members. Time and again, support group participants reported that they saw their family life in a different light "here," meaning in the support group, than at home or among family members. Invidious distinctions were drawn therefrom, many concluding that they viewed things as they really were only after having shared experiences with other caregivers in the support group. Some, of course, understandably insisted that only those who actually lived at home could know what life was like there. Those holding to versions of the two positions routinely tangled over the grounds of their respective claims in the course of discerning the domestic actualities of family living.

Although no one claimed that contexts of consideration were themselves the domains of family living, it was evident that, at the same time, households as domains were taken to be merely significative of familial realities (Gubrium & Lynott, 1985b). What organizational embeddedness did was to provide formal locations for revealing family living, the familial cultures of the institutions supplying a stock of interpretive compasses for virtually aiming households toward reasonable senses of their internal affairs. In and about these formal locations, there were regularly discovered versions of familial realities, no matter where or what their respective domestic affairs ostensibly seemed to be.

## Conclusion

What bearing does the consideration of organizational embeddedness have on what is known about the experience of the familial and what implication for assessment and planning? First, it is evident in deliberations over family affairs that there are more hands involved than those of family members proper. Although there have always been persons, in and out of households, who have concerned themselves with familial particulars, formal organizations, especially long-term care facilities, charge their staffs with official responsibility. The organizations not only house, care for, and treat family members, but maintain standing positions and committees whose primary functions include the articulation and amelioration of family matters. As such, organizational embeddedness serves to widen the network of claims for familial interpretation, family order thereby being securely tied to the official work of nonmembers.

Second, as going concerns, human service organizations and providers may virtually overwhelm the very subjects and ties they are charged with helping. The professionalization of familial concern, from family physicians and psychologists to social workers and home-care nurses, offers their spokespersons formal and highly rationalized understandings of the familial, which compete with the informal articulations of family members for familial claims. Whether the question is who, what, or where is family, embeddedness not only widens the scope of claimants of family knowledge but serves to distinguish their credibility.

Third, service organizations that deal with the long-term care of family members can become, if not biological or legal, nonetheless virtual working components of family living. In the course of residing in a long-term care facility, one's familial affairs are not only defined by family members for staffers and others, but, in the time available, are regularly scrutinized and affected by nonmembers officially assigned the duties. Long-term, as opposed to short-term, care serves to routinize, ramify, and confound organizational and familial ties. It is not that the family is dissolved into organizational contingencies in the long run, but that familial experience engages the organizational time and apparatus sufficient to diffuse it far beyond its conventional domain as a social form.

Fourth, as long-term care embeds family life, the interpretation of domestic affairs as a locus of assessment and planning is crystallized around the diverse agendas that emerge out of related jobs. The question of what is family is variously engaged by prevailing organizational treatment orientations and professional commitments. What the family is, say, for behaviorally oriented providers would not be cast likewise by Freudians. A behaviorist would be obliged to locate it less in the family's emotional history than in the conditional structure of existing domestic environments. Embeddedness suggests that what we know about the experience of the familial cannot be separated from the manifold work obligations that otherwise, in a manner of speaking, are not at all family business.

Who, what, and where family is, then, are more than just questions of proper membership, function, and domesticity. They are practical, interpretive issues, tied to the varied conditions of familial understanding. Organizational embeddedness formally secures understanding, thereby regulating the formation of familial experience. This suggests, fifth, that related questions of assessment, organization, and planning in long-term care cannot be separated from organizational cultures and processes. As those concerned—social workers, psychologists, physicians, nurses, aides, speech therapists, geriatricians, physical and occupational therapists—understandably attempt to refine and standardize their professional technology for assessing those in care, across the variety of residential settings, they simultaneously elaborate the very organizational conditions they otherwise wish to avoid in attaining objective accounts. Yet social organization is treated, optimally, as a minimal consideration in care. This behooves us to systematically consider how assessment, organization, and planning, in their own right, enter into the very realities they are meant only to represent and to ameliorate.

# 3

# A Structural Approach
# to Families

SHELDON S. TOBIN

Much attention has been given to the complimentary roles of formal services and informal supports, specifically family, in the long-term care of the elderly (see, for example, Litwak, 1985). Similarly, attention has been focused upon the kinds of services, as well as the models, for service arrangements needed to enhance the mutually enhancing roles of formal service providers and the family (see, for example, Tobin & Toseland, 1985). Additionally, the importance of the quality of the psychosocial environment for maintaining the well-being of the chronically impaired elderly is well documented (see, for example, Lieberman & Tobin, 1983). Yet a serious lacunae exists in the literature regarding the psychodynamics of family caring and, in turn, how to use an understanding of family psychodynamics to develop new structural approaches to maximizing the complimentary roles of family members and formal service providers.

One attempt to fill this lacunae was made at Drexel Home for the Aged, a home known for its experimenting approach to institutional care for the elderly. The structural approach implemented at Drexel Home simply consisted of assigning a one half-time BA-level worker to each unit of 40 or so residents. Of critical importance, however, was the reorientation of staff to the families of residents. That is, BA-level workers were selected and trained to be perceived by family members as all-loving and all-giving caregivers to the elderly resident and, in turn, administrative staff were encouraged to let themselves be targets for hostile expressions by family members regarding the dereliction of the home in caring for their relatives.

Why did the Drexel Home for the Aged, a home of excellent quality adopt this structural change? What was the rationale for the reorganization and reorientation of staff? We must begin with an understanding of intragenerational family psychodynamics; of the effects on the elderly when becoming institutionalized in even the best of contemporary nursing homes; and also of the unique psychology of the very old. An understanding of the unique psychology of the very old is particularly important for the development of long-term care programs. Unless there is an understanding of how seemingly dysfunctional psychological processes are actually functional to the adaptation of the elderly, family and formal service providers will misinterpret normative adaptive processes to be pathological. Knowledge of family dynamics, the effects of becoming institutionalized, and the unique psychology of the very old can be used in a variety of ways to enhance the lives of elderly through maximizing the quality of interaction with family members. Our structural approach in a long-term care facility is obviously only one of many ways. After discussing the background to the program, details of the structural approach will be expanded upon.

## Family Psychodynamics

The importance of family members to the elderly is critical to the well-being of the older person whether he or she is living independently in the community, being cared for by family, or residing in an institution. Their importance, for example, was revealed in our studies (Tobin & Kulys, 1980) of the very old and their "responsible others," the persons they designated when asked, "If you were admitted to the hospital and had to name someone who would be responsible for you and your affairs, whom would you choose?" We (Kulys & Tobin, 1980-1981) have reported, for example, that the 10% or so of the elderly who worry about adverse future changes are likely not to have viable responsible others, particularly familial supports. If the presence of familial supports reduces preoccupations with the future, it is understandable why so few elderly do worry. Because of event uncertainty and the uncertainty of timing of events ("anything can happen at anytime"), to worry about what will happen is actually to be preoccupied; and it is the presence and availability of responsible family members that reduces dysfunctional preoccupations.

To explore the role of the family further, we also interviewed the person designated as the responsible other. For 50 dyads composed of elderly parents and adult children, well-being of parents was related to their ability to say that the responsible child would take their wishes into account if a decision needed to be made for future care (Schlesinger et al., 1981). Also, the extent of personal care services of which the child had knowledge was associated with parental well-being because, apparently, knowledge of concrete services by children provides the necessary reassurance to elderly parents that meaningful and appropriate concern will be given when the need arises. When we also asked the parent and responsible child to describe themselves and also to describe the other as they think the other would describe him- or herself, elderly parents were better able to describe their adult children in the same way children described themselves than were children able to describe their parents in the way parents described themselves. One obvious interpretation of this finding is that it is very important for parents to perceive accurately those adult children who are to be responsible for their future care.

The role of families in the well-being of elderly members obviously extends throughout the period when caregiving at home is needed. Families respond heroically. Indeed, for every elderly individual in a long-term care facility there are at least twice as many elderly with the same physical and mental status residing in the community, which is only possible if families provide care at home.

Families continue to retain their meaningfulness after a member enters a long-term care facility (Tobin & Kulys, 1980). Many nursing homes, however, discourage family visiting. Care is easier for nursing home personnel when families do not "interfere." Obviously overworked staff, particularly aides who do the most onerous and distasteful tasks, cannot respond immediately to residents' requests. For example, all residents who have urine-soaked bed clothing when they awake cannot be bathed at the same time. Nor can the home provide the kinds of foods that each resident wishes. Thus staff at every level are likely to hear from families about these, and many other, complaints. It is, therefore, most efficient for the home as an instrumental organization to communicate to families its humane commitment to the care of its beloved residents while simultaneously discouraging visiting.

Families, in turn, can usually be discouraged from visiting and will often disengage from their institutionalized family member if assured that adequate care is being given. Yet families are needed to reinforce the sense of emotional security of the elderly resident and, also, to assist staff in perceiving the resident as a real person. The withdrawal of family, however, is understandable. A decision to institutionalize an elderly family member is never taken lightly. By the time it occurs, the family often feels relieved but not without feelings of heightened inadequacy and, moreover, great rage; that is, rage at oneself for being inadequate and rage toward the elderly person for inducing feelings of inadequacy. Too often workers focus on the family's feelings of guilt, rather than on the accompanying feelings of inadequacy and rage, as well as sense of relief, after institutionalization.

### Effects of Becoming Institutionalized

Given this mixture of painful feelings, it is expected that reassurances of competent care by personnel in facilities would be welcomed by families; and also welcomed would be subtle, and not so subtle, messages that it is not necessary to visit so much. It is indeed painful to visit a mother who is quickly deteriorating and may not recognize you. Visits by family members, however, are particularly important because of the effects of becoming institutionalized when old. What are these effects? When do they begin? And what is the role and meaning of family throughout the process? As will become apparent, effects begin before the actual entering and living in the facility and these effects are inseparable from the meaning of family to the elderly person.

In our study of becoming institutionalized when old (Tobin & Lieberman, 1976), elderly were followed from before admission through entering and then living in three homes for the aged, one of which was Drexel Home for the Aged. The primary sample consisted of 85 elderly (mean age, 79) who were interviewed, on the average, 4 months before actually entering sectarian homes for the aged, and who were on waiting lists after applying and being accepted to enter the homes. These respondents were interviewed again 2 months after admission, and then interviewed once more 1 year after admission. The selection of sectarian homes was purposeful. We chose the best of contemporary long-term care facilities because we were interested in the irreducible effects of institutional life. The choice of a longitudinal design was also purposeful because in previous studies, cross-sectional comparisons between community and institutional samples have resulted in differences between the 2 samples being attributed to living in the institution, whereas other factors may be of even greater importance, such as population differences, effects during the process before admission, and relocation effects.

To assess the fears of becoming institutionalized, Kuypers (1969) developed an interview guide that permitted the assessment of latent, as well as manifest, attitudes toward the home. The sample of 14 had a rather positive appraisal of Drexel Home, the sectarian institution to which they would apply if institutionalization became necessary. For example, they felt that old-age homes were necessary, that the staff met the needs of the residents, that a resident could maintain self-respect, and that the home provided companionship. To them, "people who went into the homes were different from themselves." If they themselves were no longer independent "the home would be a necessary alternative." The focused interview that followed the questionnaire, however, revealed more latent attitudes. For 12 of the 14 respondents, entering the home would be a calamity. One respondent said "it would be giving up everything" and that she would go "only if helpless," another compared it to "a jail," and a third, to "a place to die." Although it may be giving up everything, a jail, and a death house, they would enter a sectarian home such as Drexel Home, as have others before them, to assure survival.

Given the attitude of elderly toward these homes before admission is contemplated, it is not at all surprising that if admission is later sought, the resident-to-be becomes depressed and withdrawn before actually entering and living in the home. Also not surprising was that this deteriorating psychological portrait, that is, a portrait usually attributed to living in a total institution, was accompanied by a feeling of being abandoned by their family, as revealed, for example, by their reconstruction of earlier memories (Tobin, 1972; Tobin & Etigson, 1968). Feelings of abandonment can best be understood if institutionalization is considered a family process. Indeed families, as noted earlier, go to extremes to avoid institutionalizing a member. Although a disproportionate percentage of those who reside in long-term care facilities may be without nuclear family members, most do have families. Among those elderly who do have family members involved in the decison-making process to seek institutional care, the situation evokes problems in family relationships that are persistent, but often veiled, and the family manifests, according to Brody (1977), "internalized guilt-inducing injunctions against placing an elderly spouse or parent regardless of the most reality-based determinants of that placement" (p. 115). More recently Brody (1985) attributed the myth of how previous generations cared better for their elderly members to these kinds of feelings. Cath (1972) labeled the institutionalization of a parent "a nadir of life" because one of the most unhappy times in life may be when a child must make a decision to institutionalize a parent.

When we examined the change from preadmission to two months postadmission there was remarkable stability. We did, however, find a shift toward less friendliness, and even more hostility, toward others. These feelings were directed toward elderly peers in the homes and not toward their families. Actually there was an amelioration in feelings of abandonment (see also Smith & Bengtson, 1979) and, moreover, there was a mythicizing of adult living children. The exaggerated response is probably reinforced by the institutional environment in which the coin of the realm is family offspring who are attentive and caring and where family attention provides leverages for personal prestige and also for more attentive staff caring. Family members, however, are present not only in memories and conversations with other residents and with staff but also as visitors. Visiting is actually more prevalent at the homes we studied because visiting depends, as noted by Dobroff (1976), "in part on the degree to which the institution and its staff made the families feel welcome in the institution and encouraged their efforts on behalf of aged-relatives" (p. vii). These homes indeed welcome visitors. The family is thus not only involved in the process of entering homes but also involved afterward.

## The Unique Psychology of the Very Old

Although the family is always important, their role and meaningfulness shifts from before institutionalization until afterward, particularly if caregiving at home occurred before admission. The prevalent feelings of being abandoned by family during the anticipatory period may lessen, with, however, images of past family life apparently becoming more important and face-to-face contact of great importance in the potentially depersonalizing environment. Of course, the use of familiar family members to reaffirm the self obviously also occurs outside of institutional settings. The movie *On Golden Pond* poignantly captured this phenomenon. When Norman, the retired professor who was one day away from his eightieth birthday, becomes disoriented in the woods behind his summer home he panics and, after running in circles, arrives at his cottage with a great sense of relief. Out of breath and with obviously frightening heart palpitations, he tenderly says to his wife, with a voice strained with a mixture of anxiety and relief, "When I look into your face I can be *myself* again."

Face-to-face contact with families thus provides images for recapturing the eternal self that transcends the here and now. That is, the elderly are able to retain a remarkable consistency in identity by reaffirming the content of the self through using memories from the past in which the past and the present become interchangeable. In turn, the past is mythicized and made vivid to reaffirm the uniqueness of self (Revere & Tobin, 1980-1981). Specifically, important to adapting to institutionalization is the magical quality of transforming the decision to relocate to a home into a voluntary personal choice and perceiving the relocation environment as congruent with an ideally preferred environment, distortions that appear dysfunctional but are not. Also, aggressiveness, even suspiciousness and nastiness, facilitate adaptation to relocation (Lieberman & Tobin, 1983; Tobin & Lieberman, 1976).

Distortions reflecting magical mastery and also aggressiveness, psychological processes considered indicators of poor mental health for younger persons, are indeed troublesome to family. Only through educating families and providers about adaptational usefulness can such seemingly dysfunctional processes be perceived as helpful. Most essential is to understand how the process relates to the family. Families assist in the preservation of the self through their meanings. For the elderly the reconstruction of reminiscence that reinforces the sense of self is largely a reconstruction of family interaction. When an elderly person is institutionalized in a long-term facility, this potentially de-selfing process can be attenuated, in part, by interaction with family members. One common example is the importance of family visits to the seemingly intractably confused elderly resident of an institution. The elderly person may seem to be totally unaware of the family visitor at the time of the visit. Shortly after the visit, however, the elderly resident may become quite agitated, reflecting an awareness at some level of the visit. Often organized reminiscence replaces psychoticlike ramblings. Notwithstanding its importance to the resident, the visit can be quite upsetting to the family visitor and may serve only to heighten the previously discussed feelings of guilt, impotence, and rage. Unless someone explains to the family the specific meaningfulness of the visit, the family may reduce their visiting, which can be quite harmful to the elderly resident.

## The Structured Program

Drexel Home, in common with the best of homes, has always encouraged family visiting. As with many homes, however, as the residential population deteriorated, becoming more impaired physically and mentally, it became apparent that although family members visited the home, there was a tendency for lessened visiting of family members. Attempts to maintain visiting patterns through family groups, such as family members of new residents or Friends of Drexel Home (which was formed to raise money for special projects), did keep families involved in the home. Yet, as Safford (1980) found, family members of more confused residents participated in these groups but did not necessarily visit either the floor of their resident family member or the resident him- or herself. In withdrawing from interaction with deteriorating residents, some family members simply deny that their visiting has lessened, while others become terribly upset with themselves and their inability to tolerate the deterioration, and still others vociferously blame the home for causing the deterioration. Ubiquitous, as always, among all families was the anger toward themselves and toward the resident that is displaced onto the home.

The extreme pain in passively watching the deterioration of a loved one is quite evident. As noted earlier, families would have welcomed relief from their psychological pain through being encouraged not to visit. Occasionally, of course, family members were not encouraged to visit if it was too upsetting to them or to the resident. Surely, however, a general discouragement of family visiting would have provided great relief to families but certainly would have been dysfunctional for residents in reducing the maintenance of their identities and diminishing the perception of their uniqueness by staff. Thus our task was to develop an approach to families that would encourage their presence on residents' floors and, also, encourage face-to-face contact with even the most intractably confused family member.

Another kind of observation was important to our developing a structural approach. That is, those family members who continued to visit a slowly deteriorating resident until the time of death were less likely to have a protracted mourning process following the death of the resident. These family members, however, were not without feelings of inadequacy and rage during stages of deterioration. Thus our approach would have to allow for displaced rage that we knew was more beneficial to family members than rage turned inward causing heightened depression and, certainly, better than rage expressed toward the resident.

Fortunately, the home had a long history of acceptance of anger expressed by both residents and family members. Aggressiveness by residents, expressed by staff in such terms as "complaining" and "griping," and sometimes as "bitchiness," was perceived as facilitating adaptation and, when absent, as cause for alarm. Unless complaining was tolerated, or even encouraged, staff would become complacent and administrative needs would outweigh resident needs.

From another perspective, we were aware that an institutional relationship, or transference, is developed by families that includes both positive and negative projections. The home, that is, becomes both the life-sustaining all-giving other and also the life-impeding other that is the cause of the present, as well as further, deterioration in their family member. To direct this institutional transference (for discussions of institutional transference, see Reider, 1953; Wilmer, 1962; Safirstein, 1967; Van Eck, 1972; Gendel & Reiser, 1981) into usefulness for the resident, the structured approach to the institutional psychosocial environment was developed in which a split transference occurred wherein a BA-level unit social worker became the all-giving, all-loving other, and administrative personnel the life-impeding others.

The hiring of the BA-level workers was a careful process in which persons were sought who were genuinely altruistic and giving individuals. With the unit BA-level worker, family members discussed the concrete needs of the resident. When, for example, a cherished 40-year-old threadbare and torn sweater was missing, the social worker could assure a family member who was totally convinced that it was stolen or lost in the laundry that every means would be taken to recover it. Often, of course, the confused resident had misplaced it or, at other times, the ancient garment had simply dissolved in the process of being cleaned and had been replaced by housekeeping with a sweater in better repair. After the BA-level worker's assurance, the family could leave the home knowing that the worker would devote him- or herself to searching for the missing cherished sweater. The sense of personal inadequacy and guilt thus become in part alleviated through projection onto the worker of feelings and actions of unconditional caring and loving for the family member in the home.

The psychodynamics in the relationship between family member and BA-level worker is indeed complex. This relationship does not exist during the process of becoming institutionalized when the resident-to-be feels abandoned and the family members feel they are abandoning a loved one. The resident-to-be must repress or suppress feelings of abandonment and focus on how the home will assure survival, as well as provide opportunities for activities and socializing with peers. If the older person does not respond passively to the current situation and impending institutionalizations and also transforms the relocation into a voluntary decision and the home into a rather ideal environment for meeting needs, intact survivorship will be facilitated (Lieberman & Tobin, 1983). In turn, family members must also be assured that "it's time"; that is, that "it's time to live in a nursing home." By placement in a facility of excellent quality, guilt becomes assuaged and staff of the home, particularly intake social workers, are perceived as assuring that the correct decision for placement has been made and that the home will appropriately respond to their elderly family member's needs.

After admission, however, families observe in their member, who is now a resident of the home, the vicissitudes of the first-month syndrome. The *first-month syndrome* (the label developed by Dr. Jerome Grunes, psychoanalyst consultant to the Drexel Home) refers to the marked deterioration manifested during the first weeks after admission by lucid residents. Some become extremely depressed, some very anxious, others quite agitated, and still others frankly psychotic. Most new residents rebound from the first-month syndrome and by six weeks or so after admission the change from preadmission is some greater amount of hopelessness as well as greater preoccupation with illness and body.

During this early postadmission phase, relief from caregiving is joined by the home becoming perceived by families as more impersonal in its caring than when their member was accepted for admission. The family member, in turn, becomes observed as only one of many sick and deteriorating elderly for whom the home provides care. Into this disillusioning process the BA-level worker is inserted, so that fantasies of the home's special concern and caring for "my husband," "my wife," "my mother," "my father," "my aunt," "my uncle," "my grandma," or "my grandpa" becomes reestablished. The BA-level worker is perceived as different from all other workers in the home. He or she is perceived as taking a special interest in the family member.

For most, the rationalization for the special interest, concern, and care of the BA-level worker is because "mama after all is a special person," when mama may actually be only a shell of her former self and not very lucid. A concurrent rationalization is that "I am a special person because of all I have done for mama." Thus the BA-level worker is perceived as an extension of self who is not unlike an ideal family member who is not only always at mother's bedside but who loves mother in such a way that her or his attention and caring is from unconditional love and, certainly, not because it is paid employment. The BA-level worker, because of this love, can tolerate the deterioration of mama. Thus for some family members the BA-level worker becomes the perfect child whereas the daughter herself is the imperfect one. Thus there is a sense of satisfaction that mother's needs are being met with tender loving care.

Rage displaced toward the home may subside somewhat but it is not completely extinguished. The BA-level worker can assist in containing the rage through her or his own actions and, also, through explanations regarding how good the home truly is. Yet the displaced rage never subsides completely because the anger toward oneself for abandoning mother never dissolves, nor does the anger toward mother for evoking feelings of inadequacy, shame, and guilt. The rage does not become directed toward the all-loving and all-caring BA-level worker but rather toward an authority figure; toward possibly the charge nurse, the chief of social services, the associate director, or executive director who became the "bad" other who is causing all their woes. The covert feelings about these authority figures is that "if they only cared enough, they would make her well again." Such projections often take the form of irrational tirades, particularly when a symbiotic relationship exists between daughter and mother. If the professional judgment is that interaction between daughter and mother is helpful for the maintenance of the mother's sense of self-identity, such verbal abuses of staff become tolerable. The staff can learn to understand and to appreciate that the irrational abuse is an expression of the daughter's internal state, particularly her own fear of personal dissolution, when observing deterioration in her mother. This is not an easy task! It can be accomplished only if staff themselves are supported and nourished by administration so that they can withstand personal abuse.

Although a formal evaluation of the program was not undertaken, there was a consensus among all levels of staff that the restructuring of services was a great improvement. The long tradition of centralized social services and activity programs increasingly made less sense as the residential population deteriorated. More activities on floors lessened the burden of floor staff, but did not lessen anguish and anger of families. The presence and responsibilities of the BA-level workers, in turn, not only provided a buffer between families and floor staff but also relieved staff in meaningful ways. Daily contact with families was channeled through the BA-level worker, who not only discussed the status and problems of their family member but incorporated them into the service plan and sometimes into assisting with caregiving. Emerging from the program was a project on how to help families have successful visits with their family member.

A significant shift occurred over time from perceiving the social service department as part of administration and separate from the daily care of all residents to perceiving the department as intimately related to even the most tedious of nursing procedures. When the

BA-level worker assumed responsibility for explaining to a daughter why mother was not bathed immediately on wetting her undergarments, but had to wait a short while for the aide, who was then busy, all floor staff appreciated the assistance. Also appreciative were personnel in housekeeping and dietary services, who formerly were approached by families primarily to be criticized. Interpretations by the BA-level workers of the duties and concerns of these personnel led to a better relationship with families, as well as between these personnel and administrative staff.

With the apparent success of the program, those administrative staff who were the targets of criticism, and sometimes vociferous verbal abuse, by families were better able to tolerate these behaviors. Sharing of information among the BA-level workers and administrative staff led to a sense of partnership in which each set of personnel could perceive and understand their role in encouraging successful visiting and in humanizing care. Clearly, more families were involved not only with their resident family member but also with more staff members of the home.

When Drexel Home closed in the fall of 1981 (because the population it served no longer lived in the geographical area) we had the opportunity to examine further the split transference. Most residents were transferred to a new facility, but 22 were relocated to a variety of other facilities, predominantly proprietary (for-profit) nursing homes. Although the split transference was dissolved, we fortunately were able to retain the chief of social services to ease the transition and to remain as the caseworker after relocation. The former split transference was observable and during the transition was manifested, as expected, in some grossly exaggerated forms (see Tobin, in press, for a case study).

### Implications

Satisfactions from caregiving are rarely discussed. The daughter who leaves the institution in tears because mother did not recognize her but became agitated when she left may never be told her visit was a meaningful one for her mother. When the BA-level worker explains the meaningfulness of the visit, it is possible for family members to understand that their presence helps in the retention of a sense of self. Lyons (1982), a caseworker in a home for the aged, in reporting on his personal experience in caring for his wife (who was afflicted with Alzheimer's disease) poignantly described his frustrations in caring. Because of his background, however, he understood not only some of the principles in providing assurance of care but also how to help his wife's internal feelings. He wrote the following as if these words were hers: "You only know me from the outside, through my 'abnormal behavior.' Will you see me inside, struggling to maintain my assaulted personhood? Will you mistake my struggle to retain some dignity, some feeling of self, for organic disease rather than its consequences?" (pp. 3-4). Needed, therefore, are approaches in long-term care that accept the painful feelings of families and that build on their potential satisfactions as they remain in intimate contact with debilitated family members. To do so may necessitate structural changes within long-term care and, certainly, education of staff of facilities to the meaningfulness of family interaction, as well as to the process of becoming institutionalized when old and to the unique psychology of the very old.

# PART II

# *Families as Caregivers*

# 4

# Perceived
# Caregiving Effectiveness

## The Impact of Parental Impairment,
## Community Resources, and
## Caregiver Characteristics

LINDA S. NOELKER
ALOEN L. TOWNSEND

Although the importance of family care for impaired elderly has been empirically substantiated (Comptroller General of the United States, 1977; Crossman & Kaljian, 1984; Shanas, 1979a), it can have a variety of negative consequences for family members. Included among these are emotional and physical health deterioration, restricted personal time and social activities, financial burdens, and disrupted family relationships (Archbold, 1982a; Brody, 1985; Cantor, 1983; George, 1984; Noelker & Wallace, 1985). Furthermore, over recent decades there has been an increase in the number of very old persons (85+) in the U.S. population, a decrease in family size, an increase in divorce, and an increase in working women. These sociodemographic trends, together with the more widely known strains and burdens of caregiving, are believed to presage a decline in the ability and willingness of families to assist their frail and impaired elder members (Cicirelli, 1983; Furstenberg, 1981; Treas, 1977). Should this occur, it is presumed that insurmountable demands to care for the elderly will be placed on the public sector, because shrinking resources and decreased funding of health and welfare programs are dictating greater rather than less family responsibility.

Instead of regarding family and public responsibility for the aged's care as a duality, it seems more efficacious to view them as having complementary functions. Several social scientists have, in fact, proposed models conceptualizing the nature of the relationship between the aged's informal and formal support systems in this manner (Cantor, 1979; Litwak, 1985; Sussman, 1977). Our research, however, which is presented in this chapter and the next, draws more heavily from a model proposing that a delicate balance exists between the impaired elderly's needs and demands, the family's resources, and the community's resources and supports (Perlman & Giele, 1982). If a shift occurs in any of these three key elements, readjustments must be made in the other two so that a balance is restored to the system.

Although this model accords primacy to family resources as the fulcrum in the system, we believe that the resources of the individual family caregiver must be differentiated from those of the family unit. Recent research on family caregiving, along with clinical studies, lends support to this approach. In this chapter, therefore, we will examine the differential effects of parental impairment, community supports, and the caregiving child's characteristics on caregiving effectiveness. In the next chapter, we will explore the impact of the parental impairment, community supports, and family relationships on caregiving effectiveness.

## Caregiving Outcomes

Prior research has uncovered a plethora of strains and burdens that befall caregiving families, ranging from health deterioration, employment difficulties, income loss, marital discord, and household disruption to sleeplessness, social isolation, and physical abuse (Archbold, 1982a; Brody, 1985; Cantor, 1983; Frankfather et al., 1981; George, 1984; Johnson & Catalano, 1983; Noelker & Wallace, 1985; Robinson & Thurnher, 1979; Steinmetz & Amsden, 1983). In recent years, however, studies have begun to differentiate between caregiving's more objective, negative effects and subjective care-related burdens (Montgomery et al., 1985; Poulshock & Deimling, 1984). The objective impact of caregiving refers to its adverse effects on employment, finances, health, leisure and recreational activities, and other negative changes in social roles, life events, or living situations. In contrast, subjective burden refers to attitudes or feelings resulting from one's personal interpretation and intrapsychic response to caregiving demands and consequences. Some manifestations of subjective burden are reports of emotional difficulties (for example, anxiety, depression) and such feelings as helplessness, deprivation, anger, resentment, or frustration attributed to caregiving. Although objective and subjective burdens are related, they are conceptually distinct and have different correlates or predictors.

A review of the literature on caregiving consequences may lead to the conclusion that caring for an elder relative is inevitably stressful and deleterious to the caregiver's well-being. Within recent years, however, a shift in perspective is occurring about the capacity of families to care for dependent members without negative effects on the family's health and well-being. Data from recent studies, using nonclinical samples and/or panel designs, indicate that a significant portion of the elderly's family caregivers evidence no or minimal levels of care-related strains or stress effects (Noelker & Wallace, 1985; Noelker et al., 1984). These studies emphasize the coping abilities of families and their capacity to marshal strengths and resources that enable them to withstand the stress of caregiving.

Family theorists have developed conceptual frameworks premised on these notions (Klein & Hill, 1979; Kuypers & Bengtson, 1983; Olson et al., 1983). One posits that families vary in their effectiveness at solving problems in relation to certain elements in the family's structure and functioning, such as qualitative aspects of their relationships (for example, cohesiveness), the nature of decision-making interaction, and their ability to set realistic goals and develop appropriate means to achieve them (Klein & Hill, 1979). In our research the outcome variable of interest is the degree to which adult children perceive that the parents' care needs are met satisfactorily. More specifically, caregiving effectiveness was conceptualized as the children's perceived satisfaction with the elder's care arrangements, family decision making about the impaired elder, and the accomplishment of care-related goals.

Using this approach, it was possible to differentiate adult children who viewed their family as more or less effective at caregiving, as well as to identify predictors of caregiving effectiveness.

## Correlates of
## Caregiving Strain and Burden

### Elder Impairment

The accumulation of research findings on family care has resulted in the emergence of conceptual categories useful for better understanding the caregiving process, along with evidence about their differential importance in explaining caregiving's outcomes. Studies have consistently reported that the nature and severity of the elder's impairments have the major influence on caregiver burden or stress effects and on the use of community services (Coulton & Frost, 1982; McAuley & Arling, 1984; Perlman & Giele, 1982; Safford, 1980; Sainsbury & Grad de Alarcon, 1970). One explanation offered for the centrality of the elder's impairment in explaining caregiving outcomes is due to its "cascade effect" (Johnson & Catalano, 1983). That is, the elder's functional impairments produce a negative change in mood and outlook which, in turn, have an adverse effect on the elder-caregiver relationship. As impairment and related care needs escalate and the elder-caregiver relationship deteriorates, the caregiver experiences a greater sense of burden.

Specific types of elder impairment also appear as more burdensome to caregivers than others. Mental impairment, particularly when manifested in deviant or disruptive behaviors, is associated with more severe stress effects in the caregiver (Cath, 1972; Deimling & Bass, under review; Eyde & Rich, 1983; Poulshock & Deimling, 1984). Certain physical impairments that translate into more numerous, time-consuming, or difficult care tasks (for example, lifting, toileting) are also more problematic for family caregivers (Fengler & Goodrich, 1979; Montgomery et al. 1985). In view of the empirically established importance of the elder's impairment in relation to the type and amount of care provided and caregiving outcomes, it was given priority in this research as the primary predictor of family caregiving effectiveness.

The elderly person's relationship to the caregiver and the household context in which care is provided also affect caregiver strain and burden (Brubaker, 1983; Cantor, 1983; Johnson & Catalano, 1983; Noelker & Wallace, 1985; Soldo & Myllylouma, 1983). Spouses, for example, typically evidence more numerous and severe care-related stress effects than adult children or other kin, and a shared household-caregiving arrangement is generally more stressful than one in which the impaired elder and the caregiver live separately. It should be noted, however, that the elderly's living arrangements (separate or shared) tend to be confounded with their functional limitations and care needs, both of which are strongly associated with caregiver burden. In other words, aged persons with multiple and serious functional limitations, particularly mental impairments necessitating regular supervision, are likely to require assistance with a wider range of tasks and are unlikely to live independently. Because all respondents in this research were adult children who lived in households separate from their parents, both the elder-caregiver relationship and their living arrangements were invariant by virtue of the study's sampling criteria.

**Use of Community Resources**

A second conceptual category relevant to explanations of the care-giving process and its outcomes is community supports. The use of community services is viewed as important in helping to maintain and enhance the efforts of family caregivers and thereby prevent or delay institutional placement of impaired elderly (Frankfather et al., 1981; Perlman & Giele, 1982). Surveys of community aged have consistently shown that the chief predictor of service utilization is the elderly's level of disability (Coulton & Frost, 1982; McAuley & Arling, 1984), suggesting that services are sought by and/or targeted to the most frail and impaired. Recent research has also indicated that the needs of the family caregiver (that is, his or her level of care-related burdens), as well as the impaired elder's needs for assistance, are significant predictors of in-home service use (Bass & Noelker, 1985).

In general, however, survey research and clinical studies have shown that community health and social services are relatively unused and, in fact, tend to be resisted by the aged and their family caregivers (Frankfather et al., 1981; Getzel, 1982; Hess & Soldo,

1985; Krout, 1983; Noelker & Wallace, 1985). Some reasons are an unwillingness to become involved with bureaucracies and related feelings of a loss of control over the care situation, reservations about the quality of care from agencies, and a belief that the preferred types of assistance will not be the ones provided.

Discrepant findings about the use and value of community services may be related to the inconsistent and incomplete manner in which they have been conceptualized and measured. For example, studies have generally neglected to consider the types of providers, the payment sources, and the combination of assistance sources (Bass & Noelker, 1985; McAuley & Arling, 1984). Because it has been shown that home care service users, compared to nonusers, have more assistance from both formal and informal care providers, it appears that the two systems function in a complementary rather than an alternate manner (Chappell, 1985).

In light of these research findings, community resources in this study were more broadly conceptualized to include assistance with personal care or daily activities from nuclear and extended kin, friends or neighbors, and service providers whether paid or unpaid. Thus our measure of community supports was based on the notion that impaired aged tend to have a combination of care sources that function interdependently to meet their assistance needs. This approach also reflects the fact that a sizable number of the study's elderly did have diverse sources of assistance and, when formal service providers were used, they disproportionately included paid housekeepers, aides, or companions rather than professional or agency service providers.

## Caregiver Characteristics

A third conceptual category related to family care includes the characteristics of the caregiving family member. Included among these are the caregivers' age, sex, and health status, all of which have been shown to affect their capacity to provide care on a long-term basis and the care-related burdens they experience (Brody, 1981; Montgomery et al., 1985; Noelker & Wallace, 1985; Pinkston & Linsk, 1984). Caregivers of more advanced age and with chronic health conditions, for example, have more difficulty sustaining long-term caregiving, and an alternative care arrangement (for example, institutional placement of the elder) or greater use of home care services often results. In contrast, younger caregivers (for example, adult children) report more subjective burdens related to caregiving, such as feelings of anxiety, depression, guilt, helplessness, and excessive worrying (Archbold, 1982a; Brody, 1985; Cicirelli, 1983). Sometimes these feelings are associated with negative changes in the parent-child relationship, as evidenced by anger or resentment on the part of the child and by excessive demands or dependency and manipulativeness on the part of the parent (Breslau, 1984; Poulshock & Deimling, 1984; Johnson & Catalano, 1983; Zarit et al., 1980).

Additional aspects of subjective burden include the children's personal evaluation of the care situation and their perceived capacity to respond to it (Horejsi, 1983; Kuypers & Bengtson, 1983). When children define the care situation as unpredictable, uncontrollable, or as providing few options for meeting the parent's care needs, they impose restrictions on the extent to which they, and probably their family, can be effective at caregiving. Correspondingly, a more negative view of the care situation is likely to be associated with subjective perceptions of restricted or diminished capacity to deal with it. Children with these perceptions typically report that they lack the personal or psychic resources (for example, income, time, energy) to respond to the situation's demands.

The extent to which subjective or intrapsychic burdens are experienced by caregiving adult children is of major concern for two reasons. These difficulties are likely to have deleterious effects on the personal well-being of adult children (Lazarus & Folkman, 1984), thus parent caring would occur at the expense of the child's mental or emotional health. Second, the caregiver's level of subjective burden is also associated with disrupted care arrangements and a relinquishment of caregiving responsibilities (Frankfather et al., 1981; Smith & Bengtson, 1979; Townsend, 1965). Consequently, in an effort to sustain adult children's care of aged parents without endangering their personal health, their subjective response to the care situation is increasingly regarded as a primary consideration in research and practice.

## Methods

### Sample

Data for this research were drawn from a larger panel study, funded by the National Institute of Mental Health and titled "Caring for Elders and the Mental Health of Family Members." In this investigation, the data used were gathered during the second of three interviews with the adult children. In order to be included in the sample, an adult child had to meet the following criteria: (1) have a parent aged 60 or over in the metropolitan Cleveland area who was either married and living with a spouse or female, widowed, and living alone; and (2) the parent required assistance with personal care or daily activities.

At the second wave of data collection, 153 adult children from 109 families (82 with widowed mothers and 27 with married parents) were interviewed. In our analyses, the subset of 109 adult children who reported themselves as part of the elder's helping network are of primary concern, because a major purpose of our research is to determine the relationship between the personal characteristics of adult-child caregivers and their perception of the family's effectiveness at caregiving. Of the 109 caregiving children, 18 reported themselves as the parent's primary caregiver. The remaining 44 children stated they did not help their impaired parent with personal care or daily activities. They are used only for comparative purposes in an attempt to identify demographic or other differences that may explain why some adult children are caregivers and others are not.

**Measures**

The key variables used in these analyses reflect the study's conceptual framework which posits that a balance must be maintained between the elder's level of impairment, the caregiver's personal characteristics, and the use of community resources in order to sustain family care without deleterious consequences. The following measures were used to tap each of these three domains as well as the study's outcome variable, caregiving effectiveness.

*Caregiving effectiveness.* The outcome variable (CAREGIVING EFFECTIVENESS) in this research was a composite measure created from summated scores on three items:

(1) How satisfied are you with the present arrangement for caring for your parent? (Codes ranged from not satisfied at all = 0 to very satisfied = 3.)

(2) How successful do you think you've been in achieving your goals in caring for your parent? (Codes ranged from not successful at all = 0 to very successful = 3.)

(3) How satisfied are you with the way in which decisions concerning your parent are made? (Codes ranged from not satisfied at all = 0 to very satisfied = 3.)

The alpha coefficient of reliability for this indicator was .64 and the scale ranged from 0 to 9.

*The elder parent's impairments.* Four measures were used to assess the nature and extent of the parent's functional limitations. The first (PERSONAL CARE DEPENDENCIES) was an adapted version of the Physical Self-Maintenance Scale (Lawton & Brody, 1969) that asked adult children whether or not their parent was able to perform 6 personal care tasks: toileting, eating, dressing, grooming, physical ambulation, and bathing. The scale range was from 0 (completely dependent in personal care) to 6 (completely independent in personal care).

The parent's dependence in daily activities (DAILY ACTIVITY LIMITATIONS) was assessed using an adapted version of the Instrumental Activities of Daily Living Scale (Lawton & Brody, 1969). The 8 activities included in this scale were the parent's ability to do the following: answer the phone, shop, use transportation, take medication, handle finances, prepare a meal, do laundry, and manage light housekeeping tasks. A score of 8 indicated complete independence in daily activities and a score of 0 indicated that the parent was completely dependent in daily activities.

If the adult children reported that their parent had physical health problems or mental impairments (for example, confusion), they were also asked to rate the extent to which they perceived that these limited their parent's functioning (PHYSICAL AND MENTAL LIMITATIONS). The two items were worded as follows: How much do your parent's (physical/mental) impairments interfere with (his/her) ability to do things for (him/her)self? Answer categories ranged from 0 (not applicable, no impairment) to 3 (a great deal).

Study data indicated that, on average, the adult children reported their parent as having two personal care dependencies and three dependencies in daily activities. Slightly more than half the children (53%) perceived the parent as somewhat limited physically, and only 31% felt the parent had mental limitations that interfered with his or her ability to do things independently.

*Community resources.* There were two measures that assessed the use of community resources by the impaired elder. One (BOTH INFORMAL/FORMAL HELP) was constructed from four dichotomous items measuring whether or not the elder parent had the following types of help in the last six months: overnight care in the home of a family member or friend, help from family or friends, paid help (for example, housekeeper), or help from community agencies. A dichotomous measure was created from these items with a score of 1 indicating the elder parent had all four types of help in the last 6 months and 0 including all other responses to the items. By virtue of its construction, then, this measure specifically emphasized the caregiving children whose parent made widest use of informal and formal supports from those with less diverse support networks.

The second measure of community resources (DIFFICULTY FINDING AGENCY HELP) was a single dichotomous item asking the adult child whether or not there were any difficulties finding or using health or social services from community agencies. Approximately 1 out of 10 of the caregiving adult children reported this as a problem.

*Caregiver characteristics.* In addition to items assessing the adult-child caregivers' age, sex, marital and employment status, they were asked to report their income in categories ranging from 1 (0-$4,999) to 9 ($70,000 or more).

The adult children's well-being was measured using the Zung (1965) Self-Rated Depression Scale and Bradburn's (1969) Affect Balance Scale. There were also two self-rated items, ranging from very poor (1) to excellent (5), that assessed their physical and emotional health status (SELF-RATED PHYSICAL AND MENTAL HEALTH).

A number of items were used to measure what have been referred to as the intrapsychic tensions (Brody, 1985) or subjective burdens (Montgomery et al., 1985; Poulshock & Deimling, 1984) of an adult child caring for an aged parent. In this research, one measure was an index consisting of seven summated items constructed to assess the extent to which adult children defined the caregiving situation in a negative manner (NEGATIVE PERCEPTION OF CARE SITUATION). These items were as follows:

(1) I think of this situation as a problem that will only become more serious with time.
(2) It's upsetting not to know what the future will bring for my parent.
(3) I'm troubled by not having many choices available about ways to meet my parent's care needs.
(4) Most people aren't faced with this situation so they have no idea what I'm going through.
(5) I never know what to expect from day to day in this situation.
(6) This is the most difficult problem that I've ever had to face.
(7) It's easy to feel overwhelmed in a situation like this.

The response categories for each item were strongly agree, agree, disagree, and strongly disagree. The scale range was from 0 to 21 and the alpha coefficient of reliability for this indicator was .77.

Additionally, the adult children were asked whether or not they had any of the following three difficulties because of the parent's impairments and care needs: not being able to provide the parent with all the care he or she needed, too many demands made on the child, and not getting enough rest. The adult children were also asked whether or not one of their goals in caring for their parent was to avoid feeling guilty about this situation. Each of these variables was coded dichotomously (0, 1) and treated as a dummy variable in the correlational and regression analyses. From a more positive perspective, adult children were asked the extent to which they agreed that they had all the time and energy needed to devote to their parent's care (coded 1 = strongly agree to 4 = strongly disagree).

Approximately one-third of the caregiving adult children felt they could not meet all the parent's care needs, 28% reported that too many demands were made on them, and 16% said they were not getting enough rest. A substantially larger percentage (45%) agreed that one of their goals was to avoid feeling guilty about this situation. Only 18% of the caregiving children agreed they had all the time and energy needed to devote to their parent's care.

### Analysis Plan

An unanswered question in the family care literature is why some children assist their elderly parent(s) and others do not (Brody, 1985; Noelker & Shaffer, in press). Because this study attempted to interview all adult children who resided near the parent regardless of whether they were caregivers or not, some preliminary data can be offered to account for this phenomenon.

To ascertain whether or not there were differences between the socio-demographic and well-being characteristics of adult children who were and were not caregivers, chi-square and t-tests were used. Pearson product moment correlation coefficients were used to analyze the strength of the relationships among the parental impairment, community resources, caregiver characteristics, and caregiving effectiveness variables. Finally, hierarchical multiple regression analysis assessed the relative importance of parental impairment, community resources, and caregiver characteristics in predicting caregiving effectiveness. In the regression analysis, the impairment and community resource variables were entered as a block, followed by the caregiver characteristics in stepwise fashion using a .15 tolerance level.

## Results

### Involvement in Parent Caring

As Table 4.1 shows, the only significant demographic differences between the caregiving and noncaregiving children in this research were related to their gender and employment status. Although virtually all daughters (92%) were caregivers, less than two-thirds of the sons were. The majority (82%) of unemployed children were also caregivers compared to only 65% who were employed. Furthermore, data (not shown in the table) suggested that gender and employment status have an interactive effect on caregiving, because 96% of the employed daughters were caregivers in contrast to only 35% of the employed sons, and 88% of the unemployed daughters were caregivers compared to only 54% of the unemployed sons ($\chi^2 = 51.73$, $df = 3$, $p < .001$). Regardless of whether or not a woman works, she is likely to be involved in parent caring, but employment appears to reduce a son's involvement to a substantially greater extent.

Although the negative consequences of parent caring for the health and well-being of adult children have been widely reported (Archbold, 1982a; Brody, 1985; Cantor, 1983; Johnson & Catalano, 1983; Robinson & Thurnher, 1979), data in Table 4.1 show

TABLE 4.1

Personal Characteristics of Adult-Child Caregivers (N = 109)
and Noncaregivers (N = 44)

| | Caregivers | | Noncaregivers | | |
|---|---|---|---|---|---|
| Personal Characteristics | % | N | % | N | |
| Sex | | | | | |
| female | 92 | 87 | 8 | 8 | |
| male | 62 | 36 | 38 | 22 | $\chi^2$ (1) = 50.59, $p <$ .001 |
| Marital status | | | | | |
| unmarried | 79 | 23 | 21 | 6 | |
| married | 69 | 86 | 31 | 38 | $\chi^2$ (1) = 1.14, $p$ = ns |
| Employment | | | | | |
| unemployed | 82 | 49 | 18 | 11 | |
| employed | 65 | 60 | 35 | 32 | $\chi^2$ (1) = 4.48, $p <$ .05 |
| Age ($\bar{X}$) | 48.26 | | 45.23 | | $t$(151) = −1.53, $p$ = ns |
| Income category ($\bar{X}$)[a] | 5.35 | | 5.58 | | $t$(136) = .68, $p$ = ns |
| Zung depression scores ($\bar{X}$) | 38.62 | | 37.47 | | $t$(151) = −.70, $p$ = ns |
| Affect balance scores ($\bar{X}$) | 7.13 | | 7.39 | | $t$(145) = .72, $p$ = ns |
| Self-rated physical health ($\bar{X}$) | 4.07 | | 4.11 | | $t$(151) = 29, $p$ = ns |
| Self-rated emotional health ($\bar{X}$) | 4.01 | | 4.18 | | $t$(151) = 1.23, $p$ = ns |
| Family effectiveness at caregiving ($\bar{X}$) | 6.86 | | 7.53 | | $t$(150) = 2.07, $p <$ .05 |

a. The income categories represented by these mean scores are $20,000-$29,000 (5)
and $30,000-$39,000 (6).

no significant differences between the caregiving and noncaregiving children in their mean scores on the depression, affect balance,
or self-rated physical and emotional health measures. Average
scores were high for both groups, with the majority rating their
physical and emotional health as good or excellent and evidencing
no or minimal signs of depression or negative affect.

It is possible that the level of the parents' impairment and conse-
quent care needs were not severe enough to have an adverse affect
on the general health status of the caregiving children. Alternatively, the elderly parents in this research had relatively extensive
support networks (see Townsend & Poulshock, 1986, for a detailed
analysis), which may have had a buffering effect on any care-
related stress experienced by these children. Other studies also

indicate that children with personal difficulties or obligations (for example, illness, dependent children) may be legitimately exempt from parent care (Calkins, 1972; Ikels, 1983). Thus it may be that the noncaregiving children in this study were not involved in parent caring because of other responsibilities or life events that consumed their time and energy and simultaneously resulted in well-being scores comparable to their caregiving siblings.

Although no differences were found in the general health and well-being of these two groups, noncaregiving children tended to feel that the family was more effective at caregiving than children who were involved in parent caring. One might suspect that their absence from the parent's helping network made them somewhat oblivious to certain aspects of the care situation or to the difficulties of caregiving. However, study data showed no significant differences between the noncaregiving and caregiving children in their perceptions of the parent's type or level of impairment, the reported use of community resources, and intrapsychic difficulties associated with the parent's impairments and care needs. Thus it may have been that the noncaregiving children's more positive view of caregiving effectiveness justified their absence from the parent's helping network (that is, their help was not needed).

## Correlates of Caregiving Effectiveness

The results of correlational analysis, included in Table 4.2, showed that virtually all key variables were significantly related to the study's outcome. The relationships between the variables in each category and the outcome variable were also in the expected direction. The strongest correlates of caregiving effectiveness were in the category of caregiver characteristics. Caregiving children who viewed the care situation more negatively, who felt unable to meet all the parent's care needs, who sought to avoid feeling guilty, who rated their physical health more negatively, and who had higher depression scores also perceived that the family was less effective at caregiving. Also, caregiving children who viewed the care situation more negatively perceived the parent as more physically and mentally impaired and had difficulty finding or using agency help.

It is also interesting to note that the children's ratings of the parents' physical and mental impairments had slightly stronger relationships to family caregiving effectiveness and caregiver characteristics than the scale scores for the parent's personal care and

## TABLE 4.2
### Zero-Order Correlation Matrix for Caregiving Effectiveness, Elder Impairment, Community Resources, and Adult-Child Caregiver Variables (N = 109)

| | 1 | 2 | 3 | 4 | 5 | 6 | 7 | 8 | 9 | 10 | 11 | 12 | 13 | 14 | 15 | 16 | 17 | X̄ | SD |
|---|---|---|---|---|---|---|---|---|---|---|---|---|---|---|---|---|---|---|---|
| 1. Caregiving effectiveness | 1.00 | .18 | .29[b] | -.32[c] | -.37[c] | -.31[c] | .25[b] | .53[c] | .39[c] | -.27[b] | -.43[c] | -.24[b] | -.30[c] | -.42[c] | .33[c] | .41[c] | .35[c] | 6.86 | 1. |
| 2. Elder's personal care dependencies | | 1.00 | .79[c] | -.44[c] | -.42[c] | -.27[b] | -.24[b] | -.45[c] | .14 | .11 | -.20[a] | -.03 | -.05 | -.24[b] | .15 | .07 | .25[b] | 4.11 | 1. |
| 3. Elder's daily activity limitations | | | 1.00 | -.42[c] | -.59[c] | -.30[c] | -.10 | -.51[c] | .17 | -.01 | -.25[b] | -.02 | -.09 | -.29[b] | .15 | .12 | .26[b] | 5.29 | 2. |
| 4. Elder's physical limitations | | | | 1.00 | -.27[b] | .26[b] | .18 | .51[c] | -.21[a] | .06 | .29[b] | .20[a] | .20[a] | .34[c] | -.24[b] | -.24[b] | -.25[b] | 2.38 | 1. |
| 5. Elder's mental limitations | | | | | 1.00 | .21 | .02 | .57 | .25 | .23 | .16 | .06 | .24 | .19 | .20 | .07 | .31 | .85 | 1. |
| 6. Difficulty finding agency help | | | | | | 1.00 | -.04 | .40[c] | -.10 | .01 | .39[c] | .17 | .21[a] | .22[a] | -.18 | -.16 | -.14 | .09 | . |
| 7. Both informal/formal help | | | | | | | 1.00 | -.01 | -.02 | -.12 | .00 | -.14 | -.06 | -.17 | .01 | .10 | .08 | .36 | . |
| 8. Negative perception of care situation | | | | | | | | 1.00 | -.30[c] | .20[a] | .32[c] | .28[b] | .23[a] | .35[c] | -.26[b] | -.24[b] | -.38[c] | 11.52 | 3. |
| 9. Seeks to avoid guilt | | | | | | | | | 1.00 | -.19[a] | -.15 | -.36[c] | -.02 | -.09 | .18 | .18 | .28[b] | 1.55 | . |
| 10. Too many demands | | | | | | | | | | 1.00 | .31[c] | .14 | .36[c] | .12 | -.26[b] | -.11 | -.19[a] | .28 | . |
| 11. Can't meet elder's care needs | | | | | | | | | | | 1.00 | .17 | .34[c] | .38[c] | -.48[c] | -.32[c] | -.24[b] | .33 | . |
| 12. Has all time/energy needed | | | | | | | | | | | | 1.00 | .12 | .14 | -.14 | -.25[b] | -.11 | 3.09 | . |
| 13. Doesn't get enough rest | | | | | | | | | | | | | 1.00 | .15 | -.25[b] | -.17 | -.26[b] | .16 | . |
| 14. Zung depression score | | | | | | | | | | | | | | 1.00 | -.61[c] | -.52[c] | -.38[c] | 38.62 | 9. |
| 15. Affect balance score | | | | | | | | | | | | | | | 1.00 | .37[c] | .33[c] | 7.13 | 2. |
| 16. Self-rated physical health | | | | | | | | | | | | | | | | 1.00 | .48[c] | 4.07 | . |
| 17. Self-rated emotional health | | | | | | | | | | | | | | | | | 1.00 | 4.01 | . |

a. $p < .05$;  b. $p < .01$;  c. $p < .001$.

daily activity dependencies. Possibly, the items included in these two scales were not sufficiently comprehensive, or the parents' ability to perform the scale tasks was of less consequence than their actual performance or the facility with which they performed the tasks. Alternatively, some children may tend to magnify the parent's functional limitations as a result of their "filial anxiety," and correspondingly perceive the care situation and its outcomes more negatively (Cicirelli, 1983). The latter interpretation has some support from the strong bivariate correlations between children's perceptions of the elder's limitations and their negative perceptions of the care situation.

### Predictors of Caregiving Effectiveness

The selection of predictor variables from each of the three categories for the regression analyses was based on the strength of their bivariate correlations with caregiving effectiveness and their intercorrelations. Although the predictor variables were intercorrelated, the strength of the relationships was not at a level to indicate that multicollinearity was an issue.

A hierarchical multiple regression procedure was used in which variables related to the elder parent's impairment and community resources were entered first as a block, and then caregiver characteristic variables were entered in stepwise fashion. This procedure allowed us first to ascertain the independent effects of parental impairment and community resources on family caregiving effectiveness and, second, the effects of the caregivers' characteristics after controlling for the parents' impairments and the use of community resources.

As data presented in Table 4.1 (Model 1) show, both elder impairment variables made a significant and unique contribution to the explained variance (17%) in family caregiving effectiveness. The inclusion of community resources in the equation also had a significant effect and added 8% to the explained variance in the study's outcome.

As Model 2 in Table 4.3 shows, all four caregiver variables made a significant contribution and, together with the other predictor variables, accounted for 44% of the variance in caregiving effectiveness. Findings thus indicate when the parent's helping network did not include a mix of informal (family, friends, and neighbors) and formal supports, children perceived the family as less effec-

TABLE 4.3

Regression of Caregiving Effectiveness with Elder Impairment,
Community Resource, and Caregiver Variables

| Domain/Variable | Model 1 | | | Model 2 | | |
|---|---|---|---|---|---|---|
| | Beta[a] | $R^2$ | $R^2$ Increase | Beta[a] | $R^2$ | $R^2$ Increase |
| Elder's impairment | | | | | | |
| mental limitations | −.25** | .11 | | −.05 | | |
| physical limitations | −.30** | .17 | .06 | −.07 | | |
| Community resources | | | | | | |
| informal and formal | .29** | .25 | .08 | .24** | .25 | |
| Caregiver characteristics | | | | | | |
| can't meet all elder's care needs | | | | −.21** | .34 | .09 |
| negative perceptions of care situation | | | | −.28** | .40 | .06 |
| seek to avoid guilt | | | | .21** | .45 | .05 |
| self-rated physical health | | | | .19** | .48 | .03 |
| Adjusted $R^2$ | | .24 | | | .45 | .20** |

a. Standardized partial regression coefficients.
*p < .05; **p < .01.

tive at caregiving. Also, when caregiving children perceived their physical health more negatively and had intrapsychic difficulties with the care situation, they viewed family care as less effective. Finally, the beta coefficients shown in Model 2 indicate that only the caregiver characteristics and community resource variable were significant predictors of caregiving effectiveness. Therefore, the children's intrapsychic difficulties and their perceptions of the use of parents' informal and formal assistance appears as more important than perceived parental impairment in predicting caregiving effectiveness.

### Discussion and Implications

Our research differs from most prior studies in that it sought to explain the adult children's perceptions of the family's effectiveness at caregiving rather than their care-related burdens or strains. Our underlying assumption was that families have the capacity to resolve problems in meeting an elderly relative's care needs effectively. However, family effectiveness varies in relation to factors such as the quality of their relationships, their ability to set realistic goals, and the manner in which the problem situation is defined. In this chapter our major objective was to ascertain the relative importance of the caregiving children's personal characteristics, such as their subjective burdens associated with parent caring, vis-à-vis their perceptions of parental impairment and the use of community resources in explaining caregiving effectiveness. We viewed these three elements and their interrelationships as focal in determining the family's ability to sustain the parent's long-term care in the community.

Study findings lent support to this approach and the results of correlational analysis showed significant relationships between parental impairment, community resources, the children's definition of the care situation, their subjective burdens, and their personal well-being. More specifically, when elderly parents were more functionally impaired, the children tended to report difficulty finding or using services from community agencies. This suggests less reluctance on the part of some families to use community health or social services than other studies have found (Frankfather et al., 1981; Montgomery et al., 1985). Instead, the availability of community health and social services may be limited, even for the more severely impaired aged, or family members may be hampered in their search for services by a lack of knowledge about community resources or by difficulties negotiating for services with an often fragmented bureaucratic system (Sussman, 1977). Alternatively, the children's reported difficulty may be attributable to their parents' reluctance to accept or use agency services despite the children's interest or encouragement.

In any case, further research is clearly needed on when community services or formal assistance are sought and by which member(s) of the family. It is possible that the *timing* of service introduction is critical. For example, elderly persons with moderate rather than severe impairments may be more amenable to using community services, possibly because they have the resources needed to adapt to service initiation and to service providers. Conversely, when the elderly incur multiple and severe impairments and family caregivers are more burdened by escalating care demands, they may be less willing to accept an unknown element into an already complex and stressful situation, or less able to muster the resources needed to develop viable relationships with the community service system and its service providers.

It is also interesting to note that study data showed three of the four parental impairment variables were unrelated to the use of more diverse types of assistance from informal caregivers as well as formal service providers. Only the parent's number of personal care dependencies was weakly and negatively associated with the use of formal and informal sources of assistance. Furthermore, the bulk of the formal service providers were paid paraprofessionals (for example, a housekeeper or companion) rather than staff from community service agencies. Given that the average income for adult children was relatively high (that is, $20,000 to $30,000 annually), families in this study may have been able to purchase assistance, and their perceived need for this help was apparently colored by factors apart from the parent's functional impairments.

It seems, then, that impaired elders and caregiving families who have the resources to purchase services may introduce them at an earlier point and for various reasons apart from the elder's personal care limitations. In contrast, community health and social service agencies often target and provide services to more impaired aged whose serious disabilities and more extensive care needs command their attention and limited resources (Coulton & Frost, 1982; McAuley & Arling, 1984). Unfortunately, the effectiveness of health and social services in preventing or slowing the impaired elder's decline may be compromised when services are introduced under these more dire circumstances.

Our findings also support those from previous studies documenting the importance of the caregivers' subjective appraisal of the care situation and their subjective or intrapsychic burdens related to caregiving. Caregiving children who defined the care situation more negatively, that is, as difficult, unpredictable, and overwhelming, felt the family was less effective at caregiving. Similarly, children who felt they could not meet all the parent's care needs, who rated their physical health more negatively, and who sought to avoid feeling guilty about the care situation also viewed family care as less effective. Feelings of guilt were not uncommon among the study's caregiving children, almost half of whom said one of their care-related goals was to avoid feeling guilty about the parent's situation and care needs.

Several explanations have been offered for the subjective burdens and intrapsychic difficulties of adult children caring for an aged parent. Blenkner (1965) attributed them to a "filial crisis" that occurs in most individuals in their forties or fifties. At this point, adult children come to realize that their parent(s) may need some support from them and can no longer simply serve as providers of support and assistance to their children. When children accept the parent's dependency needs and can be depended upon to meet them, they achieve "filial maturity." In her approach, children who do not meet their parent's dependency needs, and consequently feel guilt, should not necessarily be absolved of that guilt by mental health workers. According to Blenkner, not all guilt is neurotic and, in fact, can have salubrious effects if it serves to impel positive behavior changes (that is, behaviors that gratify the individual as well as others who are affected by the individual's behaviors).

A quite different perspective on the guilt of adult children is presented by Jarrett (1985), who attributes it to a cultural paradigm of familial togetherness and affection that may have little basis in actual family behavior. He cites several studies indicating that caregiving has a negative impact on family bonds and understandably so because caregiving demands may overextend the structural and functional capacity of today's families to provide long-term care. The proposed solution is to regard family ties as a set of formal relations that impose rights and obligations but cannot command affection. Thus affection should not be seen as the basis for caregiving because adult children who do not feel it for the parent or find it dissipated by caregiving are likely to experience guilt or despair.

Elaine Brody (1985) provides a third explanation for the guilt of adult children. In her view the children's guilt is also derived from a cultural myth, which is "Nowadays children do not take care of elderly parents as was the case in the good old days." The reason for the myth's persistence is that it contains a kernel of truth. That is, children cannot and do not care for their parents with the total commitment, devotion, and care that the parent gave to the infant and child. It is the disparity between the expectation that they should and the "unavoidable realities" of parent caring that produces guilt.

This perspective, while attempting to eliminate or at least eluci-date one cultural myth, could inadvertently perpetuate another; that is, romanticizing the early-life parent-child relationship as one of total commitment, devotion, and care. In all likelihood, elderly parents who are now recipients of care from their child(ren) occa-sionally felt anger, resentment, and frustration when they were raising and caring for their children. In essence, child rearing has certain "unavoidable realities," just as parent caring does.

It is quite possible that, in general, dependency relationships involving caregiving and continual expenditures of personal time and resources on another's behalf have the potential for eliciting negative feelings. Such feelings can be exacerbated by a host of fac-tors, some of which include personality traits of the caregiver and care recipient, the history of their relationship, competing role demands, the presence of uncooperative kin, and a lack of support-ive community services. Adult-child caregivers who experience these negative feelings may, as a result, feel guilty because they are meeting the letter of the law by performing instrumental tasks for the parent, but not its spirit. That is, the children are giving care, but without affection, with their affection for the parent sorely tried by caregiving, or without constant, unwavering affection.

The source or cause of the guilt experienced by adult children is of great interest and concern to practitioners seeking to intervene in a manner that will alleviate the intrapsychic burdens of adult chil-dren. Blenkner's functionalist stance, which regards some guilt as having a legitimate basis and as being useful to practitioners' for motivating children to fulfill their filial obligations, does not seem to be widely shared. Instead, short-term group or individual therapy with adult children that is directed to relabeling, reframing the problem, or cognitively restructuring maladaptive belief systems is more commonly advocated (Altschuler et al., 1985; Jarrett, 1985; Oliver & Bock, 1985; Pratt et al., 1985; Schmidt, 1980). Clinical reports on these interventions indicate that altering the children's perceptions of the parent and their relationship provides psychological relief and enhances the children's ability to cope with the caregiving situation more effectively.

Our results lend support to both the prevalence of intrapsychic burdens among caregiving adult children and the relationship of these burdens to lower levels of psychological well-being and care-giving effectiveness. However, caution is needed when generalizing the findings from this research in view of the restrictive nature of the study's sample. The sample was purposely limited to widows and married couples living independently with at least one proximate adult child who provided care. Furthermore, the majority of the elderly parents were not seriously impaired. Whether similar findings would occur for noncaregiving adult children, among adult children of widowers, in shared household contexts, or when the elderly parent had more numerous and severe impairments is unknown.

# 5

# The Impact of
# Family Relationships on
# Perceived Caregiving Effectiveness

ALOEN L. TOWNSEND
LINDA S. NOELKER

The previous chapter focused on the role of the parent's impairment, community resources, and the adult-child caregiver's individual characteristics in predicting the child's perceived caregiving effectiveness. This chapter also focuses on perceived caregiving effectiveness, but it examines the importance of family relationships, rather than individual characteristics, in determining effectiveness.

This interpersonal, more systemic view of caregiving is one that has often been slighted by concentration on individual caregivers, particularly primary caregivers. To a large extent, caregiving research has examined the relationship between an individual adult-child caregiver and parent rather than relationships among care providers. The evidence regarding centralization of caregiving responsibilities on one person is very limited, but suggests that even when one person assumes primary responsibility, more than one person typically helps, particularly when an adult child is the primary caregiver for a widowed parent (Johnson & Catalano, 1983; Morris & Sherwood, 1983-1984; Noelker & Wallace, 1985; Townsend & Poulshock, 1986).

Research on caregiving to impaired elders has also focused more on instrumental support than on either affective support or the quality of the relationship within which instrumental assistance is provided (Noelker & Townsend, 1985; Quinn & Keller, 1983). Yet, affective ties among primary group members are one of the major features distinguishing the primary, informal system from formal care providers (Litwak, 1985). When the caregiving system consists of more than an isolated dyad, the issue of interpersonal relationships becomes exponentially greater as the number of caregivers increases. In addition, the allocation and execution of caregiving responsibilities take on added complexity related to cooperation, coordination, and communication among care providers. Aspects of relationships that may have enhanced caregiving effectiveness in the dyadic case may become problematic when multiple family members are involved: For example, children who feel less favored by the parent may resent another child's close relationship with the elder, or a close emotional relationship between one child and the parent may inhibit seeking needed assistance from others (Breslau, 1984; Schmidt, 1980).

Such issues are critical if caregiving functions are to be shared successfully (Litwak, 1985), either within the informal system or between the informal and formal systems. For example, family relationships may influence family members' willingness or ability to seek, give, receive, or sustain family assistance; the relationships may themselves be adversely affected by caregiving, potentially jeopardizing the quality and duration of family care; or family relationships may influence elders' receptivity toward, utilization of, or interactions with formal systems.

The connection between children's perceived caregiving effectiveness and three levels of caregiving relationships are explored in this chapter: the dyadic relationship between the adult-child caregiver and the impaired parent; general family relationships, sometimes referring specifically to the child, the parent(s), and any siblings and other times leaving the term *family* undefined; and relationships among everyone involved in the elder's care, including the parent, family and nonfamily informal helpers, and formal care providers.

### Older Parent-Adult Child Relationships

As the older population has grown and concerns about family care to older persons have mounted, increasing attention has been paid to the nature of relationships between parent and adult children in later life. Still, many questions remain about the bases of these bonds, their stability or change throughout the life course, and their implications for family members' willingness or ability to undertake or sustain caregiving (Brody, 1985; Cantor, 1983; Quinn & Keller, 1983). These issues are complicated by demographic and structural changes that increase the ambiguity, complexity, or fluidity of family relationships (Riley, 1983).

There are two dimensions to adult children's relationship to an older parent that have obvious implications for children's perceived caregiving effectiveness. The first is usually labeled affection, although in this chapter we refer to this concept as affirmation, connoting attachment and positive regard. As Cantor (1983) documented, this general feeling of emotional closeness or positive connection does not necessarily mean the child and parent get along well on a daily basis, however.

Bonds of affirmation or affection are often mentioned as at least part of adult children's motivation in caring for an impaired parent (Cicirelli, 1983; Horowitz & Shindelman, 1983; Morris & Sherwood, 1983-1984). Several authors have pointed out, though, that some children provide care in the absence of positive affective bonds (Horowitz & Shindelman, 1983; Ikels, 1983; Jarrett, 1985) or even to try to reverse or atone for an ambivalent or negative relationship (Schmidt, 1980). Robinson and Thurnher (1979) reported about equal numbers of adult-child caregivers describing their relationship to the parent as predominantly positive, neutral, or predominantly negative.

Other work suggests that even if affection is not necessary for the assumption of caregiving responsibilities, affection or affirmation may mediate caregiving stress (Cantor, 1983; Cicirelli, 1983; Horowitz & Shindelman, 1983) or otherwise affect the child's commitment to sustained caregiving (Litwak, 1985). Even this intervening role of affection has been challenged, however (Jarrett, 1985).

Brody (1985) has argued that caregiving is more likely to exacerbate or reactivate old conflicts than to cause new ones. Although some work suggests that caregiving by adult children—particularly when coupled with competing obligations sustained over a long period of time, or when involving serious physical or mental impairment of the parent—has a negative impact on affection between parent and child (Johnson & Catalano, 1983; Noelker & Wallace, 1985; Poulshock & Deimling, 1984; Robinson & Thurnher, 1979), other authors have found most children reporting an improvement in the relationship, which the children attributed to caregiving (Archbold, 1982; Horowitz & Shindelman, 1983; Reece et al., 1983).

The second dimension of the dyadic parent-child relationship with implications for children's perceived caregiving effectiveness is variously labeled filial obligation or reciprocity. Several authors have argued that this dimension, referred to in this chapter as *parent-child responsibility,* is at least as important as affirmation in initiating and sustaining adult children's caregiving efforts (Blenkner, 1965; Horowitz & Shindelman, 1983; Jarrett, 1985; Morris & Sherwood, 1983-1984).

Filial responsibility toward the parent can stem either from general familial norms or from a more personal sense of duty to repay the parent for previous care given to the child (Cantor, 1983; Ikels, 1983; Johnson, 1983). The precise nature of the responsibility, however, is often diffuse and ill-defined, as are its limits (Johnson, 1983; Riley, 1983). Furthermore, filial responsibilities frequently place the adult child in a position of conflict with other norms or values, such as independence, individuation, or obligations to others (Blenkner, 1965; Brody, 1985; Johnson, 1983; Kirschner, 1985).

Four situations appear to be particularly stressful for adult children trying to implement or negotiate their caregiving responsibilities: when the parent is perceived to be too dependent, too demanding or critical, or unappreciative of the child's efforts, and when, for various reasons, the child feels that no matter what is done, it will never be enough (Cicirelli, 1983; Noelker & Townsend, 1985; Reece et al., 1983; Zarit et al., 1980). The first three situations, in particular, highlight the mutual, reciprocal nature of the obligations and expectations involved in the caregiving exchange (for example, the parent is expected to do what she or he can independently or to express gratitude for what others do), although the literature on filial responsibility doesn't mention these counter-expectations for the parent. We do not know to what extent these complaints reflect the parent's actual behavior, the child's behavior, a maladaptive interaction between the two, or distorted expectations or beliefs held by the child.

## General Family Relationships

When there is more than one family member who is either an actual or potential caregiver, increased dependency can provoke a number of family issues. As Brody (1985) points out, this is true regardless of whether the previous family homeostasis was secure or tenuous.

One of the major issues is the allocation of caregiving responsibilities (Frankfather et al., 1981). This entails decisions about what care needs to be provided, how often, and by whom. These decisions can affect multiple family members' lifestyles, future plans, resources, and privacy (Brody, 1985). Adult-child primary caregivers frequently complain that other relatives could do more for the elder or that they do not adequately appreciate the caregiver's efforts, leading to feelings of inequity, resentment, and anger (Archbold, 1982b; Frankfather et al., 1981; Reece et al., 1983). This actual or perceived lack of support increases caregiving strain (Brody, 1985; Cantor, 1983; Zarit et al., 1980).

Not infrequently, the allocation of caregiving responsibilities or the process of making these decisions reactivates or exacerbates long-standing family conflicts, particularly among siblings (Glosser & Wexler, 1985; Hartford & Parsons, 1982; Schmidt, 1980). Fixed family roles or patterns of interaction may inhibit the ability to adjust to new circumstances (Kirschner, 1985).

Even when the allocation of care is not complicated by perceived inequities or old conflicts, poor communication patterns among family care providers can hinder effectiveness (Cicirelli, 1983; Quinn & Keller, 1983). Caregivers often seem reluctant to ask for help (Calkins, 1972; Zarit & Zarit, 1982). Other family members are often unaware of the caregiver's problems, hesitate to offer help, or are uncertain how to help (Glosser & Wexler, 1985). Efforts intended to be helpful may or may not be perceived as such by others (Rook & Dooley, 1985): For example, some adult-child caregivers report feeling bombarded by suggestions (Hartford & Parsons, 1982). Communication becomes even more essential to effective coordination when functions are shared (Litwak, 1985), especially in a situation such as parent caring in which expectations and obligations are ambiguous, contradictory, or unlikely to be consensual (Quinn & Keller, 1983; Riley, 1983).

In sum, there are many ways in which relationships among family members (caregivers as well as noncaregivers), like dyadic rela-

tionships between the parent and individual children, can either
strengthen or undermine children's perceived caregiving effectiveness by affecting the quantity, quality, or utilization of social support (Rook & Dooley, 1985).

## Relationships with Caregivers
## Beyond Immediate Family

This chapter's concentration on the importance of family relationships to perceived caregiving effectiveness is justified by the
fact that immediate family members (defined as the impaired elder's
spouse and/or adult children) are consistently shown to be the most
common, central, and committed care providers for most older
persons (Cantor, 1983; Comptroller General of the United States,
1977; McAuley & Arling, 1984; Shanas, 1979a). Nevertheless,
we should not forget that many elders in our sample, like other
studies, receive care from a variety of sources, including extended
kin, friends, neighbors, and professional or other paid services
(see previous chapter; Frankfather et al., 1981; McAuley & Arling,
1984; Townsend & Poulshock, 1986).

Many of the family factors previously mentioned as potentially
eroding children's perceived caregiving effectiveness and upsetting the caregiving balance also seem applicable to adult-child
caregivers' relationships with other informal subsystems or with
formal care systems—for example, poor communication patterns,
unclear expectations about responsibilities, and resentment over
perceived inequities. Kaye (1985) cites a number of examples of
how, from home-care workers' points of view, family members
interfere with effective care provision. Conversely, from the family
members' points of view, relationships with other care providers
may also be difficult (Frankfather et al., 1981; Krout, 1983; Sussman, 1977). In addition, Litwak's (1985) elaboration of inher-
ent differences between informal and formal systems highlights a
variety of potentially problematic areas for shared functioning.

Thus potential sources of instability in Perlman and Giele's
(1982) model of a caregiving triad of elder, family, and community
supports can be expanded to include the relationship between parent and child or between the elder and other care providers, relationships among family members, or relationships between family
members and other caregivers. The following analyses use adult

children's perceived caregiving effectiveness to evaluate the impact of these various relationships. As discussed in Chapter 4, the parent's impairment and use of community resources are critical predictors in our model of perceived effectiveness; thus, as in the previous chapter, the importance of family relationships was explored relative to these.

## Method

### Sample

The data came from the study titled "Caring for Elders and the Mental Health of Family Members," funded by the National Institute of Mental Health and described in the previous chapter. As in that previous chapter, the present analyses focus first on comparisons between the 109 adult children who were providing care to an impaired older parent and the 44 children who were not providing care. Then, the subsample of 109 caregivers is used to examine family relationship predictors of perceived caregiving effectiveness.

### Measures

*Caregiving effectiveness.* These analyses used the same dependent variable, CAREGIVING EFFECTIVENESS, as in the previous chapter.

*Elder's impairment.* A description of the measures of the parent's personal care dependencies, daily activity limitations, physical limitations, and mental limitations can be found in the previous chapter.

*Community resources.* The previous chapter also described the measure of use of both informal and formal sources of help (BOTH INFORMAL AND FORMAL) and the item assessing difficulty finding or using community services.

*Family structure.* Family structure was measured in five ways: the number of siblings, the number of siblings who live within one hour of the respondent, the number of sisters, the number of siblings in contact with the respondent at least once a week, and the respondent's birth order. Thus all of these pertain to the children's family of origin, not to their family of procreation, if any. Such structural factors were significant predictors in Klein and Hill's (1979) model of problem-solving effectiveness.

*Parent-child relationship.* The quality of the dyadic relationship between the parent and the adult child respondent was assessed in two ways. One was a three-item index of PARENT-CHILD AFFIRMATION (alpha = .72), measuring the extent to which the child agreed or disagreed that "My (parent) understands what I value most in my life," "My (parent) has always made me feel like a special person," and "Even if my (parent) and I weren't related, we'd still be close friends." Scores could range from 3 (low affirmation or strongly disagreed with all 3 items) to 12 (high affirmation or strongly agreed with all 3).

The second measure was a seven-item index of PARENT-CHILD RESPONSIBILITY (alpha = .80). The items in this index were as follows: "My (parent) is too dependent on me," "Lately I've found myself being more tactful about what I say to her/him," "Even though I do things for her/him, she/he makes me feel as if it's not enough," "I think my (parent) worries too much about her/his health or what might happen to her/him," "It seems as my (parent) grows older, I am becoming more like a parent to her/him," "I often feel upset after I have been with her/him," and "My (parent) tends to treat me as a child rather than as an adult." Scores could range from 7 (low difficulty with responsibility or strongly disagreed with all items) to 28 (high difficulty with responsibility or strongly agreed with all items). Both the affirmation and responsibility indices were formed on the basis of exploratory factor analyses of 15 items related to the adult child's relationship with the parent.

*Family relationships.* Three measures were employed to represent global relationships among family members. One was reported difficulty with tension or strain between the respondent and other family members, and the second was reported difficulty getting family members to cooperate in caring for the parent (both items coded 1 = yes or 0 = no). The third item restricted the definition of family to the adult child respondent, any siblings, and the child's parent(s). This measure asks respondents to reply yes (coded 0) or no (coded 1) to the statement, "If you disagree with someone in our family, they're likely to get angry."

*General caregiver relationships.* The last two variables referred to everyone helping the elder, not just family members. The first was the respondent's response to the statement, "Everyone involved in this situation cooperates to make sure my [parent] gets the care she/he needs" (coded 1 = strongly agree, 2 = agree, 3 = disagree, or 4 = strongly disagree). The second measure was reported difficulty getting the elder to cooperate with people who help (coded 1 = yes or 0 = no).

**Analysis Plan**

Differences between caregiving and noncaregiving adult children in their family structure and family relationships were examined with $t$-tests and $\chi^2$ tests. Bivariate relationships among family characteristics and elders' impairment, community resources, and caregiving effectiveness were addressed with Pearson zero-order correlation coefficients. Hierarchical multiple regression analysis was used to assess the importance of family characteristics, relative to impairment and community resources, in predicting effectiveness. Impairment and community resources were entered first, as a block, then family characteristics were entered in a stepwise fashion using a .15 tolerance level. The importance of family characteristics relative to the individual caregiver's characteristics, as well as to the elder's impairment and community resources, was also assessed with a hierarchical multiple regression analysis. In this analysis, impairment, community resources, and caregiver characteristics were entered first, as a block, then family characteristics were entered in a stepwise fashion with a .15 tolerance level. For discussion of how the impairment, community resources, and caregiver characteristics variables used in these regression analyses were selected, see the previous chapter.

*Results*

**Family Characteristics of Caregiving
Versus Noncaregiving Children**

The first question was whether children who were not helping care for the parent differed from those who were in their family relationships or configuration. Data shown in Table 5.1 indicate only one statistically significant difference between adult-child care-

TABLE 5.1
Family Characteristics of Adult-Child Caregivers (N = 109)
and Noncaregivers (N = 44)

| Family Characteristics | Caregivers | Noncaregivers | |
|---|---|---|---|
| Family structure | | | |
| number of siblings ($\bar{X}$)[a] | 1.51 | 1.61 | $t(107) = 0.30$ |
| number of proximate siblings ($\bar{X}$)[a] | 1.30 | 1.10 | $t(107) = 0.60$ |
| number of sisters ($\bar{X}$)[a] | 0.88 | 1.05 | $t(107) = 0.69$ |
| number of siblings in frequent contact ($\bar{X}$)[a] | 0.63 | 0.50 | $t(107) = -0.58$ |
| birth order (%) | | | $\chi^2 (3) = 0.87$ |
| only child | 17.43 | 20.45 | |
| oldest | 33.03 | 27.27 | |
| middle | 20.18 | 25.00 | |
| youngest | 29.36 | 27.27 | |
| Parent-child relationship | | | |
| affirmation ($\bar{X}$) | 8.68 | 8.34 | $t(139) = 1.04$ |
| responsibility ($\bar{X}$) | 17.22 | 16.36 | $t(143) = 1.17$ |
| Family relationships | | | |
| difficulty with family cooperation (% yes) | 13.76 | 6.82 | $\chi^2 (1) = 1.46$ |
| difficulty with family tension (% yes) | 27.52 | 18.18 | $\chi^2 (1) = 1.46$ |
| disagreements bring anger (% yes) | 28.44 | 34.09 | $\chi^2 (1) = 0.48$ |
| General relationships | | | |
| everyone cooperates ($\bar{X}$) | 2.02 | 1.73 | $t(151) = 2.26^*$ |
| difficulty with elder's cooperation (% yes) | 20.18 | 25.00 | $\chi^2 (1) = 0.43$ |

a. For these measures alone, data from only one respondent per family were used. The N for caregiving children was 78 and for noncaregiving children was 31.
*$p < .05$.

givers and noncaregivers: caregivers being less likely to agree that everyone involved cooperates in caring for the parent. Both groups generally reported high affirmation from the parent, moderate difficulty with their responsibility toward the parent, and few problems with cooperation or conflict. There were no significant differences in the two groups' family structure.

## Bivariate Relationships of Family Measures

The second question was how the measures of family relationships interrelated and their correlation with the elder's impairment, community resources, and perceived caregiving effectiveness. Because of this chapter's focus on the quality of family relationships and low correlations between family structure and perceived effectiveness (data not shown), the measures of family structure were not included in this or subsequent analyses. Because caregiving and noncaregiving children differed significantly in their perceived caregiving effectiveness (see the previous chapter), these correlational analyses and the subsequent multivariate analyses, like the previous chapter, were performed only on the 109 caregiving adult children.

As shown in Table 5.2, most family relationship measures have low correlations with the parent's impairment. The exceptions are statistically significant correlations between the parent-child responsibility index and the parent's physical and mental functioning, between reported difficulty getting the parent to cooperate and all of the measures of impairment, and between family tension and mental impairment.

Family relationships also showed little association with use of community resources. Only difficulty getting the elder to cooperate was positively related to difficulty finding or using community services, and high parent-child affirmation and not reporting difficulty with family cooperation were both related to the use of informal and formal help.

More covariation was evident among the measures of family relationships themselves. The two parent-child relationship measures were most highly correlated, with high affirmation related to lower difficulty with responsibilities toward the parent. Affirmation also correlated significantly but less strongly with the other family measures (except the parent's cooperativeness), and responsibility correlated significantly with all of them, particularly reports of family tension. Problems with family cooperation, tension, and anger were significantly intercorrelated and also related to overall caregiver cooperation.

Last, the parent-child relationship, family relationships, and general caregiver relationships all correlated significantly with perceived caregiving effectiveness, the two parent-child indices hav-

# TABLE 5.2
### Zero-Order Correlation Matrix for Caregiving Effectiveness, Elder Impairment, Community Resources, and Family Relationships (N = 109)

| | 1 | 2 | 3 | 4 | 5 | 6 | 7 | 8 | 9 | 10 | 11 | 12 | 13 | 14 | X̄ | SD |
|---|---|---|---|---|---|---|---|---|---|---|---|---|---|---|---|---|
| 1. Caregiving effectiveness | 1.00 | .18 | .29[b] | -.32[c] | -.37[c] | -.31[c] | .25[b] | .48[c] | -.56[c] | -.34[c] | -.36[c] | -.26[b] | -.33[c] | -.34[c] | 6.86 | 1.88 |
| 2. Elder's personal care dependencies | | 1.00 | .79[c] | -.44[c] | -.42[c] | -.27[b] | -.24[b] | -.04 | -.03 | .04 | .00 | -.03 | .08 | -.32[c] | 4.11 | 1.89 |
| 3. Elder's daily activity limitations | | | 1.00 | -.42[c] | -.59[c] | -.30[c] | -.10 | -.01 | -.12 | .04 | -.09 | .00 | .05 | -.39[c] | 5.29 | 2.38 |
| 4. Elder's physical limitations | | | | 1.00 | -.27[b] | .26[b] | .18 | -.15 | .31[c] | .07 | .09 | -.01 | -.07 | .25[b] | 2.38 | 0.63 |
| 5. Elder's mental limitations | | | | | 1.00 | .21[a] | -.02 | -.10 | .29[b] | -.04 | .21[a] | -.08 | .03 | .36[c] | 0.85 | 1.11 |
| 6. Difficulty finding agency help | | | | | | 1.00 | -.04 | -.06 | .12 | -.03 | .16 | -.08 | .08 | .24[b] | 0.09 | 0.29 |
| 7. Both informal/formal help | | | | | | | 1.00 | .24[a] | -.16 | -.24[b] | -.12 | .17 | -.09 | -.04 | 0.36 | 0.48 |
| 8. Parent-child affirmation | | | | | | | | 1.00 | -.59[c] | -.21[a] | -.38[c] | .33[c] | -.26[b] | -.16 | 8.68 | 1.73 |
| 9. Parent-child responsibility | | | | | | | | | 1.00 | -.29[b] | .50[c] | -.29[b] | .24[a] | .28[b] | 17.22 | 4.21 |
| 10. Difficulty with family cooperation | | | | | | | | | | 1.00 | .35[c] | -.22[a] | .45[c] | .13 | 0.14 | 0.35 |
| 11. Family tension | | | | | | | | | | | 1.00 | -.48[c] | .20[a] | -.23[a] | 0.28 | 0.45 |
| 12. Disagreement brings anger | | | | | | | | | | | | 1.00 | -.23[a] | -.09 | 0.72 | 0.45 |
| 13. Everyone cooperates | | | | | | | | | | | | | 1.00 | .05 | 2.02 | 0.76 |
| 14. Difficulty with elder's cooperation | | | | | | | | | | | | | | 1.00 | 0.20 | 0.40 |

a. $p < .05$; b. $p < .01$; c. $p < .001$.

91

ing the strongest correlations. Thus on a bivariate basis caregiving effectiveness was significantly related to affirmation from the parent, less difficulty with parent-child responsibilities, fewer reports of difficulty getting caregivers or the elder to cooperate, and less family tension and anger.

## Multivariate Analyses

The third question, the importance of family relationships to perceived caregiving effectiveness relative to the elder's impairment and the use of informal and formal help, was assessed through a hierarchical multiple regression. Based on the correlational analysis and our interest in both parent-child and more general family relationships, four measures were included: the two dyadic indices (PARENT-CHILD AFFIRMATION and RESPONSIBILITY), general cooperation among caregivers (EVERYONE COOPERATES), and the elder's cooperativeness (ELDER COOPERATES).

The results of this regression are shown in Table 5.3. To reiterate briefly the results from the previous chapter, the model including the elder's impairment and use of informal and formal services (Model 1) accounted for 25% of the variance in perceived caregiving effectiveness. The elder's mental and physical limitations and the use of community resources all accounted for significant variance.

When family relationships were added to this model (Model 2), the explained variance substantially increased (to 48%). Five of the seven measures had significant beta coefficients: the elder's physical limitations, use of informal and formal help, parent-child responsibility, and cooperation from both the elder and caregivers. Affirmation came close to statistical significance ($p = .06$). Adjusted for the different number of predictors in the two models, the inclusion of family relationships accounted for 21% more variance than measures of impairment and community resources alone, a significant increase.

Although family relationships clearly account for a significant portion of the variance in perceived caregiving effectiveness, controlling for both the parent's impairment and the use of informal and formal help, the fourth question of interest is the importance of family relationships relative to individual characteristics of the caregiver. The results of a hierarchical multiple regression analy-

TABLE 5.3

Hierarchical Multiple Regression of Caregiving Effectiveness on
Elder's Impairment, Community Resources and Family Relationships

| | Model | | | | | |
|---|---|---|---|---|---|---|
| | 1 | | | 2 | | |
| Domain/Variable | Beta[a] | $R^2$ | $R^2$ Increase | Beta[a] | $R^2$ | $R^2$ Increase |
| Elder's impairment | | | | | | |
| mental limitations | −.25** | .11 | | −.14 | | |
| physical limitations | −.30** | .17 | .06 | −.18* | | |
| Community resources | | | | | | |
| informal and formal | .29** | .25 | .08 | .17* | .25 | |
| Family relations | | | | | | |
| parent-child responsibility | | | | −.21* | .38 | .13 |
| everyone cooperates | | | | −.23** | .44 | .06 |
| elder cooperates | | | | −.17* | .46 | .02 |
| parent-child affirmation | | | | .19 | .48 | .02 |
| Adjusted $R^2$ | | .24 | | | .45 | .21** |

a. Standardized regression coefficients.
*$p < .05$; **$p < .01$.

sis addressing this issue are shown in Table 5.4. The first model in
this table reprises the relative importance of the elder's impairment,
use of informal and formal help, and the caregiver's characteristics
described in the previous chapter. These 7 measures accounted for
48% of the variance in caregiving effectiveness.

The second model, adding the measures of family relationships,
accounted for 58% of the variance in perceived caregiving effectiveness. Only 3 measures contributed significantly: use of informal and formal help, the caregiver's perception that the elder's
care needs can be fully met, and the sense that everyone involved in
the elder's care cooperates. Comparison of the adjusted $R^2$ values
for the two models, however, indicates that addition of the family
relationship measures does not significantly increase the variance
explained in caregiving effectiveness, beyond that accounted for by
impairment, community resources, and the caregiver's characteristics. Correlations between the measures of family relationships
and caregivers' subjective perceptions of caregiving (data not
shown), and other analyses of our data (Noelker et al., 1984), sug-

TABLE 5.4

Hierarchical Multiple Regression of Caregiving Effectiveness
on Elder's Impairment, Community Resources, Caregiver
Characteristics, and Family Relationships

| | Model | | | | | |
|---|---|---|---|---|---|---|
| | 1 | | | 2 | | |
| Domain/Variable | Beta[a] | $R^2$ | $R^2$ Increase | Beta[a] | $R^2$ | $R^2$ Increase |
| Elder's impairment | | | | | | |
| mental limitations | −.07 | | | −.08 | | |
| physical limitations | −.05 | | | −.06 | | |
| Community resources | | | | | | |
| informal and formal | .24** | .25 | | .17* | | |
| Caregiver characteristics | | | | | | |
| can't meet care needs | −.21** | .34 | .09 | −.24** | | |
| negative perception | −.28** | .40 | .06 | −.14 | | |
| avoid guilt | .21** | .45 | .05 | .15 | | |
| physical health | .19* | .48 | .03 | .11 | .48 | |
| Family relationships | | | | | | |
| parent-child affirmation | | | | .14 | .53 | .04 |
| everyone cooperates | | | | −.17* | .56 | .03 |
| parent-child responsibility | | | | −.15 | .58 | .02 |
| elder cooperates[b] | | | | | | |
| Adjusted $R^2$ | | .45 | | | .54 | .09 |

a. Standardized regression coefficients.
b. Variable that failed to reach required tolerance level for entry.
*$p < .05$; **$p < .01$.

gest that family relationships may have more indirect impact on
perceived effectiveness than these results indicate, through their
effects on caregiver strain.

## Discussion and Implications

Our first notable finding was that caregiving adult children did
not differ in family structure from children who were not providing
care to their parent. This is counter to Ikels's (1983) finding that

caregivers were more likely to be the only or only proximate child. In our sample, there was typically one other sibling in the proximate area who could, potentially, be a caregiver. This discrepancy may reflect the differences in the two samples, however, since Ikels (1983) interviewed adult children of Irish or Chinese ancestry living in the greater Boston area.

Our finding that caregiving children also did not differ from noncaregiving children in their relationship with the parent was consistent, however, with suggestions that the quality of the parent-child relationship is less important than demographic factors in determining the selection of caregivers (Ikels, 1983), that obligation may be as potent a motivation for caregiving as affection (Cicirelli, 1983; Jarrett, 1985), or that some children take on caregiving responsibilities to reverse or overcome long-standing problems with the parent (Schmidt, 1980). Because our data were cross-sectional and obtained after caregiving had been under way for five years, on average, we have no way of knowing whether this parent-child relationship has been affected, either positively or negatively, by caregiving or not caregiving.

If caregiving responsibilities need to change, this lack of difference implies that any barriers to increasing noncaregivers' responsibilities toward the parent more likely will be due to children's individual characteristics, such as their gender and employment status (see Chapter 4), than to their relationship with the elder. Indeed, the most common reason given by our respondents for why someone wasn't on the caregiving network was other responsibilities. This is not to say that the parent-child relationship is unrelated to willingness to care for the parent, but that it is no more or less a factor with the noncaregiving children than with those already providing care in this sample.

The one area in which caregiving and noncaregiving children did differ, though, was that caregiving children were less likely to agree that everyone cooperates to meet the elder's care needs. Several explanations for this difference are plausible. For one thing, caregivers may simply be more aware of difficulties because of their personal involvement in trying to organize and coordinate the parent's care. Particularly when a family contains both caregiving and noncaregiving children, caregivers may also resent what they perceive to be an inequitable situation (Frankfather et al., 1981; Reece et al., 1983). Conversely, noncaregivers may minimize problems with cooperation to rationalize their own nonparticipation or to compensate for guilt.

A second possible explanation for caregivers' greater reports of difficulty getting cooperation could be differences between caregivers and noncaregivers in the size or composition of the parent's caregiving network. However, in this study, caregivers and noncaregivers did not differ in the number of people providing care nor in the use of informal and formal care sources.

Thus these data, combined with those in the previous chapter, showed few differences between caregiving and noncaregiving children. The reasons some children with impaired elderly parents do not directly provide care are clearly in need of further study. They are a group that prior research on family caregiving has overlooked, with few exceptions (Archbold, 1982; Cicirelli, 1983), remaining an unknown factor in the delicate balance of family care.

Turning to our correlational analyses, family relationships generally were uncorrelated with the elder's impairment. The notable exception was the significant relationship between difficulty getting the elder to cooperate with caregivers and all the measures of physical and mental impairment. This finding suggests that home health care for the elder and rehabilitative services to maintain the elder's functioning, when possible, or behavioral therapy (Pinkston & Linsk, 1984) may help alleviate some adult-child caregivers' complaints about getting the elder to cooperate. Adult-child caregivers are often poorly informed about aging in general or their parent's specific health problems and prognosis in particular, and counseling, educational programs, and support groups have been proposed to help caregivers form more realistic expectations of the parent (Hartford & Parsons, 1982; Oliver & Bock, 1985; Robinson & Thurnher, 1979).

Within the measures of family relationships, the strongest bivariate correlation was between high parent-child affirmation and fewer difficulties with parent-child responsibilities. Although our cross-sectional analyses cannot address the causal order between these two, the correlation suggests that responsibilities for an increasingly dependent parent may be easier for the child to assume when the parent-child relationship is a positive, affirmative one or, conversely, successful renegotiation of responsibilities provides interactions that convince children of their competence and value in the parent's eyes.

Our bivariate results also suggested that some aspects of the parent-child relationship may be more sensitive to shifts in the parent's impairments than others. Responsibility was more highly correlated with the elder's physical and mental limitations, for example, than affirmation was. Longitudinal research on this is clearly needed.

The quality of family relationships often has been overlooked by family care research's focus on instrumental assistance (Quinn & Keller, 1983). In our analyses, all the family relationship measures, but particularly those pertaining to the parent-child relationship, were significantly correlated with perceived caregiving effectiveness. Furthermore, the relative importance of family relationships to caregiving effectiveness was evident in the first multiple regression analysis. These results signified that caregiving effectiveness could be undermined by increased physical dependence of the elder, by a change in the mix of informal and formal caregivers, by increased difficulty between parent and child over responsibilities, or by increased problems getting either the parent or others to cooperate.

As discussed in the prior chapter, individual characteristics of caregivers are a critical element in the family caregiving equation. Hence, it is not surprising that research on parent care has concentrated so heavily on understanding these individual-level factors. Our results, however, clearly indicate that future research needs to extend its focus to include the broader context within which individual family members provide assistance. Thus our final results revealed that adult children's perceived caregiving effectiveness depended on a sharing of caregiving responsibilities between the informal and formal systems, the perception that everyone involved cooperated to care for the elder, and the perception that these care arrangements were adequate to meet the parent's need for care.

Although several authors have proposed shared caregiving functions between informal and formal systems (Litwak, 1985; Sussman, 1977), little attention has been paid to family caregivers' evaluations of the quality of such interactions, to determinants of family caregivers' perceptions of the effectiveness of various care arrangements, or to the issue of how family caregivers' expectations and perceptions may compare with those of formal care providers. Our results argue that the process or quality of interaction between informal and formal systems may be as important in determining effective caregiving efforts as the form and structure of their division of labor. What facets of family relationships do our results imply services need to target in order to prevent or ameliorate an erosion of adult-child caregivers' perceived effectiveness? Foremost is the issue of cooperation. Clearly, more information is needed about what caregivers meant by difficulty getting cooperation, because this could refer to behaviors as diverse as someone's lack of involvement, actively refusing to do something, disagreeing about what should be done or how, when, or by whom, or failure to coordinate activities with others. Also, who is seen as the uncooperative party, and what attributions do caregivers make about the causes for this?

Armed with this information, a variety of interventions such as individual or group counseling with caregivers, family counseling, and case conferences between informal and formal care providers seem called for. Depending on the situation, these interventions might try to enhance cooperation through better communication among care providers, clarification or alteration of expectations about who should do what or about what the elder's care needs are, redistribution of tasks, or recruitment and integration of new caregivers.

The second family issue needing attention is the dyadic relationship between older parent and adult child, especially the responsibilities of the child toward the parent. This conclusion is consistent with observations that adult-children's perceptions of later-life responsibilities toward the parent are often ambiguous (Quinn & Keller, 1983), ambivalent (Johnson, 1983), unrealistic (Hartford & Parsons, 1982; Oliver & Bock, 1985), colored by lifelong interpersonal conflicts (Brody, 1985; Brubaker, 1983), or fraught with guilt (Oliver & Bock, 1985). Professional counseling with individual caregivers or with groups of caregivers, as well as caregiver mutual support groups, have been proposed as mechanisms for redefining, renegotiating, or otherwise coping with the parent-child relationship (Brubaker, 1983; Hartford & Parsons, 1982; Oliver & Bock, 1985; Zarit & Zarit, 1982). We would add to this joint counseling with the parent and child, analogous to marital therapy with couples, where appropriate.

In conclusion, some words of caution are in order about the generalizability of our results. First, by design, our sample was restricted to families in which at least one adult child was both alive and living within one hour of the elderly parent. Our conclusions cannot be generalized to elders without children or without proximate children. Second, we limited our analyses to children providing at least some care to the parent; we do not know whether noncaregiving adult children with impaired elderly parents would show similar results.

Third, also by design, the elders were living alone or with their spouses, in a separate household from the adult child. Studies of caregivers living with an impaired parent (Noelker & Wallace, 1985; Soldo & Myllylouma, 1983) suggest the determinants of perceived caregiving effectiveness for interhousehold care may be very different from those for intrahousehold care. Fourth, as described in the previous chapter (Noelker & Townsend), the elders in our study were, for the most part, not severely impaired physically or mentally. More serious impairment, particularly mental impairment, may have more negative impact on family relationships (Poulshock & Deimling, 1984; Zarit et al., 1980).

Fifth, we presented data only from adult children, and comparisons of adult-child caregivers and elderly spouse caregivers (Cantor, 1983; Noelker et al., 1984) suggest that our conclusions, particularly about the role of family relationships, need to be tested with other types of caregivers. Finally, our study, like most others, either focused on a particular subset of family members or used the term *family* very broadly. Considerable work is needed to understand how families and other care providers define significant family members and the relevance of these distinctions for perceived caregiving effectiveness.

# PART III

# Community-Based Services

## 6

# Homemaker-Home Health Care and Family Involvement

## ELLIE BRUBAKER

Elderly individuals receiving home health care attempt to remain in the community and, to the greatest possible extent, maintain continuity of physical functioning and lifestyle. For many older persons, continuity of lifestyle would indicate a continued relationship with family members. Do home health care agencies acknowledge the involvement of family members when initiating services with older clients?

Within this chapter the assessment process completed by homemaker-home health care agencies will be examined. Findings are reported concerning attention to family involvement when determining older clients' needs for services.

### *Literature Review*

The majority of older persons have relationships with family members (Shanas, 1979b). Even those who require formal services have likely sought and received help from their families prior to requesting formal services (O'Brien & Wagner, 1980). Most elderly individuals prefer to receive help from their families prior to requesting formal services. In addition, most family members expect to and do provide needed help to their older members (Seelbach & Sauer, 1977). Consequently, at the time that home health care services are initiated for elderly clients, the older clients and their families may be involved in meeting the aged person's needs. If services are begun, the home health aide may be one part of a trio providing services to the elderly client.

The home health care agency seeking to provide appropriate services to clients cannot do so without information regarding specific services needed. In order to obtain this information, the service provider must assess the situation in which the client is involved. For example, knowledge about a client's social support system provides information about factors contributing to the client's problems as well as about potential resources to deal with those problems. If service providers lack information about clients' social environments, their assessment of the needs of clients may be limited to the confines of their knowledge. In the case of the elderly, if the homemaker-home health care agency believes that the old do not have informal resource systems, questions concerning supports from family are unlikely to be asked.

The extent to which home-care workers assess older family relationships may be influenced by various factors. Although the literature does not provide information concerning this issue, characteristics of the practitioner and agency-related factors may be related to a practitioner's assessment procedures. The literature does not deal with the influence of agency-related factors on homemaker-home health agencies' assessment procedures.

Although assessment is an ongoing aspect of service provision, assessment prior to intervention will likely determine what services will be provided and how they will be carried out. Since the goal of assessment is "to facilitate intervention, it seems logical that the bulk of the assessment efforts fit in toward the beginning of the intervention process" (Fischer, 1978: 249). Because of its impact on subsequent service provision, assessment discussed in this chapter will refer to investigation as it takes place prior to the plan for and delivery of services.

Lowy (1985) states that the purpose of assessment is to determine what "goals" need to be set and what "action" needs to be taken by the practitioner. In gathering information prior to providing services to the client, the practitioner will examine the situation to determine what unmet needs or problems exist, what causes those needs, and how those needs can be met or prevented.

In order to examine the causes of problems, the professional must investigate the client's situation, including relationships to significant others. To assume that a complete assessment can take place without utilizing an ecological approach is to assume that clients exist without being influenced by their environments. This, unfortunately, is the approach of some professionals. For example, Hartman (1981) laments the lack of a sociological perspective on the part of social workers even after a thorough assessment has taken place. If service providers, as Hartman suggests, ignore others significant to the client following a thorough investigation, they are certainly likely to do so if attention was not directed to those individuals during the assessment process.

Because the elderly client is influenced by informal relationships and the majority of older persons do have informal support systems (usually extended family), assessment of family relationships and helping patterns is important. Without assessing the context of the client's situation, the practitioner may be unable to deal with problems as they arise. Consequently, the homemaker-home health agency requires information concerning those with whom the client relates. For example, the service provider may question the client about help received from children but not discover that the older client's siblings are involved in meeting the client's needs. Research indicates that siblings of the elderly do meet needs (Scott, 1983). Without this information, an existing resource system may be interfered with or a potential resource system may not be activated.

The older clients' needs generally have been influenced by and influenced others to whom they relate. The informal networks that the elderly have formed cannot help but be related to their functioning in some way. It is beneficial for professionals to view the elderly person as someone "who has lived through the process of life in a family unit" (Kelly et al., 1977).

In addition to an awareness that older clients often do interact with family members, the practitioner must gain information about what those relationships involve. Snow and Gordon (1980) emphasize that the transactions between clients' social networks are important and if examined, can reveal a good deal of information about the individuals involved in those transactions. For the service provider seeking to gain a complete picture of clients and their environments, the fact that older individuals have family relationships is not enough information. The client must be viewed as an individual with unique relationships and idiosyncratic ways of handling those relationships. The practitioner who lacks this perspective when intervening with older clients may be unable to provide services appropriately.

> Attempts at change—must be approached with the recognition that networks, as well as individuals, are set in a complex structure, and that not to address this complexity may seriously limit our interventions or render them harmful or ineffective. . . . In addition, network manipulations carry with them risk as well as benefits, for naive intrusions into the social world can unwittingly cause more harm than good, especially if we do not take the individuals' view and experiences into account. (Snow & Gordon, 1980: 465-466)

Unless the homemaker-home health caregiver has information about the extent of family involvement and its content, necessary other information, such as support provided or family history, will not be obtained.

Family problems can be more successfully dealt with, and services more accurately planned, when specific information is gained. In order to gain the information necessary to guide service provision, both older clients and their family members can be contacted. Rosen (1975) describes how information gained from elderly clients concerning their relationships with their families facilitated services provided to those clients.

In addition to questioning older clients about their support systems, it is also possible for the homemaker-home health care agency to request permission to contact the family. It may be that the older person has overstated or understated the amount of help received from informal support systems. For example, the older client could report that the family is providing help when in fact little help is forthcoming (Brody et al., 1978). This may occur out of loyalty to the family so that the practitioner will not realize that the family has not provided the help expected by the older client. The elderly client may state that the family is not helping when in fact they are providing support. This could occur if the support is less than expected by the elderly person or if the older person misunderstands the service provider's questions. The older client may have family who are willing to provide help to their elderly relative, but are unaware that help is needed. The aged relative may dislike the thought of becoming more dependent or may have difficulty asking family members to provide help. However, if help is indicated, the older individual may prefer that family members provide it as opposed to professionals. Without gaining information from significant family members, these issues cannot be clarified. In addition, gathering information from the family allows them to express their concerns. Blazer (1978) refers to the importance of facilitating family members in handling their reactions to the aging process. Family members can benefit from the chance to express their feelings within a professional-client relationship. Roozman-Weignesberg and Fox (1980) report successful groups for adult children who were allowed to deal with feelings regarding aged parents.

Leonard and Kelly (1975: 115) describe a mental health program which, when dealing with community-based elderly clients, involves in the assessment process family and professionals whom the older client knows. They report that this practice has two functions: "(1) it is helpful for the patient to have people whom he knows and trusts involved in what may turn out to be the plan for the rest of his life; (2) it extends the responsibility and ultimate solution to those most able to assist the patient." Consequently, attention to the family and client during the assessment phase of service provision has numerous benefits to both of those parties as well as to the practitioner in providing services.

Perhaps the most important aspect of assessment involves a determination of potential informal resource systems to provide for the needs of elderly clients. Without this information, the practitioner cannot plan for service delivery with the assurance that formal services are on target or even necessary. The provider may be duplicating services planned by the family, possibly increasing costs to taxpayers as well as violating the expectations of older families. Lack of information in this area also interferes with the ability of service providers and family members to plan services jointly, thus hampering service delivery tailored to the individual needs of the older clients and their families.

One of the greatest difficulties for the service provider lacking information about family-helping patterns is that service providers and family members may not come together to provide services to older individuals in the community successfully (Blenkner, 1969).

Service providers who do not contact family or who contact only spouses or children may be unable to work with supportive others significant to the elderly client. For example, a sibling may be providing care and wish to continue that, but find their services taken over by a formal agency. Without contacting the sibling, the chance of coordinating services with that family member may be lost.

The literature points to the advantages of service providers sharing responsibilities for service tasks with clients' informal support systems. Streib (1972) recommends that practitioners and family members join together to "share functions" of service delivery. Tiejen (1980) points to the benefits of service providers working with clients' social networks. Services jointly provided allow the practitioner, older client, and adult family members to meet together, determine the needs of elderly clients and their relatives and to distribute tasks based on resources and ability to meet older clients' needs. This approach has benefits for the older client, the family, and the service provider.

Hayslip et al. (1980: 177) suggest that when home-care needs occur, social service "agencies, rather than attempting to displace the family, might provide in-home counseling for individuals and/ or families, thus integrating the agency into this informal network." Stafford (1980) describes a program in which families were provided information about their elderly relatives, with the outcome of some shared responsibilities between family and practitioners. "Incentives" can also be provided (i.e., financial help, "respite care") to families of older persons in order to help them take responsibility for their older members in need (Lebowitz, 1979). Litwak (1965) indicates that families can fulfill affective needs and agencies complete instrumental tasks. Johnson and Bursk (1977) state that help to families will increase involvement between older parents and their children.

Hartman (1981: 8) notes that "the family is, in a sense, located between the individual and these larger systems that the family must negotiate to meet the needs of its individual members." The family can be utilized successfully only when the formal agency is aware of its involvement and coordination of services exists. Trager (1980a: 4) suggests that "coordination involves a balanced and harmonious interaction of services directed to effective and smoothly functioning care in an equitable and systematic delivery system." Those services may include help provided by the older client, the family, and a formal service agency.

Services provided by an agency without help from an informal support system may be lacking. Stephens et al. (1978: 40) report that "the picture of a withdrawn and alienated oldster—not unlike our stereotypical view of the aged—is due more to the declining availability of informal support systems than to the aging process itself." It has been suggested that families and other informal social systems have the ability to provide stimulation for older individuals with senile dementia as well as help to continue mental health in the older person (Kelly et al., 1977; Stephens et al., 1978). In addition, Unger and Powell (1980) indicate that informal support systems can provide a client with information about formal supports. The family can act as a "link between the older person and formal community supports. No matter how many community services and supports are provided for older persons, these services only supplement the emotional ties and support from the families" (Silverman & Brache, 1979: 77).

If practitioners and families are to work together successfully in providing services to the elderly in need, their work must be coordinated. The fact that community-based services to the elderly are often disorganized and require coordination has been noted in the literature (Lawton et al., 1985; Friedman & Kaye, 1980; Bradshaw et al., 1980). Lack of attention to the strengths and weaknesses of each helping party prohibits maximization of the benefits of sharing service tasks. Friedman and Kaye (1980: 119) discuss a study of elderly receiving home care from professionals as well as from family. They report:

> That families remain involved with their elderly is clear; nonetheless, in none of the cases monitored did the provider agency evidence any commitment to prepare the family for their role in the homecare relationship, or to draw upon strengths in the maintenance of the plan. In 19% of the cases mentioned, this resulted in disruptive family influences upon the homecare plan.

The disruptions referred to above came from many sources, including the family becoming overly directive due to guilt feelings that someone else was providing services. Families also demonstrated inappropriate expectations as to what the homecare worker would do (Friedman & Kaye, 1980).

Once established and organized, case coordination could be less involved than attempting to provide all the needed direct services for the client. This might reduce the practitioner's immediate workload as well as help clients and families learn to deal with problems on their own so that families could remain involved when future problems occur.

## Sample and Methodology

In order to examine homemaker-home health agencies assessment practices, telephone interviews were conducted with home health care supervisors in a large midwestern state whose agencies are funded through Title III and Aid to Independent Living funds. Supervisors were interviewed because it is generally the agency supervisor who administers policy within an agency. Homemaker-home health agencies funded by Title III and Aid to Independent Living funds were chosen because these agencies provide services to the elderly.

The interview schedule gathered information concerning the respondents, including age, sex, professional training, position within the agency, number of aides supervised, and number of aides within the agency. In addition, questions relative to the respondents' actual practice in assessing family relationships were asked.

The interview schedule requested respondents to respond positively or negatively to six items concerning their assessment procedures. The following items were used to ascertain the respondents' assessment procedures.

(1) When investigating a referral, do you routinely contact the client's spouse (if the client is married); the client's children (if the client has children); or other relatives of the client?
(2) Before you work with older clients, do you routinely assess spouses' reports of older clients' needs; children's reports of older clients' needs; or other relatives' reports of older clients' needs?
(3) As part of your agency's intake process, do you routinely ask for information such as names, addresses, or telephone numbers of spouses of older clients; children of older clients; or other relatives of older clients?
(4) During assessment of older clients' needs, do you routinely question spouses of older clients; children of older clients; or other relatives of older clients?
(5) If family is providing homemaking help to an older client who is referred to your agency, do you ask the family if they want you to help them?

(6) Prior to providing services to an older client referred to your agency, do you attempt to assess how well the client relates to his or her family members?

The possible responses to items 1 through 6 are yes or no. Items 1, 2, 3 and 4 are coded 1 for an answer of yes on each subitem and 0 for a response of no on each subitem. Items 5 and 6 were coded 1 for a response of yes and 0 for a response of no. The theoretical range of values is 1 through 14. The higher the score, the more the respondent attends to information about the family in the assessment process. Conversely, the lower the score, the less the family is attended to in the assessment process. A low score is defined as 0 through 9. A high score would be in the range of 10 to 14.

Answers to the above questions provide a measure of the extent to which homemaker-home health aide supervisors assess family members' involvement with aged clients during the assessment phase of service provision. For example, the supervisor who does not get either the telephone number or address of family members is unlikely to involve those individuals in developing a program to meet the needs of older clients. Specific questions about various family members (spouse, children) provides information about the supervisors' definition of family and about whom they gain information from prior to service delivery.

In addition to the above index, respondents were asked an open-ended question: "When an older person has been referred to your agency for services, what areas do you assess prior to delivering services?" Responses to this question were categorized by the following areas: basic background information; physical/medical; psycho social; and assessment of family and/or clients' perception of need.

*Findings*

The findings indicate that the average supervisor interviewed is in her forties. Most of the supervisors are registered nurses and/or college graduates who have taken one or more workshops or courses in aging. The majority of supervisors have between one and five years of experience as a homemaker-home health aid supervisor. The average supervisor is responsible for five aides. The range of aides employed by the supervisors' agencies is one to 64. Most of the aides within the supervisors' agencies have a high school education.

*Supervisor's scores in the assessment index.* When supervisors were questioned about their assessment of extended family as a helping resource during the assessment process, the range of responses indicating assessment of family helping patterns is 2 through 14. The mean score is 8.83 and the median is 9.00. Of the supervisors, 57% scored in the low category on the assessment index. It appears that the majority of the supervisors' assessment of older family involvement is not thorough. The supervisors' scores are slightly skewed toward less thorough assessment.

*Assessment correlated with age.* When supervisors' assessment of older family involvement is correlated with their age, a significant, negative relationship between these two variables is indicated ($r = -.281$; see Table 6.1). This finding reveals that younger supervisors assess for the existence of older family involvement more thoroughly than do older supervisors. The extent to which the supervisors assess, then, is related to the age of the supervisors.

*Assessment by gerontology courses of workshops taken.* Supervisors' scores on the assessment index were crosstabulated with courses or workshops taken in the area of gerontology. A chi-square analysis reveals that supervisors' scores on the assessment index and their participation in gerontology courses are not significantly related when Yates's correction is applied (see Table 6.2). The phi coefficient (.05) indicates a weak association between assessment scores and courses or workshops taken.

*Assessment correlated with number of aides supervised.* Supervisors' scores on the assessment index were correlated with the number of homemaker-home health aides supervised (see Table 6.1). A significant relationship exists between assessment and number of aides supervised. This relationship is inverse ($r = -.298$). The findings indicate that the fewer the aides the supervisor is responsible for, the more thoroughly she assesses the help extended families give their older relatives. Number of aides supervised is related to the supervisors' assessment.

*Assessment correlated with number of aides within the agency.* Does the number of aides employed by the supervisors' agency influence the thoroughness of her assessment of older family helping patterns? The total number of aides employed by the agency was

TABLE 6.1

Correlation Coefficients of Assessment with Supervisor's Age,
Number of Aides Supervised, and Number of Aides in the Agency

|  | Supervisor's Age | Number of Aides Supervised | Number of Aides in Agency |
|---|---|---|---|
| Assessment | −.2818* | −.2982* | −.2581 |

*Significant at .05.

TABLE 6.2

Assessment by Gerontology Courses

| Assessment | No | | Yes | | | |
|---|---|---|---|---|---|---|
|  | N | % | N | % | N | % |
| Low (0-9) | 6 | 60.0 | 19 | 54.3 | 25 | 55.6 |
| High (10-14) | 4 | 40.0 | 16 | 45.7 | 20 | 44.4 |
|  | 10 | 22.2 | 35 | 77.8 | 45 | 100.0 |

NOTE: Corrected chi-square = 0.00; phi = .05; significance = 1.0.

correlated with the supervisors' scores on the assessment index. There is a significant relationship between assessment and the number of aides within the employing agency (r = .258; see Table 6.1). This is a negative relationship. Therefore, the fewer aides within the agency, the more thoroughly the supervisor assesses older family helping patterns.

*Supervisors' responses to an open-ended assessment question.* When asked what areas they assessed prior to delivering services to older clients, 13 supervisors stated that they ask the older client basic background information (for example, financial status). A total of 41 of the respondents indicated that they question the client about physical/medical information. There were 28 supervisors who responded that their assessment process involves a psychosocial evaluation, and 9 of the supervisors question family and/or older clients to determine their perception of need. It appears, then, that the supervisors' questions focus on physical/medical information to a greater extent than they do on the client's social support systems during the assessment process.

In addition, the respondents indicated that the referral source often influences the questions they ask and whom they contact. For example, supervisors are more likely to talk with family and to determine their input if the family is the referral source than if a physician is the referral source.

*Summary of findings.* The above findings indicate that the home-maker-home health aide supervisors interviewed assess for older family involvement in a less than thorough manner. Three variables are found to be related to the thoroughness of the supervisors' assessments: the supervisor's age, the number of aides supervised, and the number of aides employed by the supervisor's agency. The relationships between assessment and these three variables are all inverse.

## Conclusions and Summary

The literature review indicates the importance of thorough assessment prior to service provision. It is suggested that the lack of a thorough assessment may mitigate against the involvement of family members. If the homemaker-home health agency is unaware of actual or potential family service delivery to older clients, several results may occur: inappropriate intrusion upon family caregiving, ignoring potential family services that are needed by the older client, and/or lack of coordination of services provided to the elderly client. The findings described above have implications for service delivery to older clients and their families, as well as for gerontological education and policy.

The fact that the majority of supervisors did not score within the high category on the assessment index may be related to various factors. Supervisors' assessments were shown to be related inversely to their age, the number of aides they supervise, and the number of aides within their agencies. The fact that older supervisors assess for family involvement less than do younger supervisors may be the result of beliefs by the older age cohort that families are not involved with their elderly members. By the same token, a younger cohort may be more informed concerning this subject. This finding would indicate that the services provided to older clients served by agencies with younger respondents are more likely to provide for greater coordination of formal and informal services, and perhaps less likely to intrude upon established family relationships. This finding has implications for in-service training for homemaker-home health aide supervisors. In-service training that can equalize knowledge of supervisors and encourage them to put information about extended family relationships into practice may result in more older clients receiving successfully combined formal and informal services.

The inverse relationship between number of aides supervised and number of aides within the agency and assessment may point to the fact that an agency with fewer resources is going to look for resources for their clients outside of the agency. It may be that those resources would include family members of the older clients. This suggestion is based on the assumption that the demand for services exceeds the resources of agencies with few aides. However, regardless of the needs of the agency, it is to the benefit of older clients and their extended families that helping relationships are assessed prior to the development of service plans.

The weak relationship between gerontology courses and workshops taken and the extent of assessment of family involvement was not expected. It is assumed that instructors of gerontology courses and workshops provide information about the informal help available within the social networks of older adults. If this information is presented, why is it not incorporated into the practice of workshop participants? This finding suggests the importance of instruction in gerontology being directed toward knowledge for use. If the service provider does not apply information gained from the educational process to practice, it has little benefit for the older clients served. Perhaps the use of experience with academic training may make education more applicable to practice.

The open-ended question dealing with the assessment practices of homemaker-home health aide supervisors indicates that the respondents' agencies do not always have formal procedures for assessing client need. When asked what areas they do assess, some of the supervisors stated that their assessment is based on their referral source. In other words, the type of referral source directs the areas dealt with in the assessment process and may influence thoroughness of assessment. Some supervisors indicated that if a physician referred a client, their assessment would focus more strongly on medical aspects, while if the family was the referral source, assessment might focus on social aspects. However, it is unlikely that an elderly client with medical needs has fewer family caregivers than does an elderly client with another referral source.

Also, needs of older clients do not appear to be assessed uniformly across agencies. For example, only 28 of the supervisors questioned indicated that they request psychosocial information from clients and only 9 supervisors stated that their agencies talked to families. As a result, equality of service provision in this area does not exist in the state in which homemaker-home health supervisors were interviewed. For instance, agency A may question clients for psychosocial information and agency B may not. Therefore, the older client being served by agency A may have family involvement that the service provider acknowledges and works into the service plan. The older client served by agency B may also have family help, but if this help is not assessed, continuation of family services and/or coordination of services provided by the client, family and homemaker-home health agency may be hampered. The client served by agency B, then, may be receiving less appropriate services than is the client served by agency A. The lack of uniform assessment can result in unequal service provision, with duplication of services to some clients and gaps in service to others.

The need for a policy concerning assessment of family involvement by service providers working with the elderly seems apparent. The lack of a stated policy concerning this may in fact have become a policy in itself, a policy that advocates a lack of uniformity in combining informal and formal service provision to the elderly. The effects of this, of course, are to the detriment of elderly service recipients, caregiving families, and formal service providers.

# 7

# Long-Term Care
# Community Services and
# Family Caregiving

JILL QUADAGNO
CEBRA SIMS
D. ANN SQUIER
GEORGIA WALKER

In recent years research has become increasingly focused on the problem of providing adequate long-term care for older persons in need of services, either in institutions or in a community setting. This topic has become a central research concern because of changes in society, which have made it more difficult for families to care for the elderly without intervention by outside agencies. Both Weihl (1977) and Rosenmayr (1977) note that as family care has become less available, the need for well-trained and well-motivated people to perform caregiving services for the elderly has increased. The problem, however, is that the bureaucracy often has neither the resources nor the potential to train personnel to provide the type of care required by the elderly. Because the bureaucracy responds to its own imperatives, its effectiveness in responding to human needs is limited (Weihl, 1977; Smolic-Krkovic, 1977; Munnichs, 1977). In summarizing the main agenda for future research, Streib (1977: 212-213) argues that the important question of how efficiently the bureaucracy serves the client has not received systematic attention.

Subsequent research investigating various aspects of family caregiving and bureaucratic intervention has tended to concentrate on two themes. One group of studies takes the bureaucracy and its goals as the central agenda. This body of research has tended to focus on the bureaucratic goal of reducing costs and improving efficiency of services with delayed institutionalization as a secondary consideration, either for therapeutic reasons or as it relates to cost effectiveness (Davies & Challis, 1980; Applebaum et al., 1980; Eggert et al., 1980; Hodgson & Quinn, 1980; Taber et al., 1980; Zawadski & Ansak, 1983; Yordi & Waldman, 1985). As Applebaum et al. (1980: 350) describe the goals of an evaluation of the Wisconsin Community Care Organization: "Testing whether or not a coordinated community based home care system could reduce expenditures for nursing home institutionalization was a prime evaluation objective."

A second group of studies has concentrated on the burdens of family caregiving (Masciocchi et al., 1984; Montgomery et al., 1985; Johnson & Catalano, 1983). All have found a great sense of burden among those who care for impaired elderly family members. Several of these studies also have pointed to a strong desire for outside assistance among family caregivers (Reece et al., 1983; Cantor, 1983). Yet when formal services have been provided by bureaucracies, they have not proved adequate in significantly reducing burden among family caregivers, and in many instances "the dumping of impaired and frail elderly upon families by professionals has resulted in a mutually disastrous experience" (Sussman, 1985: 440).

The problem is that one set of studies has concentrated on the performance of the bureaucracy, while another has focused on the subjective sense of burden among family caregivers. What is lacking is a systematic investigation of how services provided through a bureaucracy intervene in family caregiving. Do formal services, which caregivers say they desire, truly contribute to a lessening of caregiver burden? If so, exactly what type of services provide relief from burden? For example, do formal services remove the strains of daily care? Do they enhance the ability of caregivers to continue to lead active lives within their communities? If not, why don't they work more effectively? What is there in the structure of the bureaucracy or in the nature of burden that impedes formal services from efficiently performing these tasks?

What is also lacking in much of the literature on family caregiving and bureaucratic intervention is a concern for the elderly themselves, the clients of the bureaucracy. As Landsberger (1985: 5) states, "The heart of the matter [is] the reactions of this generation of elderly individuals whose needs are to be met by the care." The purpose of this study is to investigate how a community-based services program interacts with family caregiving, both from the perspective of the family caregivers and from that of the elderly clients of the bureaucracy.

*Research Methods*

In 1982 the state of Kansas received a waiver of certain Medicaid statutory limitations, allowing it to "finance through the federal-state Medicaid Program non-institutional services for elderly and disabled persons who would otherwise require care in Title XIX certified institutions" (State of Kansas, 1982: i). Under the Medicaid waiver the state was authorized to establish a Home and Community Based-Services Program (HCBS), to be administered by the Department of Social and Rehabilitative Services (SRS) as an alternative to institutional care. Clients applying to Medicaid for assistance were to be evaluated by a team, consisting of a licensed social worker and a registered nurse, who would assess each client's medical and social needs along with his or her functional capabilities and compose an individualized plan of care (State of Kansas, 1982: 27; Squier, 1984: 52). Services to be offered included case management, adult day health services, homemaker services, home health aide services, habilitation services, respite care, personal care services, and hospice care (P.L. 97-35, Sec. 2176 (c) (4) (B); Squier, 1984: 40). The primary purpose of HCBS from the government's perspective was to provide a cost-effective alternative to nursing home care by offering a package of services.

Although some potential clients approached the SRS office for help themselves, in most instances families called upon the Medicaid program because they no longer felt able to care for their elderly family members and planned to institutionalize them. The evaluation team subsequently made the decision either to send the client to a nursing home or to offer them services through the HCBS program. Thus the choice of nursing home care as opposed to HCBS services was made by the evaluation team, not by the clients or their families.

As part of an evaluation of the HCBS program, interviews were conducted with both the client and the client's primary caregiver when they first entered the program (T1). Primary caregiver was defined as the person who assumed the most responsibility for the care of the individual applying for Medicaid assistance. The client assessment instrument included basic demographic information and a group of questions concerning service needs. The caregiver assessment instrument included basic demographic information, questions concerning the caregiver's impression of services the client needed, and four scales measuring various aspects of the caregiver's relationship to the client. The four scales, adapted from Kosberg et al. (in press), included a 7-item Sociability Scale, a 16-item Mental Impairment Scale, a 10-item Interpersonal Relationship Scale, and a 7-item Change in Lifestyle Scale.

Between 12 and 15 months after the first interview, both clients and caregivers were reinterviewed. In addition to the questions included on the first interview schedule, clients at Time 2 (T2) were asked a series of questions relating to the HCBS program. Questions included a listing and evaluation of services received, and several open-ended questions concerning client satisfaction with the program. The caregiver questionnaire at T2 also contained the questions asked at T1, including the four scales plus a detailed assessment of service provision. The focus of these questions was on who provided the services in order to compare those services provided by a professional caregiver from the HCBS program with those provided informally by the informal support network. Caregivers also were asked to evaluate the HCBS program. The interviews were conducted in five counties in Kansas, in six cities, and in surrounding rural areas in those counties.

## Description of the Subjects

### Clients

In the first phase of the study, 109 clients were interviewed, but the total number of clients interviewed at both T1 and T2 was only 43. The high attrition rate was caused by several factors. Some clients died in the 12 to 15 months between interviews; others either dropped out of the program or were removed because of changes in health or in income; some refused to be interviewed a second time; in others their health had declined so significantly that it was impossible to conduct an interview with them.

The clients ranged in age from 22 to 96, with a mean age of 67. The few younger individuals who came under the jurisdiction of the HCBS program were mentally retarded. A total of 78% of the clients were female and 22% were male. In terms of race, 63% were white, 35% were black, and one individual was a Native American. Of the clients, 61% were widowed, 16% married, 7% divorced, and 13% never married.

The three major health problems of the clients (nearly 66%), as reported by their primary caregiver, were senility, stroke, and arthritis. In addition, 38.5% were reported to have heart trouble, 23.1% had a recent fracture, and 23.1% were reported to be at least partially paralyzed.

The vast majority of the clients (69.6%) lived with their primary caregiver. Another 4.3% lived in an adult care home, and 26.1% lived in their own residence.

### Caregivers

In the first phase of the study 53 caregivers were interviewed. There were 23 caregivers interviewed at both T1 and T2. The mean caregiver age was 57, with a range from 21 to 86. A total of 82% were female. In regard to marital status, 39% were married, 17% widowed, 4% divorced, 22% separated, and 17% never married. In terms of labor force participation, 56.5% worked outside of the home. Of those who worked outside the home, 38.5% worked full time and 61.5% were employed on a part-time basis.

Income among the caregivers was low, with 60.9% having a total family income of less than $10,000 per year. This is probably because a very high percentage were single heads of household. Wages, social security, or a combination of the two were the main income sources in these families. In response to the question, "Would you say your household income is adequate to cover the monthly expenses?" nearly 35% responded "rarely" or "never." Thus many of the caregivers were a relatively powerless group of women living with constrained resources, a situation likely to minimize their ability to pay for outside help in taking care of a dependent family member or to bargain effectively with the bureaucracy on behalf of the client.

One-third (33.3%) of the primary caregivers were daughters. Sisters (23.8%) made up the second most significant category of caregivers, with wives and mothers (14.3% each) also accounting for some caregivers. Another 14.4% received help from other relatives. It should be noted that 21 of the clients either had no primary caregiver or did not have a primary caregiver who was willing to be interviewed.

## Results

Although 11 different services are supposed to be available to clients of the HCBS program, as Table 7.1 shows, most of the clients received only one type of service, that of nonmedical attendant. Over 78% had a nonmedical attendant come to their home on a daily basis, and another 15% received the service several times a week. Most of these clients lived in urban areas. Thus it is likely that these figures overestimate the diversity of services received, because Squier (1984) has already shown that even fewer services are offered from the Kansas HCBS program in rural areas.

In spite of the lack of a full program of services, both clients and caregivers expressed overall satisfaction with the program. For those clients with a nonmedical attendant, 81.8% rated the service as "excellent" and 18.2% rated it as "fair." Among the caregivers, 85% rated the nonmedical attendant service as excellent, 5% rated it as "good," and another 10% rated it as "fair" or "poor."

What accounts for the high degree of client and caregiver satisfaction given that the program is not fulfilling its bureaucratically defined goals of providing a package of services? For the clients one factor overwhelmingly overrode all others in explaining their satisfaction with the program: They believed that it allowed them to remain in their own home rather than having to go to an institution. As Table 7.2 shows, in response to the question, "What do you like best about the HCBS program?" 47.6% of the clients answered, "It allows me to remain in my own home." Second to this was the companionship provided, and all other reasons were of only minimal consequence.

TABLE 7.1

HCBS Services Actually Received by Program Clients

| Type of Service | Percentage Receiving Service (N = 42) |
|---|---|
| Chore services | 00.0 |
| Home maintenance | 00.0 |
| Nonmedical attendant | 90.1 |
| Night support | 00.0 |
| Medical alert | 00.0 |
| Hospice care | 00.0 |
| Wellness monitoring | 9.1 |
| Home health aid | 4.5 |
| Adult day care | 9.1 |
| Habilitation | 4.5 |
| Respite care | 00.0 |

TABLE 7.2

What Clients Like Best About the HCBS Program

| Client Response | Percentage (N = 42) |
|---|---|
| Able to remain home | 47.6 |
| Companionship | 21.4 |
| Gives my family help | 9.5 |
| Help with personal hygiene | 7.1 |
| Feel independent | 7.1 |
| Get meals | 4.8 |
| Have cleaner place to live | 2.4 |

In general, caregivers agreed that the major benefit of the program for their family member was that it kept them out of an institution. In response to the question, "How has HCBS helped your relative the most?" 55% responded that it allowed them to remain at home, another 30% stated that it gave them better care than they had previously been receiving, and 5% stated that it increased family contacts.

Caregivers also received personal benefits from the HCBS program. In response to the question, "How has HCBS helped you the most?" 33.3% said they couldn't do it alone, 19% said it gave them time to do other tasks, and 9.5% said it gave them peace of mind.

HCBS services also generally improved family relationships.

As Table 7.3 shows, in response to a question about how the program had affected family relationships, 66% of the caregivers felt that their relationship to the client had improved since they began receiving HCBS services, 19% felt there was no change, and 14.3% felt there had been a negative impact. When clients were asked the same question, 43.6% stated that family relationships had improved, 38.5% felt they had stayed the same, and 18% felt it had a negative impact.

Caregivers' positive evaluation of the program was mostlyl predicated on the fact that the nonmedical attendants did provide real services that lessened their burden. As Table 7.4 shows, although family caregivers continued to provide a substantial amount of care in all categories, paid professionals assisted caregivers with numerous services. The services most often provided by paid professionals were those that directly eased the burden of direct care on family caregivers: grooming (70.6%), personal hygiene (75.0%), housekeeping (54.5%), meal preparation (47.4%), and supervision (31.6%). Whereas previously, aside from some help from other family members, caregivers had carried the whole burden, the nonmedical attendants provided a substantial amount of daily caregiving activities.

As noted above, four scales measuring different aspects of caregiver burden were included on the research instrument. Only a small number of caregivers answered all questions on all scales. With such a small sample, it is difficult to draw generalizations. Nonetheless, the general pattern is one of little or no change between T1 and T2 on three of the four scales.

The Sociability Scale was composed of seven questions evaluating the caregiver's feelings about how pleasant it was to spend time with his or her elderly family member. Using chi-square as a measure of significance, a comparison of caregiver's responses at T1 and T2 showed no significant difference in overall scale score. As shown in Table 7.5, at both points in time caregiver's Sociability ratings were relatively positive. Nearly three-quarters of the caregivers rated the clients as sociable "all of the time" or "most of the time" at T1, and 65% rated them this high at T2. Although there was a decline in perceptions of sociability between T1 and T2, this difference was not statistically significant.

The Mental Impairment Scale measured caregiver's perceptions of the disruptiveness of client's behavior. The results of this scale

TABLE 7.3

Impact of HCBS Program on Family Relationships

| Response | Client Percentage (N = 42) | Caregiver Percentage (N = 23) |
|---|---|---|
| Better family relationships | 43.6 | 66.7 |
| No change | 38.5 | 19.0 |
| Decreased family contact | 15.4 | 4.8 |
| Increased family friction | 2.6 | 9.5 |

TABLE 7.4

Sources of Service Provision

| Type of Service | Who Provides Service (percentage) | | | | |
|---|---|---|---|---|---|
| | CG | OF | FR | PP[a] | O |
| Transportation | 25.0 | 37.5 | 6.3 | 12.5 | 18.8 |
| Housekeeping | 31.8 | 9.1 | 4.5 | 54.5 | 00.0 |
| Minor home repairs | 23.1 | 30.8 | 15.4 | 15.4 | 15.4 |
| Home maintenance | 23.1 | 30.8 | 23.1 | 15.4 | 7.7 |
| Meal preparation | 42.1 | 10.5 | 00.0 | 47.4 | 00.0 |
| Managing money | 61.5 | 30.8 | 00.0 | 7.7 | 00.0 |
| Grooming (washing hair, shaving, and so on) | 17.6 | 11.8 | 00.0 | 70.6 | 00.0 |
| Personal hygiene (dressing, bathing) | 18.8 | 6.3 | 00.0 | 75.0 | 00.0 |
| Supervision for safety | 42.1 | 26.3 | 00.0 | 31.6 | 00.0 |

NOTE: CG = caregiver, OF = other family member, FR = friend, PP = paid professional, O = other.
a. For a few services, the category "paid professional" may have included someone other than the HCBS service provider.

are presented in Table 7.6. There was no significant difference on this scale between T1 and T2. The overall assessment by caregivers was that clients were not extremely disruptive in their behavior, although more than one-third at T1 and 43% at T2 rated them as "occasionally" disruptive. It seems likely that the slight decline in the ratings of clients on the Sociability Scale between T1 and T2 was due to a real increase in the disruptiveness of a few clients.

The Interpersonal Relationship Scale measured the caregiver's sense of psychological burden. The results from the Interpersonal Relationship Scale are depicted in Table 7.7. At T1 caregivers felt

TABLE 7.5
Caregiver's Scores on Sociability Scale, T1 and T2

| Frequency | T1 Score (N = 53) | T2 Score (N = 23) |
|---|---|---|
| All of the time | 32.1 | 30.4 |
| Most of the time | 41.5 | 34.8 |
| Occasionally | 26.4 | 17.4 |
| Rarely | 00.0 | 17.4 |
| Never | 00.0 | 00.0 |

TABLE 7.6
Caregiver's Scores on Mental Impairment Scale, T1 and T2

| Frequency | T1 Score (N = 47) | T2 Score (N = 23) |
|---|---|---|
| Often | 00.0 | 00.0 |
| Occasionally | 34.0 | 43.5 |
| Never | 66.0 | 56.5 |

remarkably positive about their dependent family members, with 72.9% stating they "never" felt angry toward the client or resented the client. At T2 more than half (56.5%) of the caregivers still expressed very positive feelings toward clients, but there was a statistically significant change in affect between T1 and T2. At T2, 34.8% admitted to negative feelings occasionally and 8.7% often. Thus, even though the caregivers' daily burden had decreased, their sense of psychological burden had increased.

At both T1 and T2 caregivers indicated that their lives were definitely limited by the caregiving role. Because of the burden of caring for a dependent family member, they were less able to attend social functions outside the home and to have time for themselves. On the Change in Lifestyle Scale all caregivers said there were limitations on their social lives. They were less able to take part in activities, to visit with friends, and to have time for themselves than they had been before they began caring for a dependent relative.

## Discussion

Although bureaucratic directives specified a package of services that the HCBS program was supposed to offer to all clients in each

TABLE 7.7
Caregiver's Scores on Interpersonal Relationship Scale, T1 and T2

| Frequency | T1 Score (N = 48) | T2 Score (N = 23) |
|---|---|---|
| Often | 2.1 | 8.7 |
| Occasionally | 25.0 | 34.8 |
| Never | 72.9 | 56.5 |

NOTE: Chi-square = 17.75, d.f = 4, p < .001. Chi-square was calculated only from the scores of those responding to all items at T1 and T2, an n of 15.

county in the state of Kansas, most clients received only one service, help from a nonmedical attendant. In spite of this apparent failure of program objectives, HCBS was highly evaluated by both clients and primary caregivers. Client satisfaction with the program was predicated primarily on their belief that HCBS services protected them from going to a nursing home. Caregiver satisfaction stemmed from the fact that the nonmedical attendant did provide many of the services that were supposed to be offered, even though they were not formally categorized as such. Nonmedical attendants unofficially provided Chore Services, Home Maintenance, and Respite Care. These services were especially useful to the families in this study, because many of the primary caregivers were single heads of household who worked outside the home. Most were low-income women who did not have the alternative of hiring outside help available to them. Because the day-to-day burden of care was removed from the shoulders of the caregivers, both they and their elderly family members generally agreed that family relationships had improved.

When asked how the program had benefited them, a fairly high proportion of caregivers said that they couldn't do it alone. Because most caregivers applied to the Medicaid program with the intent of institutionalizing a dependent family member, these results can be interpreted to mean that the HCBS services provided by the nonmedical attendants did make it possible for them to continue to care for their relatives at home.

There were limitations on the ability of the nonmedical attendants to provide relief from the caregiving burden. Although the nonmedical attendants did provide relief for the primary caregiver from numerous daily chores, allowing the caregiver to attend to instrumental tasks, such as going to work, doing grocery shopping, and so on, caregivers' lives were still highly constrained. All of the caregivers indicated that their social worlds had shrunk since they began caring for a dependent family member. It seems likely that the increase in negative feelings toward clients, as measured by the Interpersonal Relationship Scale, may be attributed to an increased sense of burden on the part of the caregivers. Caring for a dependent family member for a short period of time is unlikely to strain interpersonal relationships, but an extended period of care clearly does cause strain and an increased sense of burden.

## Conclusion

There are several conclusions that can be drawn from this study. One important issue concerns measures of burden. The results of this research indicate that burden includes at least two separate and independent components. First, there is the burden of day-to-day caregiving that can be relieved by the provision of services. The instrumental type of services provided by paid professionals free caregivers and provides them with the time to fulfill their usual tasks. It also improves family relationships and helps keep dependent individuals out of institutions. Formal services do little, however, to relieve caregivers' subjective feelings of burden, because their lives are still severely constrained by the caregiver role. It is burden in this second sense, of having one's social world shrink through the long-term responsibility of caring for a dependent relative, that cannot be relieved by formal service provision.

The positive feelings of the caregivers toward the program also have to be interpreted somewhat cautiously. Many previous studies of burden among family caregivers have focused on middle-class women who sometimes quit jobs to assume the caregiving role. In contrast, the caregivers in this study were mostly poor women who did not have the option of quitting work to care for a dependent family member and resume a traditional woman's role. Although the program reduced their instrumental burden, their positive evaluation of it must be taken in the context of the fact that they are powerless individuals with few alternatives to those offered by the bureaucracy. The bureaucracy certainly provided them with an incentive, that of marginal support, to care for a dependent family member at home, but it also forced them to continue to assume a large burden. Some of their increased sense of burden may have stemmed from a feeling of helplessness that there was no longer any chance that their life situations could be improved.

# 8

# Supporting Family Caregiving Through Adult Day-Care Services

## PEGGYE DILWORTH-ANDERSON

In the early 1970s, as a result of the escalating cost of nursing home and hospital care for the elderly, the government began developing a wider variety of community-based long-term care options for the elderly and their families. Among such options emerged the concept of adult day care, which is generally viewed as an alternative to or substitute for institutionalization. Therefore, in the 1970s pilot programs funded through the Social Security Act, the Older Americans Act, the Housing and Human Development Act, and state or local governments began offering adult day-care services on an experimental basis. Although these pilot programs were at the forefront of providing another long-term care option, they nevertheless were developed under a range of mandates and administrative expectations. Thus, as Mace and Rabins (1984) assert, the development of day care was not a part of a comprehensive plan for geriatric services nor has there been a single or formalized model for them.

In general, day services are viewed as a community-based program designed to meet the needs of functionally impaired adults through an individualized plan of care. Day care provides health, rehabilitative, and/or social services to groups of chronically impaired individuals in a central location during daytime hours. The purpose of day care is to maintain, restore, or improve physical and/or mental functioning (National Institute on Adult Day Care, 1984). It usually complements family care and provides relief to families (Arling et al., 1984: 226).

Although it has been suggested that classifying day-care programs into models misrepresents what they are about, some researchers have used their delineations as a reference to help us understand the range of services provided through day care. Weissert (1976), for example, classifies day-care programs into two categories: Model I and Model II. Model I day care provides professionally administered rehabilitative, physical, occupational, and speech and hearing therapy. Model II provides social and psychosocial services such as individual and group counseling, reality therapy, social activities, and arts and crafts. O'Brien (1982) describes day-care programs as having four different models and emphasizes that they are not necessarily mutually exclusive. Model I (rehabilitative) is for the most severely disabled who are provided extensive medical care; Model II (restorative) provides medical and social services to the chronically ill who have mental and physical disabilities; Model III (maintenance) is for those who need supportive health services; and Model IV (protective) is for those elderly with minimal impairments who are in need of basic health and psychosocial support services.

The concept of adult day care in the form of the psychiatric day hospital dates back as early as 1945 in this country (O'Brien, 1982). In 1973, however, fewer than 15 day-care programs were available (Trager, 1980b). According to the Director of the National Institute on Adult Day Care (NIAD), there are about 1,500 programs currently operating, and they serve 10,000 to 15,000 people daily (Ransom, 1985). These programs are dispersed throughout this country, with the fewest in states such as Montana and Wyoming, where there are very few older people. States with a large number of older people, such as Florida, Pennsylvania, Illinois, and California, have the greatest number of day-care programs.

In 1980 the Subcommittee on Health and Long-Term Care of the U.S. House of Representatives Select Committee on Aging conducted a survey to gather general information on day-care programs. Questionnaires were sent to every Medical Assistance Office in all 50 states and to Puerto Rico, Guam, the Virgin Islands, and the District of Columbia. A total of 32 states responded, of which

4 indicated they had no day-care programs. However, among the remaining 28 states in the study, the number of day-care programs available ranged from 1 to 204. Of the 28 states, 93% said their programs are funded by Title XX, 25% are funded by Title XIX, and 25% by both plans. Although the findings from the survey show that only 11 of the 28 states in the study had done a needs assessment on day-care programs, 93% of them claimed that with full funding they could return a large percentage of the current nursing home population to their communities. A total of 50% indicated they have standards for adult day care, 39% have standards for licensure, and 21% have standards for both. The states listed 24 different services they provide the elderly through adult day care. In order of frequency, providing nutrition, social services, health services, and transportation were mentioned by at least three-fourths of the states. Those clients receiving these services have a median age of 75, the majority are women, and their most frequent occurring health problems include mental disorders, heart disease, strokes, arthritis, blindness, and hearing impairments.

Because approximately two million Americans are victims of Alzheimer's disease or related disorders and most of these are elderly, Mace and Rabins (1984) conducted a survey to determine how and to what extent day-care programs address these clients. Included in the study were 346 day-care programs serving various proportions of mentally impaired clients. These programs provide a variety of services to the elderly and their families. Over 75% of them provide family counseling, nursing assessment, activities of daily living assessment, psychosocial assessment, and nursing care. At least 40% of them offer physical, art, and music therapy. The results from the study show that family demands for a respite resource encouraged the day-care providers to establish services for clients who suffer from different types and degrees of mental impairments. The findings also show that programs with the most disabled clients tend to accept or keep the most severely impaired people.

Although it is obvious that there has been an increase in the number of day-care services since the early 1970s, Goldstein (1982: 157) asserts that program development, adequate funding, standards, and regulations have been slow to develop and erratic in meeting the needs in the community. In 1984, NIAD developed and published national standards for adult day care. Although

NIAD states that it is not a governing body, the day-care standards were developed in response to the growing number of programs and the diversity and disparity among existing state standards. Under the section on services-essential components of care, NIAD's standards mention addressing the needs of the elderly and their families. Specific services to the elderly include personal care, social leisure, physical and educational activities, health monitoring, nutrition, transportation, emergency services, counseling, and community referral. Essential services to families include counseling and community information and referral. NIAD suggests that counseling should be made available to all clients and appropriate family members and that it should be provided on an individual and group basis. Support groups for families are also under the heading of providing counseling services to families. In regard to community relationships NIAD standards point out that through information and referral, clients and families can be assisted in learning of and using community resources to meet their needs.

### The Need for Day-Care Services

The relationship between advancing age and disabling chronic diseases in later life clearly creates a demand for different types of long-term care, especially services such as adult day-care programs. This demand becomes even more important in light of the fact that both the actual number and proportion of older people have significantly increased in the last 20 years. Just in the last decade alone, when the general population increased by 6.3%, there was a 23% increase in the number of older people, with the largest amount of this growth in the age group 75 years old and over (U.S. Bureau of Census, 1980). This growth is expected to increase for the rest of the century: People aged 64-75 will increase by 23%, those 75-84 by 57%, and those 85 and over will increase by 91% (Brotman, 1980). Therefore, although in 1983 the elderly represented 11.7% of the population, by the year 2000 this number is expected to change to 13%.

As our society grows older—due in great part to advancing medical science, which has decreased deaths resulting from infectious and acute illnesses—we have created a society of people who live longer but suffer from many more chronic diseases. However, only

5% of the elderly are institutionalized, and in 1980 the percentage increased dramatically with age, ranging from 2% for persons 65-74 years and 23% for persons 85 and older. Among the noninstitutionalized at least 30% suffer from chronic disabling diseases that require them to have some degree of long-term care and support (Comptroller General of the United States, 1977). It is suggested that the majority of potential day clients are found within the 30% of noninstitutionalized elderly people who are mentally and physically dependent. A large proportion of this segment are women, their median age is in the 70s, and they suffer from major chronic diseases that greatly impair their level of functioning and independence.

Regardless of whether or not day-care services are available to meet the needs of those older people described above, most of the dependent elderly receive a substantial amount of care and support from their families (Brody, 1981; Shanas, 1979a, 1980; Streib & Shanas, 1965; Weeks & Cuellar, 1981). The high level of support families provide the elderly is in part reflective of the availability of family. At least two-thirds of those 65 and older have children; 94% of those with children have grandchildren; 46% are great grandparents (Shanas, 1980). Several researchers (Barney, 1977; Brody et al., 1978; Maddox, 1975) have found that the presence of the family in providing support to chronically ill older people is a determining factor in delaying and often in preventing institutionalization. All of the support families give to their frail and chronically ill older members, however, is not without stress and strain.

Cicirelli (1981) reports that a substantial portion of the caregivers in his study experienced some degree of personal strain and/or feelings of guilt. He also found that some adult children reported feeling stressed even when they were providing little or no help. Cicirelli describes these feelings as filial anxiety, which results from adult children anticipating their parents' dependency and need for support. He also notes that as older parents become more dependent, adult children monitor their parents' well-being, which often results in them becoming worried and stressed. Cantor's (1983) findings, similar to those made by Cicirelli, show that because the children and spouses of the frail elderly provide them with the greatest amount of care and because of the close bond between them, they generally experience more stress in their caregiving role than other family members. Brody (1985: 19) states that "parent care has become a normative but stressful experience for individuals and families and that its nature, scope, and consequences are not fully understood." She further contends that filial care of the elderly often affects the entire family and that the demands of parent care frequently exceed the adult child's abilities to deal with the ever-present demands. She also asserts that adult daughters, as opposed to others in the family, are especially vulnerable to caregiver stress because they are the elderly's principal caregivers, and they more often share their homes with older relatives when they can no longer manage on their own.

Monk (1983) and Moroney (1976) report that there is a persistent willingness of families to continue being the primary caregivers for their older dependent family members. Brody (1985) suggests that families have always been willing to care for their older dependent members, and the family invented long-term care before the government and formal organizations began providing it to the chronically ill. Montgomery et al. (1985) note that the willingness of families to take care of their own keeps the dependent out of publicly supported services. It is further suggested that the willingness of families to support their older dependent members also diverts attention from caregiver strain and burnout. Brody (1985) also reports that the strains families experience are not completely preventable or remediable but that policy interventions through the formal system, in this case day care, can create a workable partnership with willing and persistent family caregivers. She further asserts that social policy can strengthen the informal support of the family and therefore would keep the formal system from being overwhelmed.

Adult day care, according to Rathbone-McCuan (1976), is one type of service that can provide assistance to families caring for an older dependent sick member. Her research findings on adult day care and family issues indicate that this service not only helps provide assistance to and maintain the older person, it also helps the psychological functioning of families. She states that day care benefits families in three ways: (1) They provide an organized service unit that can share significantly in the physical burden of daily care and supervision of aged persons, (2) they provide psychological support in the knowledge that the aged family member is involved in a social-health environment that allows him or her to have supervised peer interaction, and (3) they provide a means by which the family is able to fulfill the desire to keep the aged person at home for as long as possible.

Zimmerman's (1985) research, like that of Rathbone-McCuan, shows that adult day care is a viable resource to families. Day-care services allow families to care for the older person at home and allow caregivers to attend to their own needs better as well as help reduce general caregiver stress and strain. Goldstein (1983) also suggests that day care serves as a tension releaser for both the elderly and their primary caregivers. The day-care setting provides a place to discuss family problems and concerns that help alleviate pressures in the family.

To further our understanding of how and to what extent day care supports family caregiving by addressing the needs of the elderly and their primary caregivers, the remainder of this discussion is based on research in which two major questions were addressed: (1) What long-term care provisions do day-care programs provide the elderly and their families? (2) What types of psychosocial supports are provided to family caregivers by day care?

### The Method of Study

The administrators at 32 of the 33 day-care programs in the Chicago metropolitan area were interviewed by telephone. One administrator refused to be interviewed. I chose to interview only the chief administrators because of their decision- and policymaking roles in the organization. The interview was conducted by telephone because of the geographic dispersion of the sample and because of cost containment. Also, the telephone allowed more efficient follow-up on incomplete interviews. The 26-item interview schedule with both open- and closed-ended questions was designed to assess what types of day-care programs are available in the Chicago metropolitan area, how they are funded, and the emphasis of care through program orientation or philosophy. Questions also focused on assessing the characteristics of the staff and those of the clients served at the day-care programs. Information was also collected on the needs of the caregivers of the older day-care clients, and how the administrators were attempting to address these needs. Further, the findings collected through this interview are intended to provide insight into how day-care programs can include address-

ing the needs of families and assist them in caring for their older
dependent members. Therefore, the findings from this study are
discussed in view of the types of support given in relation to the
needs of day-care clients and their families.

## Findings

### The Day-Care Programs, Staff, and Clients

The 32 day-care programs in this study represent 99% of those
in the Chicago metropolitan area and 65% of those in the state of
Illinois. Of these, 10 (35%) are privately funded, 5 (14%) are publicly funded, and 17 (55%) are funded through both private and
public monies.

The administrators were asked to describe the basic philosophies of their programs. Although there was some overlap in their
responses, four major themes were found: (1) maintaining the
elderly through different support mechanisms, (2) providing the
elderly with a stimulating and interactive environment, (3) alleviating or delaying the institutionalization of the elderly, and (4) providing respite care to families. Of these four themes, maintaining
and stimulating the elderly were mentioned most often, with providing respite care to families mentioned the least.

The different philosophies of the adult-day care programs in the
Chicago metropolitan area, as well as the services provided (which
will be discussed below), indicate that these programs are a combination of Models III and IV according to O'Brien's classification of
day-care services and Model II of Weissart's classification mentioned earlier in this chapter. According to these models, adult day
care in the Chicago metropolitan area primarily provides supportive health services, protection, and psychosocial support to elderly
people who are mentally and physically impaired.

The staff members at the programs reflect the models of day care
described above. As a result, all the programs have staffs that are
similar to one another. Each program has a director or administrator. At least 50% of the programs have full- or part-time activity
directors, nurses, and social workers. Volunteers are common
components of the programs, and, according to the administrators,
they play significant roles in assisting the staff. In comparison to

national data, the staffs at the programs are like those elsewhere, particularly in reference to presence of a director, a nurse, and a social worker (Mace & Rabins, 1984).

Although the administrators indicated that their services address the needs of the frail and chronically ill elderly, sixteen (51%) of them said their clients must be ambulatory in order to attend their programs and 51% of them also mentioned that their clients must have no (or only a minimal level of) mental impairments. Five of the administrators specifically mentioned that they accept clients who suffer from some type of dementia, especially if they do not exhibit combative behavior. Only one program specifically addresses clients with cognitive or mental impairments. Further, to qualify to attend the programs, potential clients must be at least 50 years old. Although all the programs have restrictions about the types of mental and physical conditions clients can have to qualify to attend their day-care programs, there is very little consistency regarding these policies. In fact, as mentioned earlier, with the lack of standards and regulations for day care, individual providers themselves, along with other governing bodies, determine who qualifies for day-care services. However, in Illinois, standards and policies have recently been developed for vendors receiving state funds to support their programs. The requirements or codes cover a wide array of issues regarding services and who should receive them. These guidelines are beginning to help day-care providers establish standards and regulations.

The different programs serve clients who are very similar in characteristics. Of the programs, 3 have predominantly black clientele, 1 serves the Japanese, and another serves only Hispanic elderly people. The other 26 programs have a predominantly white clientele. Like other day-care clients nationally, the average age of those represented in the 32 adult day-care programs in this study is about 75; 69% of them are women and 31% are men. The average program has a daily attendance of 26 clients and at least 75% live with relatives. All of the clients are frail and chronically ill, they, like other dependent elderly, have heart disease, diabetes, arthritis, and other debilitating physical and mental impairments. They generally live in close proximity to the programs and attend them 2 to 5 days a week from approximately 8:00 a.m. to 5:00 p.m. Monday through Friday.

## Meeting the Needs of Clients

The administrators were asked to list, in order of importance, the top five needs of their clients. Other than socialization standing out as the need most frequently mentioned by the administrators, no other needs of clients were mentioned as often among the 22 that are listed in Table 8.1. However, when the list of needs was examined according to the top five mentioned, the following pattern emerged: Socialization was mentioned most often, supervision second, nutrition third, counseling fourth, and self-esteem fifth.

The programs in this study, like the majority of those nationally, provide a range of services. The administrators identified 12 different kinds of social services they provide their older clients. All of the programs provide meals and information on nutrition and diet; 87% provide transportation for the clients; 29 (93%) of the programs provide either individual and/or family counseling. In general the social services the clients receive are in response to their major needs. Therefore, among the various services the administrators provide, most of them specifically address the clients' major need for socialization.

## Meeting the Needs of Families

The needs of families were assessed by asking the administrators to list the five major needs of their clients' families as they related to caregiving. Thirteen different needs were identified, as shown in Table 8.1, and the top five among them when ranked ordered include respite, counseling, protection for parents, information and referral, and advocacy. Over three-fourths (78%) of the administrators mentioned respite care and 50% of them mentioned counseling services as major needs of their clients' caregivers. Although Mace and Rabins (1984) studied day-care programs that included only demented clients, they also found respite and counseling to be important needs of the elderly's caregivers.

As evidenced from the findings in the literature reported earlier, the family is the first source of help to the very old and impaired and there is a persistent willingness by families to continue providing assistance. Therefore, the number of administrators in the study identifying respite as a major need of their clients' families is probably indicative of the extent and long-term nature of their caregiving

TABLE 8.1
Needs of the Client and Family Caregivers

| Needs of the Client | Number of Times Mentioned by Administrators | Needs of the Family Caregivers | Number of Times Mentioned by Administrators |
|---|---|---|---|
| (1) Socialization | 22 | (1) Respite | 25 |
| (2) Supervision | 14 | (2) Counseling/support/advice | 17 |
| (3) Nutrition | 13 | (3) Safety of parents | 6 |
| (4) Mental health/counseling | 10 | (4) Referrals | 5 |
| (5) Self-worth/individuality/sense of belonging/emotional support | 9 | (5) Advocacy/intervention | 4 |
| (6) Health care monitoring | 7 | (6) Assurance that parents are being socialized and living with dignity | 4 |
| (7) Stimulation/group-interaction | 7 | (7) Supervision of parent | 3 |
| (8) Supervision of medication | 6 | (8) Parent's health maintained | 3 |
| (9) Recreational activities | 6 | (9) Assistance while working | 2 |
| (10) Exercise | 5 | (10) Caregiving education | 2 |
| (11) Medical assistance | 4 | (11) Environmental adjustments | 1 |
| (12) Education | 4 | (12) Nutrition of parent | 1 |
| (13) Family respite | 4 | (13) Alternatives to nursing home placements | 1 |
| (14) Physical health | 3 | | |
| (15) Rehabilitation | 3 | | |
| (16) Motivation | 2 | | |
| (17) Maintaining skills | 2 | | |
| (18) Transportation | 2 | | |
| (19) Advocacy | 2 | | |
| (20) Weekend assistance | 1 | | |
| (21) Institutionalization | 1 | | |
| (22) Income | | | |

roles. However, none of the administrators mentioned providing respite services to families as a major part of the orientation or philosophy of their day-care programs. In fact, none of the day-care programs provides late evening and weekend services to the elderly and their families. It appears, therefore, that there is a gap in the delivery of services through day care to support those caring for the elderly and the program orientations in the day-care setting. In view of the fact that day care was not developed as a concept in which the family was seen to be as much the client as the elderly, providing services such as respite to families would go beyond who and what day care was originally designed to address. Nevertheless, the need for long-term care services to families with older dependent sick members could be better provided if concepts such as day care were restructured to view both the primary caregivers and the elderly as the client.

The administrators also were asked if they provide social services to address the needs of families and, if so, to describe those services. A total of 24 (75%) said they provide services to help meet the needs of their clients' caregivers; 8 (25%) said they did not. Providing support group meetings for caregivers is the leading form of service the day-care programs provide families. Individual and family counseling are also major support services available to caregivers. Keys and Szpak (1983) also found support groups and counseling to be the primary services provided families in their study on day care. The administrators in the Chicago survey said they also provide case management, problem-solving interventions, and referral services to families, although to a lesser extent than support groups and counseling.

All of the programs provide social activities such as parties, dinners, open houses, and educational programs that include staff, clients, and families. These activities are designed to help families become more integrated into the day-care program so that their concerns and needs are better understood by the staff. In addition to this involvement in the day-care program helping caregivers, Mace and Rabins's (1984) findings show that there is a positive relationship between client adjustment and family's attendance at day-care program activities.

### Discussion and Policy Implications

The concept of adult day care developed in the United States in the early 1970s is viewed as another option of long-term care for the elderly. It has, however, not been a part of a comprehensive plan for geriatric services, although it is usually seen as an alternative to or substitute for nursing home care. Further, day-care providers have never had standards and regulations to help them develop programs and monitor the care their clients receive.

The lack of standards and regulations available to day-care providers regarding family issues is of particular concern. As evidenced from the information available, it is now known that the typical day-care client is over age 70, in poor health, female, widowed, economically dependent, and living with a family member, usually an adult daughter. Therefore it is the family who is generally responsible for the well-being and primary care of most day-care clients. This caregiving to the elderly is usually done willingly, it is persistent, and it creates a lot of stress and strain in the family. Adult daughters tend to experience most of the stress because they traditionally have been the major source of help to the elderly. These adult daughters, along with other family caregivers, often seek day-care services to alleviate some of the stress experienced in their caregiving role. Day care also provides additional care to the older family member by providing physical and mental health services, a protective environment, and a place for stimulation and socialization.

Specific regulations and standards for day-care providers focused on addressing supporting family caregiving to older day-care clients would provide a model with a more comprehensive approach to care for the elderly. This approach would broaden the concept of the day-care client, which would include the elderly and their primary caregivers. In 1984 the National Institute on Adult Day Care developed standards for providers that included addressing the needs of the elderly's caregivers, but because NIAD is not a governing body it cannot regulate its standards. The need for NIAD standards to be implemented is obvious given the degree and extent of care families provide their older dependent members.

The results from the survey reported on in this chapter show that both the elderly clients in day-care programs and their families are in need of supportive services. The day-care programs in the study provide a wide range of services to meet their needs. The older person's major long-term needs for socialization, nutrition, mental health care, and supervision are addressed through social activities, prepared meals, individual counseling by social workers, and the protective environment provided by the staff. The family's major need for respite is not addressed by the day-care services, although their other major need for counseling is provided by the staff. Further, an overwhelming majority of the programs provide support group meetings for families. These meetings are designed to advise, educate, and assist family caretakers. Also, families can share experiences and learn from one another in these groups.

Although some of the needs of the family are addressed through day-care services in the Chicago metropolitan area, day-care providers have not had standards or guidelines to help them. Recently, the state of Illinois developed adult day-care standards for vendors receiving state funds to support their programs. None of the regulations addresses issues pertaining to the families of the day-care clients; however, the 32 day-care programs represented in the telephone survey make up 62% of the state day-care vendors and all of the administrators of these programs identified family issues in their delivery of services as important. As previously stated, administrators have no formal policy guidelines to help them define and address family issues. Therefore, at best, supporting family caregiving to the elderly through adult day care is basically determined by individual administrators' views of the problems.

Much more research is needed on adult day care, especially in regard to family issues. Investigating how the concept of day care can be developed to include the family as the client would more realistically address long-term care and the elderly. To understand further how day-care services can assist both the elderly and their primary family caregivers, research is also needed that focuses on the issue of family policy. Research on family policy would provide some knowledge on how to address long-term care issues from a family perspective. As Zimmerman (1976) states, there is a vast array of social programs that reflect policies related to social services that may influence the family, but they were not designed to ensure the viability of the family as a social system. Because the family is the major source of support to the elderly, research on adult day care that provides insight into how this service can address the family as a social system would benefit the development of long-term care for the elderly and their families. Given this perspective, then, day care would become a social service for the family in which both the elderly and their major caregivers' needs are addressed.

# 9

# The Feasibility of Volunteers and Families Forming a Partnership for Caregiving

RHONDA J.V. MONTGOMERY
LAURIE RUSSELL HATCH

One of the most pressing social planning tasks of the decade is the need to develop coherent systems of long-term care services for the frail or disabled. Proportionately, the elderly constitute a high-risk group in these categories. The growing numbers of people at all income levels who need assistance with planning for, finding, and paying for support services have elevated the issue to a major priority of domestic policy.

In search for solutions, policy analysts have recognized the importance of the family and its central role in providing assistance to the unable or disabled. Despite changes in the structure of the American family, such as shrinking family size and increased employment of women, research has repeatedly documented that families provide the majority of long-term care services (e.g., Shanas et al., 1968; Monk, 1983; Moroney, 1983). In most cases families continue to maintain the primary responsibility for the care

AUTHORS' NOTE: This project was supported in part by award #90AM0046, from the Administration on Aging, Office of Human Development Services, Department of Health and Human Services.

of the elderly until their resources have been exhausted (Brody, 1978). Institutionalization is often the result of a lack of congruence between family resources and the needs of the elderly. Logically then, institutionalization could be prevented if intervention measures were taken to increase family resources and/or to decrease the needs of the elderly. A number of services, including education, counseling, financial assistance, and respite, have been proposed to support the continuance of the family in its caregiving role (Lebowitz, 1978; Shanas & Sussman, 1977; Sussman, 1979).

In addition, strong efforts are being made to use volunteers to assist the frail elderly. Such efforts are indicated by recent requests for proposals from federal agencies. For example, the Office of Human Development Services has called for research efforts that increase the use of volunteers and paraprofessionals (Federal Register, 1984). Researchers also have advocated the increased use of volunteers to relieve families who are providing care to elderly members (e.g., Allinson, 1982).

Currently, most programs use volunteers in institutional settings to work with elders for whom family members are not available. This chapter reports findings from a research and demonstration project in which volunteers were employed to provide respite for families caring for elderly relatives. Volunteer respite was one of four services offered to families participating in the Family Support Project. The purpose of the project was to identify the costs, benefits, and feasibility of three model programs for supporting families. An experimental design was used to determine which model, if any, could sufficiently enhance the families' resources to enable them to extend their caregiving efforts.

The focus of this chapter is on the volunteer respite service. The intent is to describe the service, to analyze the difficulties encountered in implementing the service, and to assess the impact of the service on caregivers. Attention is also given to client satisfaction and desires for alternative or additional respite services.

## Methodology

### Sample

A total of 307 family units participated in the project. Each unit consisted of an elderly person and at least one family member who was providing regular care. All elders resided in King County, Washington. The family caregivers either resided with the elder or lived within a one-hour driving distance from the older person. Families learned of the project through a wide variety of sources including newspapers, radio, television, and health and social services in the community. Many of the families obtained information about the project through multiple sources before choosing to participate in the demonstration. The 307 elderly care recipients who participated in the project are among the oldest, most frail part of the population. The median age of the elders was 80. The majority (170) of the elders reported their health to be "fair" or "not at all good." About half of the elders were reported to have a serious mental impairment, and 140 were unable to be interviewed due to speech, hearing, or mental impairments. Elders being cared for by adult children were older but healthier than those being cared for by a spouse (see Table 9.1). This difference in health status was found to be statistically significant ($p \leq .05$). In addition, many of the elders were isolated, with 61 (20%) indicating that they have no informal contact with persons other than their immediate families.

The 298 caregivers included in this study were relatives who considered themselves to have primary responsibility for attending to the elders' needs. Consistent with findings reported in the literature (Brody, 1981; Steinitz, 1981), the majority (80%) of the caregivers were female. A total of 37% (109) were spouses of the elder and 57% (170) were adult children. The majority of the caregivers reported their health to be good, very good, or perfect. Caregivers reported assisting elders with all aspects of their daily living. The amount of time spent assisting the elder differed significantly, however, between caregivers who were spouses and those who were adult children. Compared to the adult children, spouses spent an average of eight hours more per week assisting the elder with personal caregiving tasks such as bathing, dressing, and toileting. Spouses also spent more time performing other, less personal tasks. They spent an average of 14 hours more per week than the adult children helping the elder with shopping, preparing meals, cleaning, and canning food. The average number of hours spent per week helping with business matters, such as writing checks and attending to legal matters, was also higher for spouses than for children.

Each family unit was randomly assigned to one of three treatment groups or to the control group. Those families assigned to the first treatment group were eligible to receive volunteer respite ser-

TABLE 9.1

Mean Elder Health Score and Median Age at Time 1 and Time 2
by Relationship of Caregiver

|  | Time 1 (N = 307) | | Time 2 (N = 211) | |
|  | Self-Rated Health | Age | Self-Rated Health | Age |
| --- | --- | --- | --- | --- |
| Total sample | 3.64 | 82 | 3.56 | 84 |
| Spouse as caregiver | 4.19 | 73 | 4.12 | 75 |
| Child as caregiver | 3.37 | 86 | 3.29 | 88 |

NOTE: 1 = perfect, 5 = very poor health.

vices; families assigned to the second group were eligible to attend
the family education program; and families assigned to the third
treatment group were eligible for both the education program and
volunteer respite services.

Initial interviews were conducted with the elderly subjects and
their family caregivers. The interviews, which averaged 40 minutes
in length, were conducted in the homes of the subjects. In addition
to basic demographic information, data were collected concerning the elderly person's level of disability, family structure, use of
community services, quality of family relationships, and morale.
Approximately half of the elders were able to participate in the
interviews. Information on the remaining 140 elders, who suffered
from speech, hearing, or mental impairments, was collected from
the family members providing care. The 298 care providers were
asked about their family structure, the types of tasks they perform,
the amount of time spent performing tasks, the extent to which they
find caregiving burdensome, the quality of their relationship with
their elderly relative, and their morale.

A telephone interview was conducted with caregivers after families had been eligible for services for six months. Data pertaining
to the elders' activities of daily living (ADLs) and their use of long-
term care services were collected at this time.

Follow-up interviews were conducted with all subjects 12 months
after the families became eligible for services or after they were
assigned to the control group. Caregivers were again asked about
their health, caregiving tasks, morale, perception of burden, relationship with the elder, use of services, and plans for institutionalization. At this time the caregivers were asked about their

satisfaction with services provided through the project, and their reasons for using or not using services. Data were also collected about the elder's living arrangements, health, ADLs, relationship with the caregiver, morale, plans for institutionalization, and use of long-term care services.

Information concerning the volunteer respite services was obtained through two additional sources. Detailed records were kept on families' utilization of services, and informal interviews were conducted with the agency staff responsible for the implementation of the volunteer respite service.

## Services Tested

Three models of support programs were tested by the research and demonstration project. The first model consisted of the volunteer respite service. The second model offered a family education program, and the third model offered both the respite service and the education program.

*The family education program.* The family education program was composed of three services: family education seminars, support groups, and family coordination services. The family education seminars for caregivers consisted of a series of six two-hour sessions conducted weekly. The curriculum addressed a wide range of topics, including changing family roles, decision making, communication skills, health-related aspects of aging, community resources, legal concerns, and the importance of self care. Caregiver support groups were organized for family members who completed the series of seminars and wished to continue meeting with other people who were experiencing similar circumstances. Family coordination services were provided by a master's-level social worker. The family coordinator was available to help families and the elderly care recipient learn case management skills, including how to locate needed community services and how to develop a family action plan. The family coordinator did not provide ongoing counseling or direct services, but was available as a consultant to the family throughout the project.

*Volunteer respite.* The volunteer respite service was made available through a local home health agency. The goal of the volunteer respite component was to give primary caregivers temporary relief from their tasks by sending volunteer and/or paid workers into clients' homes. The intent was to offer in-home services to families on a regular and/or emergency basis. Families assigned to the respite portion of the project were to be given the opportunity to have a respite worker come into their home on a biweekly basis, for a period of up to four hours each visit. To the extent possible, respite was to be provided by volunteers. A minimal amount of funds was available to supplement the volunteer service in case of emergency or when volunteers could not be found.

A number of difficulties were encountered that prevented the project from meeting this goal and led to the implementation of a service that differed substantially from that planned. An understanding of these difficulties is as important to an assessment of the feasibility of the volunteer respite service as are the findings derived from empirical data.

## Difficulties Encountered

### Recruitment of Volunteers

First, it was learned through the home visits by the family coordinator, and later confirmed by data collected through interviews, that a large number of the families were relatively isolated and had very contracted social networks. If friends or other family members were available to assist with caregiving tasks, these persons were already doing so. Hence all volunteers for the project had to be recruited through the volunteer department of the home health agency. Unfortunately, staff soon discovered that the recruitment of a pool of volunteer respite workers large enough to serve 150 families was an impossible task.

Upon reflection, both project staff and agency staff attribute the difficulty of recruiting volunteers to a number of factors. The large size of the geographic area served by the project created a problem that was perhaps unique to the project. King County covers over 2,128 square miles and hence created difficulties of matching the geographic location of volunteers with that of families. Geography is less likely to be an issue in smaller communities or for agencies serving smaller geographic areas. Similarly, the size of the pool of volunteers that was necessary for the project created unique problems. Programs serving a smaller number of persons or programs able to recruit volunteers over a longer period of time may not encounter as many difficulties. Finally, it might be speculated that programs operating in smaller or more rural communities may be more successful at identifying sources of volunteers.

## The Nature of the Volunteer Job

A barrier to volunteer recruitment that is not unique to the project, but one that staff found to be most inhibiting, is the nature of the volunteer job and its precarious position between the formal and informal caregiving systems. It quickly became clear that volunteers who were willing to assist families on a regular basis were very different from persons who are willing to volunteer for other types of activities. To be effective, volunteer respite workers had to be very dependable, personable, and willing to commit themselves to the program for a minimum of three months. Although the commitment required of volunteers was substantial, the rewards offered by the work were fewer than those associated with many other types of volunteer activities (see Gidron, 1978; Lossing, 1979). Volunteers did not have the opportunity to socialize with other volunteers. Their work was not performed in a public arena where other people could acknowledge their efforts or where they could learn from professionals. Many times the elder with whom they stayed resisted their presence and made their tasks even more difficult. In addition, the work the volunteers performed is not given high status in our society and, in fact, often included "dirty" hands-on activities such as assisting with eating. The job certainly could not be viewed as a training ground for some higher-status paid position. Indeed, the only rewards that were possible for the volunteer were those of establishing a new friendship with the elder or the family members and of "feeling good" about him- or herself. Extrinsic rewards were absent and, as a result, grave difficulties were encountered in finding a sufficient number of volunteers.

In short, the volunteer position was difficult to fill because it requires the incumbent to operate simultaneously within a formal organization and a primary group. According to Litwak and Meyer (1966), these two types of organizations have antithetical structures that, when brought into close contact, lead to conflicts. Indeed, the volunteer position was by definition a point of tension between the family and the bureaucratic organization. On the one hand the volunteer was expected to establish a primary relationship with the family and disabled elder and thereby be able to substitute for a family member's idiosyncratic and nontechnical services. On the other hand the volunteer was expected to provide instrumental services on a regular basis as would a paid employee. Yet neither the formal nor the informal systems was able to reward the volunteer sufficiently for any of the services. As a result, it was difficult to locate volunteers willing to assume a position that was intrinsically fraught with conflicting and perhaps unrealistic expectations.

The confusion surrounding the volunteer's role also contributed to some caregivers' reluctance to utilize volunteers. Like the elders, caregivers did not always welcome volunteers. They were hesitant about anyone coming into their homes and sometimes questioned the motives of persons willing to do so. Family members often experienced a certain amount of embarrassment about exposing their private concerns to strangers and were often reluctant to ask volunteers to help with tasks that were necessary but perhaps too personal. The volunteers were not viewed by the family as members of their primary group and therefore idiosyncratic tasks were not seen as appropriate. At the same time, the role of volunteer did not correspond to a paid professional and hence, family members were also unwilling to request help with technical or routine tasks.

### Matching Volunteers with Families

Perhaps as difficult as locating volunteers was the process of matching volunteers with families. Priority was given to the goal of matching families with volunteers who would continue to provide services to the family for an extended period of time. The intent was to encourage the family-volunteer relationship to continue beyond the end of the project. Among the factors that had to be taken into consideration were: geographical locations of the volunteer and elder; the care needs of the elder; personalities and interests of the volunteer, the family member, and the elder; time schedules of families and volunteers; and, for some families, the sex of the volunteer was important. It was very difficult and time consuming to address all of these factors in a countywide program. It was necessary for the volunteer coordinator to meet with each volunteer and to visit the home of the family. The large number of

volunteers needed for the pool made this task even more difficult. The result was that volunteers were located who could not be
matched with families, and at the same time many families were
not served by volunteers.
Even when a successful match between a volunteer and a family
was made, problems sometimes arose due to rapid changes in the
health and needs of the elder. Sometimes volunteers could not safely
continue to provide care. This observation is related to another very
important finding.
Contrary to initial expectations held by the project staff, many of
the elders were severely disabled and family members were performing complex care routines. Unless close supervision and extensive training could be made available, volunteers could not perform
many difficult tasks such as bed transfers, assistance with toileting,
or administration of medications. This finding may help to explain
why the families' expectations for the use of volunteers differed
from those held by the formal organization. Families wanted and
needed help with performing rigorous caretaking tasks, but the
home health agency was unaware of the families' level of need and
expected volunteers to act primarily in a role of companionship.
Also, even with extensive training of volunteers, concerns about
the liability of the home health agency would have prevented the
use of volunteers in many cases.

**Staff Time**

The staff time needed for matching volunteers with families was
substantial and was originally underestimated. When volunteers
were located, the staff time needed to support them was substantial. Because volunteers going into private homes were not able to
discuss with their peers the problems that they encountered, they
needed the opportunity to discuss these issues with staff. However,
the volunteers were not part of a care team that included professional staff, and therefore all of the responsibility fell on the volunteer coordinator. Because the coordinator was responsible for
recruiting and training volunteers and for matching them with
families, it was difficult for her to provide the time necessary to
meet the needs of the volunteers.

**Families' Expectations**

The final difficulty encountered as the volunteer program was implemented stemmed from families' expectations for scheduling the use of respite. Many families were reluctant to use respite services on a regularly scheduled basis. These families who wanted occasional use or emergency use of services were almost impossible to accommodate with a volunteer program. Again the difficulty stemmed from the conflicting expectations placed on volunteers by families and the home health agency. In this case, the families needed idiosyncratic services but the volunteer program, as is frequently the case with formal organizations, was capable only of meeting routine or regularly scheduled needs. Volunteers frequently are limited as to the days of the week or the times of the day that they can help and are, therefore, not available to meet emergency situations. For the same reason, the project was generally unable to meet the needs of families who wanted occasional "on-call" services. This was especially true if families wanted assistance in the evening or on weekends.

Due to these many discoveries and difficulties, the original plans for the volunteer respite service were altered when the service was implemented. The small amount of funds that had been intended to be used for paid respite only in cases of emergency were used for families with elders who had severe disabilities. Respite in these cases was limited to eight hours per month. Efforts to match volunteers with families were focused first on those families requesting regular scheduled respite and second on those requesting occasional respite services.

*Findings*

Two sets of findings emerged from the project that are important in assessing the feasibility of using volunteers to provide respite. The first set of findings concerns the use of and satisfaction with the services. The second set focuses on the impacts of service on caregivers' situations.

## Use of Services

Each of the 152 families eligible for respite were sent a short questionnaire concerning their respite preferences and the health status of the elder. From these questionnaires, and, in some cases, home visits, it was determined that 20 of the families needed paid respite services; 49 families wanted and were appropriate for regular volunteer respite; 20 families wanted occasional service; 15 families wanted no respite; and 12 families were unsure about wanting any respite. A total of 22 families never returned their questionnaire even after repeated prompting and in 12 cases the elder died before the families were able to return their questionnaire.

Volunteers were matched with 25 of the families requesting regular respite. In 4 of these cases families refused to use the respite or did not follow through on using it beyond a single visit. In 1 case the volunteer did not work out, and in 9 cases the volunteers did not remain after the initial 3-month commitment. Paid respite was substituted for the volunteer in 1 case after the elder became too disabled for volunteer respite. In 13 cases the elder either died or moved to a nursing home before a match could be made. An appropriate volunteer could not be found for 16 families requesting regular respite and for 15 families requesting occasional respite.[1]

Although this distribution of outcomes is disappointing when judged in terms of numbers of clients successfully served, the distribution is very informative when interpreted as an indicator of the major issues surrounding the feasibility of volunteer respite. Together the patterns of service use and delivery provide a succinct summary of the issues with which a volunteer respite program must contend. For example, the 22 families who failed to return their questionnaires requesting service and the 12 families who were unsure about wanting respite illustrate the difficulty that was repeatedly encountered in reaching these families and in serving them. The families tend to be fiercely independent and fail to seek services until arriving at a point of crisis—a fact made all too clear by the 25 cases where the elder died or moved to a nursing home before the family was able to return the questionnaire or before a volunteer could be located.

The 21 families served by paid respite reflect the serious disability level of many elders who are being cared for by family

members in the community. In fact, on a 5-point self-report measure of health, the elders receiving paid respite services rated their
health significantly poorer (4.1) than did those receiving volunteer
services (3.4). Finally, the 31 families the project was unable to
serve are indicative of the difficulties of recruiting volunteers and
of matching them with families needing their service.

### Client Satisfaction

Despite the many difficulties encountered in the development and
implementation of the volunteer respite service, a number of families did receive services. These families overwhelmingly reported
a high satisfaction with the service. Of the families who used
respite and responded to the second interview, 70% indicated they
were very satisfied with the respite service, and another 11% indicated they were somewhat satisfied. Most of the families receiving
respite (86%) also indicated that they would have liked to have used
more had the services been available. Interestingly, 81% of caregivers who received respite and attended the education program
reported being very satisfied with the respite services, compared to
56% of the caregivers who were eligible only for the respite services. A possible explanation for this difference may be that the
education program helped families establish realistic expectations
for the respite service, and as a result they were more satisfied with
the service.

The majority of the families receiving respite through the project
would have liked to have more respite care if the services would
have been available. In addition, many of the families who received
services, as well as those who were eligible for respite but remained
unserved, indicated that they would have liked respite in alternate
forms. Almost 70% (95) indicated a preference for paid in-home
services and 45% (62) would have liked in-home overnight services.
Respite in an institution was desired by 44 (32%) of the caregivers,
and adult day care was desired by 40 (29%) of the participants.

### Impact of Volunteer Respite

Although client satisfaction is certainly important in assessing
services, perhaps the most telling evaluation of a service is its impact
on caregivers' situations. In short, to what extent did the caregivers

who received volunteer services benefit from the services? The difficulties encountered in implementing the respite program make this question even more salient to the judgment of feasibility of volunteer respite. The impact of the services was measured by looking at changes in the living arrangement of the elder, the morale of the caregiver, and the levels of objective and subjective burden experienced by caregivers. Analysis of variance with repeated measures was used to determine whether or not there were significant differences among the treatment and control groups in the amount of change in each of these variables.

Before examining the data for differences among the treatment groups in the outcome variables, it is useful to look at trends of the total sample of elders and caregivers with regard to changes in living arrangements, health status, and caregiving behaviors. As shown in Table 9.2, less than half (47.8%) of the elders were still living in their own or their caregivers' homes at the 12-month point. Almost 23% of the elders had died—a fact that underscores the frailty of the initial sample. Another 50 (16.3%) elders were residing in a nursing home, and 14 (4.5%) had moved to a congregate care setting.

It is of interest that the average health status of the 211 elders who participated in the study at time 2 was slightly better than the average health status of the total sample of 307 elders at time 1 (see Table 9.1). This pattern was also observed when the analysis was confined to only those elders continuing to live in a community setting. The pattern can most likely be attributed to death of the more severely disabled elders and the resulting change in the composition of the sample. There was also a significant decrease over the 12-month period in the average number of hours that caregivers spent performing helping tasks. To a great extent, this reduction in tasks can be attributed to the large number of cases in which the elder moved to a group or institutional setting. However, even when analyses were confined to caregivers continuing to assist an elder in a community setting, there was a decrease in the average number of hours spent performing caregiving tasks.

Consistent with the finding that the caregivers spent fewer hours performing helping tasks, the data also indicated a decrease in the average level of objective and subjective burden and an increase in the level of morale.[2] It appears that over the 12-month observation period, the most severely disabled elders moved to a nursing home

TABLE 9.2

Status of Elders at Time 2 by Service Group (N = 307)

| | Control Group | | Respite Group | | Education Group | | Respite and Education Group | | Totals | |
|---|---|---|---|---|---|---|---|---|---|---|
| | N | % | N | % | N | % | N | % | N | % |
| Elders living in the community | 33 | 42.3 | 35 | 46.1 | 45 | 58.4 | 34 | 44.7 | 147 | 47.8 |
| Elders living in retirement homes or congregate care facilities | 4 | 5.1 | 3 | 3.9 | 4 | 5.2 | 3 | 3.9 | 14 | 4.5 |
| Elders living in nursing homes | 14 | 17.9 | 11 | 14.5 | 9 | 11.7 | 16 | 21.1 | 50 | 16.3 |
| Deceased | 15 | 19.2 | 19 | 25.0 | 16 | 20.8 | 20 | 26.3 | 70 | 22.8 |
| Refused interviews | 12 | 15.4 | 8 | 10.5 | 3 | 3.9 | 3 | 3.9 | 26 | 8.4 |
| Totals | 78 | 100.0 | 76 | 100.0 | 77 | 100.0 | 76 | 100.0 | 307 | 100.0 |

or died, leaving a healthier and less needy population to be attended to in the community. As a result, many caregivers were relieved of their caregiving duties and hence reported less burden. However, this general pattern of improvement was not equally shared by the caregivers in the sample. Careful scrutiny of the data indicates that those caregivers who continued to care for an elder in a community setting showed a much smaller improvement, and in many cases an increase in burden.

Of particular interest are the differences that were observed among the treatment groups. When analysis of variance with repeated measures was performed for those persons who were still caring for an elder in the community (excluding caregivers of deceased elders and those residing in the nursing home), there was a three-way interaction among time, treatment group, and the generation of the caregiver (see Table 9.3). Further analysis indicated that there was a statistically significant decrease in objective burden for spouses who received respite (treatment groups 2 and 4) and for the children who were assigned to the control group (see Table 9.4). Given the weakness of the respite intervention, the finding that the spouses assigned to the respite treatment groups expe-

TABLE 9.3

Analysis of Variance with Repeated Measures on Objective Burden

| Source of Variation | df | F |
|---|---|---|
| Main effects | | |
| Service group | 3 | 2.1 |
| Generation (spouse or child is caregiver) | 1 | 6.9* |
| Time (change from $T_1$ to $T_2$) | 1 | 20.7* |
| 2-way interactions | | |
| Service group × generation | 3 | .7 |
| Service group × time | 3 | 1.0 |
| Generation × time | 1 | .0 |
| 3-way interactions | | |
| Service group × generation × time | 3 | 3.6* |

*$p \leq .05$.

rienced a significant decrease in objective burden certainly deserves attention. It appears that as caregivers, spouses not only perform more demanding tasks but also benefit most from respite.

Although the findings concerning spouses are intuitively satisfying, the finding that only the children in the control group had a significant decrease in objective burden is not as readily interpretable. Although any interpretation at this point is speculative, several patterns emerge from the data presented in Table 9.5 that suggest a plausible explanation. First, as noted earlier, it is clear that at both time 1 and 2, children—regardless of treatment group—care for healthier elders. Second, the children in the control group and in group 4 (respite and education) care for the healthiest elders. What is more important is the change in the average health status of the elders from time 1 to time 2. In most of the groups, the average health status of the elders at time 2 is slightly better (lower score) or slightly poorer (higher score) than at time 1. In contrast, the average health score of the elders cared for by children in the control group is not only one of the best of among the eight groups but showed a substantial improvement. The relatively good health of these elders reflects a much smaller need for assistance than most of the elders in the study. It appears that the most disabled elders being cared for by children in the control group either died or were placed in a nursing home during the 12-month interval. Unlike the

TABLE 9.4

Analyses of Variance with Repeated Measures on
Objective Burden Within Categories of Service Group
and Generation (spouse versus child as caregiver)

| Source of Vatiation | df | F |
|---|---|---|
| Control group/spouse | 1 | 0.2 |
| Control group/child | 1 | 23.5* |
| Respite only group/spouse | 1 | 6.8* |
| Respite only group/child | 1 | 0.6 |
| Education only group/spouse | 1 | 0.2 |
| Education only group/child | 1 | 0.7 |
| Education and respite/spouse | 1 | 7.0* |
| Education and respite/child | 1 | 2.4 |

*$p \leqslant .05$.

spouses who used respite to continue to care for the very disabled elders in their homes, it appears that the children in the control group tended to place these persons in a nursing home. Only those children who were caring for the least needy of elders continued the caregiving role. It is likely that the observed decrease in objective burden reflects this decrease in the average disability level of the elders.

Additional support for this interpretation was obtained by testing for a significant relationship between the generation of the caregiver and the number of persons placed in a nursing home. Given the fact that spouses were caring for less healthy and supposedly more vulnerable elders, the lack of difference in rate of placement suggests that children are less willing to care for the most disabled of elders. This tendency seems especially true for children in the control group who received no support services.

Overall, the data suggest that when respite is made available to spouses, they are not only able to continue caring for their elders but also experience a reduction in the amount of objective burden. Although there was not a corresponding reduction in the amount of burden experienced by children in the treatment groups, it appears that the lack of services for children in the control group may be related to a greater tendency to place elders in an institution. A by-product of this tendency appears to have been a decrease in objective burden that corresponded with a decrease in the average need level of the elders who continued to be cared for in the community.

TABLE 9.5

Mean Health Scores for Elders at Time 1 and Time 2, Numbers of Elders Deceased, and Numbers of Elders in Nursing Homes Within Categories of Service Group and Generation (spouse versus child as caregiver)

| Service Group | Caregiver Generation | | Elder's Time 1 Mean Health Score | Elder's Time 2 Mean Health Score | Number of Elders Deceased at Time 2 | Number of Elders Living in Nursing Homes at Time 2 |
|---|---|---|---|---|---|---|
| Control | spouse | (11) | 3.73 | 3.80 | 5 | 7 |
| Control | child | (23) | 3.57 | 3.04 | 8 | 8 |
| Respite only | spouse | (10) | 4.10 | 4.00 | 6 | 5 |
| Respite only | child | (26) | 3.00 | 3.24 | 4 | 13 |
| Education only | spouse | (13) | 4.08 | 3.54 | 6 | 6 |
| Education only | child | (32) | 3.34 | 3.31 | 3 | 9 |
| Respite and education | spouse | (14) | 4.14 | 4.43 | 4 | 12 |
| Respite and education | child | (22) | 3.09 | 3.00 | 12 | 6 |

159

## Summary and Conclusions

As the growing need for assistance among the elderly continues to place pressure on public budgets, it becomes imperative for policymakers to consider a number of alternatives for supporting families in their efforts to care for the elderly. Volunteer respite care is one of the many services that has been advocated by policy makers and service providers as a viable means of supporting families and reducing the pressure for public dollars to care for the elderly. Yet, the experiences and findings reported in this study would suggest that creating and implementing such a service is difficult and will limit the extent to which such a program will provide the prophesied benefits.

In summary, the experiences and data obtained through the Family Support Project have provided much needed insight into the viability of using volunteer respite as a means for supporting families and reducing the pressure on the public purse. The experience revealed a number of difficulties in using volunteer respite. These difficulties included the recruitment of volunteers; the nature of the volunteer job and its precarious position between the formal and informal caregiving systems; the process of matching volunteers with families; the amount of staff time required; and families' expectations for scheduling the use of respite. The findings obtained from the project suggest, however, that under the right conditions such a service can benefit caregivers, and especially spouses who are providing extensive care.

The most general conclusion is that volunteer respite services cannot meet the wide range of needs that exist among families caring for elders. Not only was it difficult to recruit a sufficient number of volunteers to allow appropriate matching of volunteers with families, but in many cases it was impossible to use volunteers to meet the needs of families. All too frequently families seek services only when they are experiencing a crisis or are at the very late stages in their caregiving career. As a result, many elders are too disabled to be served by volunteers. In other cases, the length of time necessary to recruit, train, and match volunteers with families is too great and the elder is likely to die or be moved to a nursing home before the process is completed. In still other cases, volunteers could not provide the flexibility in scheduling that families desired and needed. As a rule, volunteers could best be used as companions.

Despite the limitations of the volunteer respite, the data suggest that respite can benefit many caregivers by allowing them to continue their tasks and by relieving the level of objective burden. When both the difficulties and benefits of the volunteer respite program are taken into account it might be concluded that a volunteer respite program is most likely to be successful only when it is designed to augment a paid respite program. As part of a more extensive respite service volunteer respite is viable.

Although the experiences and findings of the project are informative, it is important that the limitations of the study be acknowledged and caution be exercised in generalizing conclusions. In particular, the Family Support Project involved a large number of families and served a very large geographic area. Many of the difficulties surrounding recruitment of volunteers and the matching of families with volunteers may have been unique to the project and associated with the size of the service area.

It is also important to note that many of the families, although eligible for respite services, did not receive them. Hence, the study provided a weak test of the impact of the respite intervention. Given this limitation, the finding that respite did benefit spouses is encouraging and should certainly prompt further research into the effects of respite care.

## NOTES

1. These figures account for 150 of the 152 *family units* eligible for respite. Two families had two elders participating in the project, and thus a total of 150 *families* were eligible for respite.

2. *Objective burden* refers to the concrete events, happenings, and activities resulting from caregiving, and was measured by a 5-point, 6-item inventory. *Subjective burden* is the feelings, attitudes, and emotions expressed about the caregiving experience, and was measured using a 5-point, 4-item inventory (see Montgomery & Borgatta, 1985a).

# 10

# Rural-Urban Differences in Service Use by Older Adults

ROSEMARY BLIESZNER
WILLIAM J. McAULEY
JANETTE K. NEWHOUSE
JAY A. MANCINI

Older adults represent not only the fastest-growing age group in the U.S. population, but also a group of very high users of health care and social services. Because of increased demand for such services and increased costs associated with providing them, national policymakers and gerontological practitioners are concerned about developing appropriate and cost-effective strategies for service delivery. Among the key factors to be considered in determining the best methods of providing services are the health, financial, social, and geographic characteristics of the client population, and whether services should be institution or community based.

Health needs and functioning dictate the requirements for long-term care facilities and services in the community. The need for long-term care services, especially for chronic conditions, will escalate with the population of elderly persons because the proportion who are very old and frail is rapidly increasing. Two alternative forms of long-term care exist for impaired elderly: institutional facilities, and community-based programs that are delivered by either professionals or a network of family and friends. The form of care and pattern of services that are used by a given older person will depend to a large extent on financial resources, health insurance, types of facilities and services available in the geographic area, availability of informal helpers, and personal preferences of the older person (McAuley & Blieszner, 1985). As pointed out so effectively by Litwak (1985), both primary groups of informal caregivers and formal organizations must cooperate in order to meet all the long-term care needs of older persons, regardless of the setting in which services are utilized.

This chapter focuses on the use of services by elders residing in the community. In-home care services are a vital component of any continuum of care for noninstitutionalized frail elders (Friedman & Kaye, 1979). The availability and use of informal, mainly familial, support is a key element in the impaired elderly person's being able to reside in the community and avoid or delay institutionalization (Barney, 1977; Brody et al., 1978; Noelker & Harel, 1978; Palmore, 1983). Older people perceive the informal network of kin, friends, and neighbors as the appropriate source of assistance and social support in most situations of need (Mancini & Simon, 1984), and typically they turn to formal organizations for help only when assistance from the informal system is unavailable or over extended. For example, older people are more likely to use help from formal sources if they are more dependent, live alone, are unmarried, and live farther from children (Cantor, 1980; Rosow, 1967; Stoller, 1982; Streib & Beck, 1980).

Community-based services can often be more cost effective, in terms of public dollars, than institutional long-term care (Jackson, 1984; Knight et al., 1982; Widmer et al., 1978). One reason for this is that the informal support system provides a substantial portion of the total care received by impaired community residents (Comptroller General of the United States, 1977). Another is that older community residents or their families are usually responsible for basic living expenses such as food, clothing, and shelter.

Consideration of the geographic location of elderly service users has been neglected in planning for older clients. Differences between rural and urban seniors are likely to exist on numerous dimensions, yet few have been empirically documented. Comparison of rural and urban elderly adults with regard to need for and use of various services is important for several reasons. First, there has been a disproportionately large population growth among older people in rural America (Longino et al., 1984). Attention must be given to the implications of the changing economic and demographic character of rural areas.

Second, in an effort to determine conditions of rural life that make it unique for older people, researchers have discovered the inadequacy of community services for them. Although rural elderly residents have more objective needs than their urban counterparts (Coward & Lee, 1985; Nelson, 1983), they have access to fewer services than the aged in urban areas. The limited economic base and sparsely distributed populations of many rural areas serve to restrict the range and coverage of services for their older citizens.

Third, rural community-based services seem to be less adequate than urban services not only in number, but also in method of delivery. Service providers and program designers often fail to consider such factors as cultural differences between rural and urban elderly persons, transportation problems in rural areas, acceptability of programs among rural subcultures, and structure of kinship and friendship networks in rural areas. Furthermore, there has been a tendency to develop models for programs and services based on research conducted in urban environments. Although these may fit the needs, lifestyles, and living arrangements of urban older people, there is no assurance that scaled-down versions of urban service delivery models will benefit rural elders (Coward, 1979).

Fourth, the research necessary to provide direction to practitioners is both methodologically limited and sparse. Attempts to study older adults in rural environments without comparing them to their urban counterparts are inadequate. On the one hand, the effects of rural residence on older people can be determined only by comparisons across rural *and* urban communities. On the other hand, not all of the characteristics of older rural Americans are necessarily attributable to their age; some (e.g., lower levels of education, lower incomes, and less adequate housing) may be common to rural residents of any age (Lee & Lassey, 1982). Thus both type of community and age must be treated as variables in order to identify factors that uniquely affect rural elderly persons' need for and use of community services.

Preliminary research suggests that both the needs of elderly people and the provision of services to meet these needs differ in important ways betweem rural and urban communities (Moen, 1978; Taietz, 1975). The data analyzed in the present study were from a representative sampling of older Virginians residing in geographic areas ranging from rural to urban. Thus it was possible to conduct a detailed examination of similarities and differences in extent of service use and sources of assistance among older adults in diverse geographic settings.

## Methods

### Data Source

Data for these analyses were taken from the 1979 Statewide Survey of Older Virginians (McAuley et al., 1980). The 2,146 respondents were selected by a multistage area probability technique designed to produce a representative sample of noninstitutionalized older persons. Screenings were made in over 93% of the sample housing units, and information was collected on approximately 87% of all individuals who were identified as age eligible. In a small proportion of cases (8%) informants provided some or all of the survey information because the target respondents were not able to participate in the interview. The interviews took about 45 minutes to complete.

Sample members were from 60 to over 85 years old, with the largest proportion (76.3%) between 60 and 74 years. Females composed 58.7% of the sample, whites were 81.3%, and married persons were 55.4%. The amount of education ranged from none to post-graduate work, and the modal years of schooling was 5 to 8 (31.5% of the sample). Annual income ranged from none to more than $40,000, with a median category of $5,000 to $6,999. This figure compares with a median of $6,032 for Virginians aged 60 or older in 1979. About one-fifth of the respondents were employed, but only slightly more than half of these worked full time. Table 10.1 summarizes the demographic characteristics of the sample. Based on 1980 census data (U.S. Bureau of the Census, 1982, 1983a), the sample distributions are equivalent to the population distributions of older adults in Virginia on age, gender, race, marital status, education, employment status, and income.

In the present study, rural areas included farms, ranches, and open countryside. The proportion of sample members from such areas was 40.5%. Towns/small cities had populations up to 100,000 people, and 30.9% of the sample resided therein. Urban

TABLE 10.1
Demographic Characteristics of the Sample and
the Population of Older Virginians

| Characteristic | Sample %[a] | Virginia %[b] |
|---|---|---|
| **Age** | | |
| 60-64 | 29.3 | 30.4 |
| 65-69 | 27.2 | 25.2 |
| 70-74 | 19.8 | 18.6 |
| 75-79 | 11.8 | 12.6 |
| 80-84 | 6.9 | 7.5 |
| 85 and older | 5.0 | 5.7 |
| **Gender** | | |
| female | 58.3 | 58.7 |
| male | 41.7 | 41.3 |
| **Race** | | |
| white | 81.3 | 81.7 |
| nonwhite | 18.7 | 18.3 |
| **Marital status** | | |
| married | 55.4 | 55.2 |
| widowed | 33.7 | 31.4 |
| divorced | 3.9 | 4.1 |
| separated | 1.6 | 3.4 |
| never married | 5.4 | 5.9 |
| **Education** | | |
| 0-4 years | 11.3 | 9.8 |
| 5-8 years | 31.5 | 33.3 |
| 1-3 years high school | 17.5 | 18.7 |
| 4 years high school | 16.0 | 18.6 |
| 1-3 years college/trade | 11.4 | 11.3 |
| 4 years college | 5.6 | 5.4 |
| 5 or more years of college | 4.6 | 2.9 |
| **Employment status** | | |
| not employed | 78.7 | 84.8 |
| employed | 21.2 | 15.2 |
| **Amount of employment** | | |
| full time | 53.5 | 57.1 |
| part time | 46.4 | 42.9 |
| **Annual income**[c] | | |
| 0-$1,999 | 5.0 | |
| $2,000-$3,999 | 24.6 | |

(continued)

TABLE 1 Continued

| Characteristic | Sample %[a] | Virginia %[b] |
|---|---|---|
| $4,000-$6,999 | 24.2 | |
| $7,000-$14,999 | 23.2 | |
| $15,000-$29,999 | 12.9 | |
| $30,000 or more | 5.2 | |
| Don't know | 4.7 | |

a. N = 2,146.
b. Virginians aged 60 or older, N = 726,370.
c. U.S. Census income categories differ from those used in the Statewide Survey of Older Virginians, so the frequency distribution of income at the state level was omitted from the table.

areas were defined as cities with populations of 100,000 or more people, or suburbs of such cities. Urban respondents composed 28.6% of the sample.

**Instrument and Measures**

The questionnaire used in the face-to-face interviews was based upon the Older Americans Resources and Services (OARS) multi-dimensional functional assessment strategy (Duke University Center for the Study of Aging and Human Development, 1978). This instrument assesses individual level of functioning on each of 5 dimensions (social, economic, mental health, physical health, and self-care capacity) and extent of utilization of 24 generically defined services (such as transportation, meals, nursing, and social services). A number of tests of validity and reliability have been carried out on various sections of the OARS instrument or its earlier version, the community service questionnaire (Duke University Center for the Study of Aging and Human Development, 1978; Fillenbaum & Smyer, 1981).

Five types of in-home care from the OARS instrument were used in the present study: personal care (assistance with physical activities of daily living, such as bathing, dressing, and toileting), nursing care (administration of prescribed treatments or medications), homemaker assistance (household chores such as cleaning and laundry), meal preparation, and continuous supervision. In all cases, respondents were asked if they had received each service within the past six months. The primary source of care was also ascertained. Each type of care could be provided by a family member, another informal caregiver (friend or neighbor), or a formal caregiver (agency, professional, or organization in the public sector).

*Results*

The analyses indicate that the vast majority of older noninstitutionalized Virginians do no receive formal or informal long-term assistance for personal care, nursing care, meals, homemaking, or continuous supervision: 79% to 94%, depending on the service and the geographic area, do not use such aid. However, when attention is turned to the data for users of such services, very interesting patterns emerge. The following results are based on analysis of the data for service users only.

Homemaking assistance was the most frequently used service across all 3 geographic areas, with 20.7% of the rural persons, 18.3% of the town/small city respondents, and 16.3% of the urban residents receiving such assistance. Meal preparation was used by 12.4%, 11.6%, and 13% of each group respectively, followed by personal care (7.6%, 6%, 8.6%), and continuous supervision (7.5%, 8.6%, 7.5%). Nursing care was used least often by all groups of respondents (6.4%, 6%, 6.8%).

Table 10.2 shows the source of each type of home-based care for residents of each geographic area. It is clear that the greatest percentage of respondents who relied on any of the five forms of assistance in the last six months received help chiefly from family members in every case. In most instances, formal organizations provided care to the second highest proportion of respondents, with a very small group receiving care primarily from friends or neighbors. Exceptions to this latter trend are in the area of personal care, in which the same proportion of rural individuals received help from informal and from formal sources, and in the case of meal preparation and continuous supervision, in which a greater proportion of town/small city residents received help mainly from informal as opposed to formal sources.

The data in Table 10.3 show the extent to which long-term care recipients rely on one or several sources of assistance. These percentages are for all five services considered together. The majority of individuals in each geographic area receive help only from family

TABLE 10.2
Persons Receiving Selected Long-Term Care Services
from Each Source, by Geographic Area

| | Geographic Area | | | | | |
| | Rural[a] | | Town/Small City[b] | | Urban[c] | |
| Type and Source of Assistance | n | % | n | % | n | % |
|---|---|---|---|---|---|---|
| Homemaking | | | | | | |
| family | 155 | 86.1 | 88 | 72.7 | 69 | 69.0 |
| informal | 10 | 5.6 | 10 | 8.3 | 9 | 9.0 |
| formal | 15 | 8.3 | 23 | 19.0 | 22 | 22.0 |
| total users | 180 | 100.0 | 121 | 100.0 | 100 | 100.0 |
| Meal preparation | | | | | | |
| family | 99 | 91.7 | 62 | 80.5 | 59 | 73.8 |
| informal | 2 | 1.9 | 8 | 10.4 | 8 | 10.0 |
| formal | 7 | 6.5 | 7 | 9.1 | 13 | 16.3 |
| total users | 108 | 100.1 | 77 | 100.0 | 80 | 100.1 |
| Personal care | | | | | | |
| family | 46 | 69.7 | 26 | 65.0 | 37 | 69.8 |
| informal | 10 | 15.2 | 4 | 10.0 | 4 | 7.6 |
| formal | 10 | 15.2 | 10 | 25.0 | 12 | 22.6 |
| total usuers | 66 | 100.1 | 40 | 100.0 | 53 | 100.0 |
| Continuous supervision | | | | | | |
| family | 60 | 92.3 | 47 | 82.5 | 40 | 87.0 |
| informal | 1 | 1.5 | 6 | 10.5 | 0 | 0 |
| formal | 4 | 6.2 | 4 | 7.0 | 6 | 13.0 |
| total users | 65 | 100.0 | 57 | 100.0 | 46 | 100.0 |
| Nursing care | | | | | | |
| family | 35 | 62.5 | 26 | 65.0 | 24 | 57.1 |
| informal | 3 | 5.4 | 5 | 12.5 | 1 | 2.4 |
| formal | 18 | 32.1 | 9 | 22.5 | 17 | 40.5 |
| total users | 56 | 100.0 | 40 | 100.0 | 42 | 100.0 |

a. Farms, ranches, and open countryside.
b. Population to 100,000.
c. Population 100,000 or more.

members. Next in order of frequency, although at a much lower rate, is assistance from formal organizations only. Next is aid from a combination of family and formal caregivers, followed by aid from informal sources alone. Although the percentages vary across geographic areas, the order is the same. In rural areas, a small pro-

TABLE 10.3
Percentage of Persons Receiving Any of the Long-Term Care Services
from One or a Combination of Sources, by Geographic Area

| Source of Assistance | Geographic Area | | |
|---|---|---|---|
| | Rural[a] | Town/Small City[b] | Urban[c] |
| Family only | 76.81 | 66.67 | 59.06 |
| Formal only | 8.21 | 14.97 | 16.54 |
| Informal only | 4.83 | 8.16 | 7.09 |
| Family and formal | 5.80 | 9.52 | 13.39 |
| Family and informal | 3.38 | .68 | 1.57 |
| Informal and formal | .48 | .00 | 1.57 |
| All three sources | .48 | .00 | .79 |

NOTE: N of service users: rural = 207, town = 147, urban = 127.
a. Farms, ranches, and open countryside.
b. Population to 100,000.
c. Population 100,000 or more.

portion of the older service recipients get help from a combination of family members and friends or neighbors, but in only a few cases does assistance come from a combination of informal and formal sources or from all three sources. In towns and small cities, only a few individuals receive assistance from the combination of family and informal sources, and no one reported receiving help from the combination of informal and formal sources or from all three sources together. In urban areas, very few persons receive assistance from the family and informal combination, the informal and formal combination, or all three sources.

## Discussion

### Informal Versus Formal Service Provision

Litwak (1985) made the point that family, friend, neighbor, and formal groups have different structures, and that each group will most effectively handle tasks that are consistent with its structure. According to his analysis of the match between support groups of older adults and services they can provide, informal groups are best able to assist with services that require proximity and long-term commitment. The present data confirm Litwak's proposition.

In general, family members were most likely to provide home-making assistance, meal preparation, and continuous supervision. These services are needed on a daily or more frequent basis, but do not require a high level of training to perform. In contrast, personal care and nursing care require more specialized skills and knowledge, such as techniques for transferring a person from bed to wheelchair to bathtub or administering injections. Litwak would argue that formal organizations are more effective than informal supports in delivering technical or specialized services. The present data support this position, because personal care and nursing care were more often provided by formal organizations than the other types of assistance. Differences in the nature of long-term care services and structure of supportive groups may at least partially explain the high proportion of individuals who receive home-making, meal preparation, and continuous supervision assistance (but not personal or nursing care) from family members, especially in rural areas.

Compared to those in rural areas, the much greater reliance on formal organizations by town/small city residents for homemaking assistance and personal care, and by urban residents for homemaking, meal, personal care, and continuous supervision assistance may reflect the greater availability of such services in nonrural areas. Not only are more services generally available in nonrural areas, they are easier to deliver. Impaired town and urban elderly persons are likely to live in more concentrated areas and to live closer to the formal service source than is the case for rural residents. This pattern may also reflect the increased likelihood that nonelderly women, who had carried out much of the family care-taking without other assistance in the past, are now employed outside of the home. Although research shows that working daughters continue to assume a great deal of responsibility for the care of their aged parents (Brody, 1981), it is possible that they do so in conjunction with formal services that they had not used in past eras.

The higher percentage of town/small city and urban dwellers, contrasted with rural elders, who receive assistance with meal preparation from informal sources suggests the advantages of having helpful friends or neighbors in close proximity. A much higher proportion of these informal helpers also provides continuous supervision and nursing care to town/small city residents than is the case for either rural or urban respondents. Perhaps friends and neighbors live closer to elderly persons in towns/small cities than to those in rural areas, and are more willing to fill in as needed. In urban areas, friends and neighbors may be aware of the availability of formal sources of assistance, and their role may be to help the impaired elderly person negotiate the bureaucracy to obtain needed services, rather than providing them directly themselves. Rural elderly adults and their informal support network members may have less knowledge about and experience with using formal services, and thus may be less skilled in advocating for their provision.

## Supporting Informal Providers

Because family members seem to be meeting so many of the long-term care needs for a majority of older adults, it is apparent that service planners and providers must assess the availability and capabilities of family when making decisions about services for older adults (Brubaker, 1983), especially in rural areas. Case management must include recurrent consideration of family resources and the effects of long-term caregiving on the family, as well as assessment of the status of the older person. Rather than assuming that formal services are not needed when strong family caregiving is observed, service providers must seek ways of supporting and supplementing the efforts of family members with appropriate professional services (Brubaker, 1983; Scott & Roberto, 1985).

*Education.* Successful long-term care partnerships among families, informal caregivers, and formal organizations are facilitated if each contributor of care understands the needs and roles of the other caregivers, as well as those of the older person. Family members and other informal caregivers should be educated about normal aging processes, the specific conditions of the frail elderly person, and effective methods of carrying out their chosen tasks. Training of professional staff must include information about aging, family roles and interaction patterns, typical sources of stress in caregiving families, and signs of impending caregiver crises. (See Goodman, 1980; Romaniuk et al., 1984; and Springer & Brubaker, 1984, for models of educational programs for families and practitioners.)

*Additional services.* A commonly voiced need of many family members is for safe, caring, convenient substitutes on an occasional basis, in the form of trained sitters or some type of organized respite care. However, it would not be valid to assume that respite care is the only supportive service that families need. Respite care will not necessarily solve every "burdened" family's problems. It may be that some families would benefit more from family counseling sessions than from any other type of intervention. Such therapy could enable them to continue their caregiving with a minimum of stress, guilt, or other debilitating emotional reaction. Other families may benefit from caregiver support groups, in which they could gain information, learn coping strategies, and receive emotional support. Financial planning sessions might help families learn to use their economic resources most effectively and plan for future needs. Time and crisis management strategies could be useful to families who are experiencing burden or distress related to caregiving and other responsibilities. Information and programs such as these are only indirectly related to particular long-term caretaking tasks, yet they could strengthen the family's ability to continue providing care to the elderly member.

*Special training for informal caregivers.* We referred previously to Litwak's (1985) suggestion that various support groups are likely to provide services that are congruent with their structure and function, and we noted that respondents in this study were less likely to receive personal or nursing assistance than other services from family, friends, and neighbors. Perhaps some family members and friends are reluctant to perform personal care and nursing activities because they feel incompetent to carry out these tasks, they do not consider the "nursing" role an appropriate one to assume, they are exhausted by contributing other forms of assistance, or personal care tasks such as assisting with bathing and toileting violate privacy and intimacy norms held by the caretaker and/or older person. One means of bolstering the informal network's ability to provide personal and nursing care services, particularly in rural areas, is to transfer to them knowledge and skills usually possessed only by formal service providers. If individuals living in close proximity to elderly persons who need personal services or nursing assistance were trained to perform these services, and were provided necessary supplies and occasional refresher training sessions, they might be less reluctant to get involved in this form of care. A telephone consultation network could provide a backup system for questions that may arise from such caretaking. Thus it is possible that personal and nursing care could be delivered in a timely and cost-efficient fashion without needing to develop or expand full-blown formal services.

## Needed Research

Our findings provide evidence, not available previously, about differences in levels of family caregiving among rural and urban residents. But they also raise many questions that signal the need for further research in this area. For instance, *why* are rural families more likely to assist elderly members than urban families? Are they more available? Do they hold a stronger sense of respect or obligation or responsibility? Or do they merely fill in for services that are unavailable from any other source because they have no choice? Do the expectations for care from family members vary between rural and urban older adults? What constellation of personal characteristics and early-life family dynamics contribute to family members' willingness to provide care to older adults?

These questions focus on the interpersonal dimensions of caring for an elderly family member, whereas previous research has emphasized quantity and type of assistance and caregivers' experiences of stress and burden. Data on motivations for assisting, attitudes about assisting, expectations of assistance, and perceived benefits of caring for an older family member might contribute useful information to the practitioner's assessment of the types of formal organization support needed by different families. This type of information could complement the existing body of technical knowledge about service delivery, for better coordination of in-home services by family and informal and formal providers.

# PART IV

# *Institutional Setting*

# 11

# Families of the Institutionalized Older Adult

## A Neglected Resource

KATHLEEN COEN BUCKWALTER
GERI RICHARDS HALL

Institutionalization of the older adult is a common occurrence, taking place hundreds of times each day across the country. It would appear that long-term care placement is a relatively simple process of locating the best possible facility to meet the needs of the dependent adult with the available funding. The family and, perhaps, the potential resident might visit the home, interviewing the administrator, director of nursing, and the director of social services. Arrangements are finalized and the new resident moves in. It all seems so simple. Not quite!

Long-term care placement is often the result of months of agonizing for the dependent adult and family and may precipitate a period of crisis. Institutionalization represents a specific environmental transition in aging in which the older adult is relocated to what is most often perceived as his or her last home. Tobin (1980) found that noninstitutionalized elderly reported few concerns about nursing home placement if they perceived family support systems to be in place. However, perceived lack of interpersonal support systems precipitated concern, anxiety, dysphoric mood, and a preoccupation with potential events. These respondents reported that nursing home placement would be "a calamity," "a place to go only to die," or compared the environment to "jail" (Tobin, 1980: 198).

Considering these attitudes, contemplating admission to a long-term care facility is an extremely stressful event. Persons on a waiting list for nursing home placement were found to be significantly more distressed than their counterparts residing in the nursing home. Potential residents were less emotionally responsive, had worsened affective states, were less intact cognitively, and suffered more negative changes in self-esteem than their matched counterparts who had completed the transition to institutionalized life (Tobin, 1980).

Anticipation of nursing home placement can be equally distressing for family members. Adult children report the placement of a parent into a nursing home as one of the most unhappy events of their lives. Studies conducted among adult children of nursing home residents demonstrate that 29% to 45% tried to avoid placement by moving the dependent adult into their home for care (Tobin, 1980). The decision to institutionalize is most often related to lack of availability of social or familial supports and resources to provide needed care, which may be misinterpreted by the potential resident as unwillingness by family members to meet obligations. These feelings can evoke guilt in adult children and feelings of abandonment by the new resident, resulting in long-term changes in family relationships (Brody, 1977).

Once placed, the process of adaptation for both residents and family members begins. The adjustment to the new environment is complicated by the effects of living within a bureaucracy. Adaptation to the nursing home environment often requires that both resident and family members assume unfamiliar and unnegotiated roles within the bureaucracy, determined solely by the nursing home. The resident is expected to rise with others, room compatibly with strangers, participate in preplanned activities (e.g., group bingo) and cheerfully adhere to the rules and implied norms of the system. Little advance notice is given of most rules and norms, leaving the dependent adult and family to "learn the ropes" by trial and error. Moreover, rules and norms may be altered unexpectedly due to changes in governmental regulations, administrative policy, or personnel.

The family is often expected to relinquish the dependent adult to the bureaucracy. The new resident may be perceived by the staff as "theirs," viewing the family as people who have entrusted the resident to the home for care (Clifford, 1985). The family becomes relegated to visitor status, assigned to bring hearing aid batteries, toiletries, and so on, and, perhaps, criticized if visits are too frequent, too long, or otherwise conflict with nursing home routines. If the family attempts to settle disagreements resulting from the placement process, they may be perceived as upsettting the new resident or others and the family may then be regarded by staff as a barrier to resident adaptation rather than an asset. All too often family and staff develop a competitive or even adversarial relationship trying to protect and care for the new resident. This competition is natural in the blending of the two systems: the family systems and the institutional bureaucracy. Successful resident adaptation requires harmony between the systems and creative use of the family to soften the impact of the bureaucracy.

This chapter examines the relationship between families and nursing homes, and addresses ways in which the family can become a valuable resource to aid their elder in adaptation to the facility through family-centered interventions and rehabilitative strategies. We begin with a brief overview of the family system and the nursing home as a bureaucracy, followed by the steps of the nursing process, through assessment, planning, intervention, and evaluation, to facilitate adaptation in long-term care settings.

*The family system.* The family is the primary unit in our society, structured to perform certain tasks, such as transmission of values, solving crises and interpersonal issues, more efficiently than a bureaucracy. These family tasks are not uniform in nature, but require individualized planning and responses. Most of the tasks require no highly specialized knowledge or technical skill (Shanas & Sussman, 1977). Much of the knowledge required is passed down through ethnic values that establish a basis for self-esteem by relating the members' productivity, work, and activities to cultural norms (Markham, 1979). The family system can interact with the bureaucracy (or nursing home system) in several ways, but in our society this interaction is seldom based on mutual support and recognition of the value of and need for the other system.

Ideally, the family role in long-term care is to facilitate linkages that will assist the dependent resident's interaction with the nursing home bureaucracy and will buffer the effects of the bureaucracy on the resident. Bureaucracies most often stress conformity, and may view ethnic/cultural diversity as undesirable. It is also unrealistic to expect the nursing home to function as a melting pot (Markham, 1979). The family must therefore continue to act as the primary group for their resident and attend to the preservation of cultural identity by participating in customs and rituals with the resident.

*The nursing home as a bureaucracy.* Long-term care facilities are bureaucracies that provide complex human services and perform uniform impersonal tasks (Sussman, 1977). They benefit groups as a whole and require specialized knowledge or skill to fulfill their tasks. Bureaucracies are minimally influenced by interpersonal variables and decisions are made slowly within the hierarchy (Sussman, 1977). Because nursing homes must deal with external and environmental variables, such as families, community organizations, ownerships, and local, federal, and state organizations, nursing home organizational structures are difficult to study and describe (O'Conner, 1981). Instead they are often mired in a state of ill-defined interconnected relationships.

Nursing homes are usually organized according to either a medical or social model. The models determine the structure of the administration, attitudes concerning residents and families, and the type of care provided as illustrated in Table 11.1.

Many nursing homes are mixed medical and social models and their organizational structures are not designed to respond quickly to individualized resident needs. In addition, due to paperwork, red tape, and reimbursement strategies, there is little incentive to experiment with alternative forms of care that might lessen the impact of the bureaucracy on the resident (O'Conner, 1981).

Organizational goals are dependent on consumer demands and on regulations. Regulations tend to define the minimum standards acceptable for care at a given rate of reimbursement. Care provided is commensurate with reimbursement. Therefore, homes may provide care at a minimally satisfactory level, avoiding falling below that level for regulatory reasons, and rising above it for resource reasons (O'Conner, 1981). This can place an additional burden on the family, that of supplementing basic care provided to residents, thereby enhancing the quality of institutional life.

*Family and institutions at the time of placement.* Successful resident adaptation to the long-term care center is multifaceted.

TABLE 11.1
Nursing Home Organizational Models

|  | Medical Model | Social Model |
|---|---|---|
| Client label | "patient" | "resident" |
| Philosophy | patients are ill and need medical and nursing care | residents have a variety of interests, drives, needs, and wants |
| Family involvement | families as visitors | families are an integral part of the resident's life |
| Community approach | facility as provider of health services, closed to community | facility is a member of community structure and participates openly with community |
| Organization | hierarchical, decisions flow upward, ultimately to the physician | hierarchical, without clear lines of decision-making, multidisciplinary approach |

Schwirian (1982) found that resident satisfaction was dependent on knowledge of and satisfaction with financial status, health status, and family relationships. This dispels the myth that the resident develops a "new family" or kinship with other residents and the nursing home staff. Such information should encourage staff to recognize the autonomy of nursing home residents, supporting and preserving family relationships whenever possible.

Family relationships are often strained at the time of placement. Few adults are enthusiastic about taking up residence in a nursing home. Months of conflict may have preceded actual placement. Family members may be indecisive about limiting the freedom of the older adult. They may be forced to confront fears of their own mortality, unresolved developmental tasks, old conflicts, and role reversals. There may be real concern about loss of resources.

Media presentations of nursing home abuses, community opinion regarding abandonment of older family members, myths about readily available, inexpensive private adult home health care services, and studies reporting high percentages of persons in long-term care being placed inappropriately have added to the crisis of placement. In addition, there are very few other situations in our society in which total strangers are mandated to share a bedroom, bath, and life's more intimate moments. The dependent adult may find him- or herself sharing a room with someone who is confused, incontinent, or dying, adding to feelings of helplessness and mortality. This is particularly true of residents in urban facilities, where everyone in the facility may be a total stranger. It is important that nursing staff not view this experience in light of their own experience with roommates at summer camp or college, as an exciting opportunity to make new friends, but for what it is, a frightening experience for an older person in crisis.

*Family as a resource.* The long-term care center staff has an obligation to assist the resident with adaptation to the nursing home environment. This includes helping the family to adapt to seeing their loved one within the environment so abandonment does not occur. Counseling family members about policies and procedures within the environment is not enough. Family members and, if possible, residents need to share in the care planning process on a regular basis. This will help to prevent misunderstandings that tend to occur with a lack of communication. The nursing and social work staff need to have an "open door" policy for residents and families for problem solving before crisis intervention is needed. Last, a family that is comfortable within the nursing home environment is a valuable asset. Utilizing family members as a resource for care planning and some care provision for the resident, as support persons and peer counselors for other families, as resource persons and adjunct therapists within the facility, and as community and public relations liaisons can provide the long-term care center with an invaluable resource while assisting both resident and family with adaptation to this new life phase.

### Preadmission Assessment

The preadmission assessment is an ideal way to start family-nursing home interaction off in a mutually supportive and complementary manner. It promotes accommodation, the support of shared goals and objectives. The nursing home and the family acknowledge that each system has expertise in performing specialized functions and that, indeed, they may need each other.

When the decision to seek information about nursing home placement is reached, the role of the professional staff begins. Regardless of whether the initial contact was made by a family, discharge planner, or community-based case manager, the long-term care center staff must begin to evaluate the potential resident and family to determine if this is the best possible placement.

A preadmission assessment is an appropriate method for gathering baseline data on the potential resident and observing the resident/family dynamics. The preadmission assessment is invaluable for explaining the facility's program and allowing the family to ask questions prior to the stress of the actual time of placement. In some facilities, the preadmission assessment is the responsibility of the social worker. In others, the nursing staff or both nursing and social worker may share the responsibility. The preadmission contact determines, ultimately, the family's interaction with the staff.

The assessment is most effective when completed in the potential resident's home. This allows the assessor to evaluate level of function within the resident's most comfortable environment, thus gaining more insight into strengths and weaknesses. This is particularly helpful when evaluating potential residents with dementing illnesses (about 50% of most nursing home residents) as when attempting to match the stimulus level of the first few days in the nursing home with their residence stimulus level to ensure an easier relocation for the demented resident and family. Although it is not always possible to complete the preadmission assessment in the home, the assessment should never be "skipped" to save time or money. The preadmission visit should assess the factors presented in Table 11.2.

The final purpose of the preadmission assessment is to assist the patient/family with the bureaucratic decision-making process. Explaining the program, procedures, and expectations of residents and family, helps to determine if the facility is the best one for the individual. However, more is needed. The family may be grappling with more fundamental issues, such as whether or not nursing home placement is really needed. In this situation, the assessor's responsibility is to provide factual information about placement that will help the family to reach a decision. Information that the family might find helpful includes the following:

(1) the anticipated prognosis of the senior's condition and functional status (i.e., after a stroke the person usually shows some improvement for about 18 months)
(2) safety needs

## TABLE 11.2
### Factors to Be Assessed During Preadmission Visit

(1) What is the adult's level of function? How much assistance will be required? Supervision? Direction? What is his or her medical status? What techniques and "tips" can the family give you concerning care of the dependent adult?

(2) What has the dependent adult been told concerning the placement? Is this a surprise? If so, how does the family expect the facility staff to assist a severely distressed new resident? How will the staff protect the resident's rights?

(3) What is the home environment? Will the older adult be distressed by noise, tidiness, or clutter within the long-term care environment? What is the activity level within the home?

(4) What are the older person's daily habits? Does he or she rise late or have specific patterns that will be problematic when interrupted?

(5) What is the social environment? Is the person used to living with other people? Does he or she socialize regularly? How are the person's social skills when meeting you?

(6) Who are the family members? Where are they located? Have any been involved in the potential resident's care? Do family members live with the person? If not, how often do they visit?

(7) Observe the interaction between the family members and the senior. Does there appear to be conflict? Is there evidence of role strain or burnout? Does the family make eye contact with the assessor? the senior? Who has the ability to make decisions? Is the senior able to participate in the decision-making process? Does the senior express an opinion?

(8) What are the other responsibilities of the family members? Do they hold jobs outside the home? Do they care for other family members on a regular basis? How far do they live from the facility?

(9) What is the senior's attitude toward placement? Is the senior aware of his or her disabilities? Is the senior able to consider the needs of family members/caretakers realistically? Is the senior concerned about finances?

(10) What is the family's attitude about placement? Are all family members in agreement? What do they expect from the staff? Is that realistic? Are they suspicious of the facility and how can you work through that? Is the family grieving? Are they concerned about finances?

(11) Will the family need a support group prior to admission? Do they have strengths that will assist in planning and providing care to their family member? Do they have potential strengths and interest in helping other families who may be adapting to the environment?

(12) How can the transition from home to long-term care center be made without creating unnecessary stress for the resident and family?

(3) the person's right to decide
(4) available community services (i.e., day care, home health services)
(5) the facility's program and services

Once the decision for placement is made, nursing staff should assume responsibility for recording and disseminating data from the assessment. Information should be validated, whenever possible, with other involved professionals such as family physicians and case managers and incorporated into the care plan.

*Planning*

Prior to the resident's arrival at the facility, the nursing staff utilizes the assessment data to determine the level of care, appropriate nursing unit, and the best possible roommate. A detailed description of the preadmission assessment data is provided to at least two shifts of nursing personnel. The rationale for communicating these assessment data are presented in Table 11.3.

Family members should be encouraged to play an active role in care planning with or for the resident. They should understand the principles underlying the program, for example, a structured routine for residents with cognitive impairment. With understanding, cooperation with the program is likely to occur rather than misinterpretation and suspicion. In this way, competence and exchange is fostered; that is, the family uses its resources to optimize care by developing, managing, and mediating interpersonal relationships and linkages in order to maximize gain for the resident.

The family may wish to participate in aspects of physical care not usually assumed by family members. This should be negotiated with the nursing staff in advance and an informed contract developed to prevent misunderstandings with other family members. Family caregivers should understand that they need not continue providing the extra care indefinitely and that nursing staff will assume needed additional responsibilities at any time without extra charge to the resident or prejudice to the resident or family.

Planning responsibilities for family members can facilitate care of the resident, family interaction, and satisfaction with the chosen facility. Planning is a critical step in developing family involvement. Sensitivity is needed by the planner to determine how much

TABLE 11.3
Rationale for Distributing Preadmission Assessment Data to Staff

Data are distributed so that nursing personnel will

(1) have input in planning and determining evaluation measures for the resident's and family's care.

(2) be aware of resident/family attitudes and concerns regarding placement and will be able to address them immediately.

(3) be comfortable with the resident exhibiting behavioral alterations and will request assistance from family members.

(4) understand the family's grieving process and need to be involved with ongoing resident care.

(5) understand resident's need to continue to remain autonomous rather than identify as a member of the "facility family."

(6) promote the family's interaction with the resident in an appropriate manner, teaching visiting skills, if needed.

(7) remain nonjudgmental regarding the family's interactions with the resident.

(8) feel free to interact and problem solve with family members, assisting them with care-related problems, conflicts, and the grieving process.

(9) offer suggestions for increasing family participation within the facility, such as support groups, family peer counseling, resident programs, and special activities.

the family is able to participate at a given point. The nurse liaison should plan and regularly reevaluate the family's need to participate or change participation styles, that is, from support group, to assisting other families. Guidance may be needed in assisting families to recognize opportunities for participatory roles within the facility and enhancing performance, as discussed in the following section.

## Family-Centered Interventions

Institutionalization of a family member is a stressful time for both the family and the elder. Health professionals must recognize the impact of long-term placement on both parties, and can then intervene to smooth the transition and sustain positive relationships. A study by Miller and Harris (1967) supports this concept of "family homeostasis." They note that with the improvement of many institutionalized elderly, there is a subsequent deterioration in the quality of family interactions. They suggest that most families will try to maintain the family system as it is, even after institutionalization. Families of the institutionalized elderly can serve as an important resource, especially in meeting the psychosocial needs of their elderly resident. But first, a sense of family equilibrium, or balance, must often be reestablished. This section begins with an examination of some *family-centered interventions* useful in promoting this balancing process; it is followed by a discussion of ways in which the family can serve as a resource in the long-term care setting through involvement in *rehabilitative strategies*.

Most elderly persons adhere to the American cultural ideals of independence and self-sufficiency and try to avoid burdening their adult children (Hirshfield & Dennis, 1979; Lowenthal & Robinson, 1977). However, in times of crisis, or when other sources of support decrease (such as loss of friends through relocation or death), the family often assumes a more significant helping role (Seelback, 1978; Shanas, 1979b). This increased reliance on family support is true for both elderly individuals living independently in the community and those residing in long-term care settings (Dobrof & Litwak, 1981).

However, increased familial support is not without problems for both the elderly person and the adult children involved. Some of the more common issues confronted in this situation may be best resolved in family counseling sessions. These single family or group sessions may deal with topics such as emotional illness in the elderly; the changing role of female caretakers; aging as a family dilemma; and the economic, physical, and emotional burdens older children, who may be coping with their own aging process, face in providing long-term care for their "old-old" relatives (Gelfand et al., 1978). Ethical dilemmas such as the rights of "old-old" parents versus the needs, values, and rights of "young-old" (ages 55 to 75) children can also be discussed (Cohen, 1983).

Many family members experience ambivalence about institutionalizing an elderly relative (Cath, 1972). Counseling can help the family to arrive at a more realistic, guilt-free placement decision (Lazarus & Weinberg, 1980). Furthermore, with relocation, the nursing home staff often assumes the role of "foster family." This sharing of the aged parent frequently produces interfamilial and intrapsychic conflicts, which are seldom adequately addressed in long-term care settings (Breslin, 1978). Although ongoing communication among administrators, staff, and family members is all too infrequent, family involvement can be a significant factor in the elderly patient's emotional well-being and can either hinder or facilitate the role of the professional staff (Breslin, 1978).

Cohen (1983: 248-249) lists five main goals for family counseling and family support groups:

(1) to provide a supportive atmosphere for families of aged persons, where feelings (such as sadness, shame, grief, anger, guilt, and relief) can be shared, and where similar as well as unique problems can be recognized and dealt with;
(2) to provide information about the aging process and adult development, as well as available resources and services;
(3) to provide assistance in and support for decision making;
(4) as a vehicle to teach self-care activities to both the elderly patients and their family members, such as assertiveness, listening, communication skills, or interpersonal skills training;
(5) to provide a "safe" setting to confront such prevalent and emotional issues as sibling rivalry, unresolved childhood conflicts, and role reversals.

The group process is of particular value in dealing with the family problems identified above. Family counseling sessions promote the sharing of information and solutions to problems, and enable participants to recognize the commonalities among the problems they face. Just talking to other elderly and their family members both during and after the family group sessions can be very therapeutic (Cohen, 1983) and can help family members to objectify and cope with their feelings.

Staff counseling with spouses who were former caretakers also has been shown to be effective in reducing staff-family conflicts, to promote a more therapeutic care environment through the sharing of vital information, and to create a more meaningful role for the family member (Goldstein, 1983). Family counseling sessions may be brief (2 hours/week) and time limited (8-10 weeks duration).

Psychotherapeutic interventions with the elderly are positively influenced by counselors working with family members (Cohen, 1983). Families may be directly involved in these counseling efforts—as in network family therapy, multiple family group work, or family support groups. Or, they may be more indirectly involved, by serving as "adjunct staff" who can be trained to approach their family member in a manner consistent with that employed by the long-term care team. Regardless of the level of involvement, family members should always be informed about the counseling approaches and treatment techniques used with their elderly loved ones (Weiner et al., 1978).

Although support groups are most often associated with family caregivers in the community, their usefulness should not be overlooked when a family member is institutionalized. Following placement, family members can still benefit from sharing similar experiences with others, can work through feelings associated with institutionalization, and establish new "protective-kin" roles (Gwyther & Blazer, 1984). The need for supportive relationships may be greatest among long-time family caregivers of demented patients, or those who have cared for a family member with multiple demanding physical problems. Often these family members have sacrificed other close interpersonal relationships to devote themselves exclusively to the care of their loved one. With institutionalization, they may feel "out of it" with respect to social and leisure-time activities. Considered by society to be neither married nor widowed, the spouse who remains in the community often develops social limitations. Rarely invited to couples events, noninstitionalized spouses find that even widowed friends do not understand their grief. Often spouses who attempt to reestablish themselves socially meet with strong criticism for "abandoning" their partners. The remaining spouse may turn naturally to spending all his or her time visiting the institutionalized family member, only to find that the nursing home bureaucracy rejects this "intrusion" in the care process. Support groups can help to reestablish the emotional balance that has been upset by the relocation of the family member to a long-term care setting, and can bridge the transition back to normal adult roles and activities for unaffected family members.

Occasionally, family members will need more professional counseling interventions to reestablish their lives following institutionalization of their loved one. Logotherapy is an effective approach, especially when the former caregiver feels that life is "empty" and that his or her value was tied to caring for the now institutionalized family member. Logotherapy assists persons to find meaning and purpose in their lives, and provides a sense of freedom and choice, culminating in the will to live (Fabry, 1968).

For some family members, meaning and purpose will continue to be found in "doing" for others and care-related activities. In these circumstances, and when a healthy relationship exists between the family and the elder, family members are an invaluable and neglected therapeutic resource and can be involved in an "adjunct staff capacity" in a variety of rehabilitative strategies. The following section describes selected patient-family interactions that build upon the strengths of the family bond and enhance staff efforts to meet patient needs in a long-term care setting.

*Family Involvement in Rehabilitative Therapies*

Too often elderly patients in long-term care settings are dismissed as hopeless by overworked staff and frustrated family members who view the aging process as a progressive and irreversible deterioration inevitably leading to custodial care (Hussian, 1981). Older patients may experience what Goffman (1961) has termed a "mortification of self", secondary to multiple losses involving roles, property, and self-identity. Desocialization occurs and results in many of the passive behaviors commonly displayed in long-term care settings: interpersonal detachment, apathy, decreased initiative and interest in the environment, family members, and the future, and deterioration of personal habits (Zusman, 1967). However, these low levels of engagement are more likely due to lack of opportunity rather than to disability (McCormack & Whitehead, 1981).

Although subjective feelings of loss of control over one's behavior and environment most often result in passivity, they may also produce inappropriate acting-out responses that label the elderly patient as "unmanageable" and "disruptive" and may create a situation of mutual withdrawal and neglect among patients, family members, and staff. This abandonment is particularly unwarranted in light of recent clinical and research evidence that suggests that a combination of psychosocial rehabilitative strategies consistently incorporated into the ongoing care program can improve behavior and have an overall positive effect on the quality of life of residents in long-term care settings. Family members can play an important role in such a care program and, in so doing, provide relief to overworked, "burned out" staff members. Of course, for this approach to be effective, the bureaucratic environment must be receptive to family involvement.

The next section presents a brief overview of several therapeutic approaches that can involve family members in an adjunct staff capacity. That is, family members can be trained to approach residents in a manner consistent with that employed by the long-term care team. For this collaborative staff-family effort to function most smoothly a "family liaison" nurse should be appointed from within the facility. Responsibilities of the "family-liaison" nurse include the following:

(1) recruitment and evaluation of family members for adjunct staff activities
(2) training of family members in selected rehabilitative strategies and techniques
(3) monitoring of family involvement (e.g., as co-group leader)
(4) referrals of family members to support groups or family counseling as needed
(5) ongoing and systematic evaluation of family involvement and participation in activities

Many strategies have been found to be efficacious in long-term care settings, including remotivation; music, movement, and psychodrama therapies; reminiscence and life review; reality orientation; attitude therapy; and sensory stimulation and training. Space limitation of this chapter permit review of only a few of these approaches.

These rehabilitative strategies are diverse, but share certain characteristics that enable knowledgeable family members and staff to counteract the more negative effects of a long-term care environment (Weiner et al., 1978). These characteristics include (1) *psychosocial stimulation,* which encourages the revitalization of the integrity and individuality of each resident; (2) *social interaction,* which can be effectively used to draw individuals out of a passive withdrawal or hostile rejection mode of behavior or channel acting out, disruptive behavior through socially acceptable and mutually rewarding interpersonal involvement; and (3) *positive reinforcement* related to growth and achievements, which builds each person's sense of self-control and heightens awareness of how to deal constructively with the reality of the situation. To be successful these approaches require consistency and caring involvement on the part of all family members and staff in contact with the resident.

*Remotivation therapy.* Remotivation therapy, a structured program of group discussion, "encourages individuals to take renewed interest in their surroundings by focusing their attention on the simple, objective features of everyday life" (Weiner et al., 1978: 65). The aims of this psychosocial rehabilitative strategy are threefold: (1) to help individuals achieve a sense of belonging and to view themselves in relationship to others; (2) to increase feelings of self-worth, self-reliance, and personal value within a social context; and (3) to assist individuals to maximize their potential through other-directed communication and stimulation of interest in the surrounding environment and people.

Remotivation is a group-oriented approach (10 to 15 patients) that consists of a series of informal meetings once or twice a week. Family members can serve as effective group leaders, and in this capacity they prepare a program of discussions from a variety of sources such as magazines, newspapers, and libraries. The group sessions are *not* educational programs. Rather than trying to teach patients content, the goal of remotivation groups is simply to stimulate their interest in the world around them. Learning, if it does occur, is regarded as a byproduct of this group process. The five steps of the remotivation group process are (1) welcoming, (2) creating a bridge to reality, (3) sharing the world we live in, (4) the world, and (5) appreciation.

The structured approach of remotivation groups has successfully reawakened the interest of regressed and apathetic patients, and thus can be an especially useful therapy in the long-term care settings. It also allows for family members to develop and maintain an increased sense of self-esteem, as they are active and contributing members of the therapeutic team (Weiner et al., 1978). Family members and staff report that the information gained from residents during a remotivation session helped them to appreciate the residents as unique individuals with varied backgrounds and experiences (Weiner et al., 1978). This proves particularly valuable when the family member is able to share these insights on a regular basis with other staff members and administrators. Remotivation therapy has potential for creating a bridge between an elderly person's self-perception and the perception of others. Remotivation groups allow the elderly to reminisce about their experiences and to identify and assert those experiences through interactions that may strengthen the concept of reality (Burnside, 1984).

*Music and movement.* Music therapy is enjoying increasing popularity as a rehabilitative strategy that can accommodate a large number of residents as well as incorporate other approaches such as reality orientation and movement therapy. Music therapy is the "controlled use of music in the treatment, rehabilitation, education and training of adults and children suffering from physical, mental, and emotional disorders" (Burnside, 1984: 199). Family members can use music in groups in the following ways: (1) listening to music, (2) having music in the environment, and (3) making music.

The goal of music therapy groups is not to teach music per se so no particular musical talent is necessary on the part of the family member. Rather, such groups can be used to (1) improve quality of life, (2) increase body movement, (3) stimulate withdrawn persons, (4) stimulate reminiscence, and (5) increase feelings of relatedness (Burnside, 1984). Research has demonstrated that music facilitates socialization, decreases aggressiveness, incontinence and hallucinatory behavior, and improves patient appearance and self-esteem. Even isolated and regressive individuals can listen to music with their family members and can be encouraged to respond nonverbally. Music can also be cathartic in that it assists older persons and their family members to get in touch with their feelings and express them in the safe environment of a group. Music therapy can be a vehicle for changing moods, promoting relaxation, and fostering a sense of group cohesiveness. Burnside (1984) highlights three ways in which music facilitates discussion and sharing in the group experience: (1) identification with feelings expressed, (2) associations that relate past experience, and (3) improvement in the perception of reality through projection.

Music can help older persons and their family members to move with more freedom and confidence, and music therapy has been combined successfully with movement therapy in long-term care facilities. One of the major deprivations in many institutional settings is lack of movement and touch. Holding hands with family members and moving with other body parts to music is one way to counteract this deprivation. Movement therapy can be emotionally satisfying, creative, and social. It can increase self-awareness and expression as well as endurance. Our youth-oriented culture has made it difficult for the elderly to feel positive about their physical self (Boots & Hogan, 1981). Movement and music therapy can help overcome this negative focus, while at the same time promoting health through breathing and relaxation and bodily activity for both the resident and family members (Boots & Hogan, 1981).

*Sensory stimulation and training.* Intensified sensory input can produce significant behavioral changes even in very old and debilitated patients (Weiner et al., 1978). Responses to sensory deprivation and environmental disengagement may result in so-called senility and other psychopathological behaviors that may be reversible. Family members can assist in stimulation and training efforts with their loved one.

Sensory training refers to a structured experience (either individual or group) that involves the five senses. The goal of this approach is to put the elderly, regressed person back in touch with his or her surroundings, improve sensitivity and responsiveness to the environment, and increase discrimination ability (Weiner et al., 1978). This strategy is particularly useful for patients who lack the socialization skills, motor coordination, and strength or attention span to participate successfully in some of the other rehabilitative activities discussed in this chapter. Thus sensory training can benefit even patients experiencing problems with perceptual motor ability, sensory input discrimination, and psychosocial performance because this approach presents the environment in its most comprehensible, elemental form through body awareness exercises and the presentation of stimuli. Examples of different types of stimuli family members can present include the following:

- *visual:* looking in the mirror
- *auditory:* listening to voice on tape
- *tactile:* touching textured objects such as velvet cloth
- *olfactory:* smelling fragrant, spicy objects
- *gustatory:* tasting sweet, sour, and bitter foods
- *kinesthetic:* moving and dancing

It is also important to keep in mind that assistive devices such as glasses, hearing aids, and large-print books may help alleviate sensory deprivation. Something as simple as removing impacted ear wax may decrease hostile and suspicious behaviors in an elderly resident. Finally, touching and bodily contact are essential aspects of this approach that convey warmth, acceptance, and humanness—qualities often lacking in the impersonal environment of many long-term care settings.

Family members can combine sensory training experiences effectively with reminiscence to stimulate memories and link the present to the past. This modification provides more meaning to the sensory training experience and adds an additional integrative function for the patient (Weiner et al., 1978).

*Reminiscence and life review.* Attempts to stimulate cognitive functioning in the elderly are worthwhile, and memories and reminiscence can provide the material needed for such activities (Hughston & Merriam, 1982). Furthermore, reminiscences are an important source of improving self-esteem among the elderly and their family members (Blau & Berezin, 1982).

Reminiscing is the processing of remembering the past, either verbally or internally. Many factors can influence what is remembered and how the memories are awakened. Often, reflections on the past are regarded as evidence of "senility" among the elderly by uninformed family members. However, in the early 1960s Butler (1963) theorized that reminiscence is part of a normal and healthy life-review process brought about by the realization of impending death. There is much research evidence that suggests reminiscence can be a beneficial activity (Brennan & Steinberg, 1983-1984). Benefits of the life-review process include (1) resolution of old conflicts, (2) personality reorganization, and (3) restoration of meaning to the elderly person's life (King, 1982). Remembering the past helps the elderly both personally and socially and provides positive growth experiences for both patients and their family members. It assists elderly persons to evaluate, understand, and accept their lives. It can also reawaken mental and emotional faculties and provide a mechanism for coping with stressors (Hamner, 1984).

Life-review therapy can be conducted by informed family members individually or in groups limited in size to 4 to 8 participants. Almost any type of elderly patient can be included (e.g., brain damaged, physically regressed, blind, mildly psychotic). Only those persons with receptive aphasia and severe psychosis should be excluded. The broad appeal of this approach is centered on the fact that this strategy utilizes the brain-impaired person's strongest cognitive asset: past memory (McMordie & Blom, 1979).

Memory-evoking techniques are varied and can include tangible reminders of the past such as family pictures, mirrors, scrapbooks, and letters brought in by family members. Groups can be time limited, that is, structured once per week for a period of ten weeks. Sessions begin with discussion of childhood memories and progress to current memories, all the while increasing the elderly patients self-esteem and reaffirming their sense of identity. Other topics that are favorably received in reminiscence groups include the Great Depression, military experiences, holiday celebrations, movie stars, and old-time songs and cars. Associating current experiences with meaningful past events reinforces memory and gives added significance to experiences shared with the group. Care must be taken to avoid anxiety and despair, lest the elderly person views his or her life as a total waste. However, most people can reconcile their lives and find meaning in the past to confront the present (Schnase, 1982).

## Evaluation

The family-liaison nurse is in the best position to evaluate the efficacy of family involvement in rehabilitative strategies and with the long-term care facility in general. Ongoing and comprehensive evaluation involves multiple components, including the following:

(1) Family and resident satisfaction measures.
(2) Does the family supply necessities (e.g., hearing-aid batteries) as well as luxuries?
(3) Do they visit on a regular basis?
(4) Does the family interact with other patients and families?
(5) Do they communicate freely with staff members?
(6) Do family members provide positive feedback to the community regarding care given in the facility, and/or promote referrals?
(7) Are family strengths and abilities used as a resource by the facility (e.g., if a resident's son is a dentist, will he provide the staff with recommendations on oral care needs)?
(8) Does the family participate in planning and implementing special activities (e.g., holiday parties)?
(9) Do they provide input for activities, programs, and special care needs?

Evaluation activities can be conducted either formally, as in a research mode, or informally, using a variety of data-gathering strategies. The family-liaison nurse may wish to use standardized satisfaction measures, such as the Family Perceptions Tool or Risser Patient Satisfaction Questionnaire (Maas & Buckwalter, 1985). In addition, observations and structured interviews will elicit valuable information on the degree and effectiveness of family involvement.

## Summary

This chapter has reviewed several family-centered interventions and rehabilitative therapies that can be employed successfully by family members with their elderly residents in concert with staff efforts in long-term care settings. Each strategy outlined has pros and cons and should be undertaken only after individual and family assessment, and with adequate training, monitoring, and evaluation of family members. Use of these approaches is suggested as a way to smooth the transition of elderly residents as they relocate from the family system to the nursing-home bureaucracy. Further, these strategies are designed to promote more positive interactions between the nursing home staff and family members such that they come to view each other as needed allies rather than adversaries. Appointment of a "family-liaison" nurse is suggested as the best way to increase family involvement in long-term care settings in a quality manner, consistent with staff efforts. Perhaps even more important than the type of approach selected is the manner in which it is delivered. Genuine concern and involvement on the part of all caregivers are paramount, and in this regard family members are often a neglected resource for the institutionalized elderly.

# 12

# The Forgotten Client

## Family Caregivers to
## Institutionalized Dementia Patients

CLARA PRATT
VICKI SCHMALL
SCOTT WRIGHT
JAN HARE

The objective difficulties and subjective sense of burden experienced by many family members who provide day-to-day care for physically and mentally impaired elders have been described by several authors (Zarit et al., 1980; Zarit & Zarit, 1982; Gwyther & Matteson, 1983; Archbold, 1982a; Brody & Lang, 1982). In fact, institutionalization of dependent elders has been linked to these burdens becoming "excessive" (Tobin & Kulys, 1981; Carrilio & Eisenberg, 1983; Morycz, 1985). Although feelings of guilt and inadequacy often accompany institutionalization of a relative (Brody, 1977; Tobin & Kulys, 1981), it is often believed that institutionalization abates the stresses of caregiving. Smith and Bengston (1979), for example, note that institutionalization of a dependent relative may alleviate the strain of "technical care" and allow families to refocus their efforts on the emotional aspects of their relationship.

Recent studies (George, 1984; Pratt et al., 1986; Wright, 1986) have specifically examined the experiences of family members of institutionalized dementia patients. Further research on such family members has been identified as an important future research area in Alzheimer's disease (Ory et al., 1985). Given current estimates that at least 50% of residents in nursing homes suffer from some type of dementing illness (National Institute of Health, 1981), it is clear that many families are affected.

Family caregivers to institutionalized dementia patients often feel a strong sense of continued responsibility after placement (George, 1984). Yet such families may face great difficulty in maintaining any sense of social relationship with the severely demented relatives who are unable to recognize or respond to them (York & Calsyn, 1977). Thus these families may not experience the sense of caregiving relief and renewal of emotional relationships described by Smith and Bengston (1979).

Several other researchers and practitioners have commented on the interface between the family caregivers to dementia patients and the institution (Brody, 1977; Eisdorfer & Cohen, 1981; Hayter, 1982; Mackay, 1983; Ricci, 1983; Lynott, 1983; Peppard, 1985). The important general responsibilities typically described for the family caregivers in the institution include providing information about the patient, regular visiting and outings, reminiscing, exercising with the patient, assisting with the implementation of care plans, and providing continued love and affection.

Yet despite this consistent interest in families' general responsibilities in institutions, two other recent studies have indicated that there may be considerable ambiguity about specific responsibilities of staffs and families for various aspects of patient care (Shuttlesworth et al., 1982; Rubin & Shuttlesworth, 1983). These researchers maintain that such ambiguity potentially creates problematic family-staff interactions and may ultimately limit the quality of patient care. The researchers state that through sensitive, ongoing communication with families, clarity about roles and responsibilities can be enhanced and that families, staffs, and particularly patients benefit.

This concern with staff actions to facilitate positive relationships with families is one that is found throughout the literature. Implicitly or explicitly building upon Litwak's (1981) theory of shared functions and balanced coordination, authors recognize that there are clear impediments to patient care when confusion exists over respective family-staff responsibilities. To some degree all of the authors cited above as supporting family involvement in institutions suggest that families' feelings of guilt and confusion over their new roles require responsive, supportive action from the institution staff. Similarly, Dobrof (1981) maintained that institutional barriers must be removed and families actively encouraged if they are to be positively involved in long-term care institutions.

Despite this frequent call for positive interactions between family and the family and the institution, such interactions may not readily occur. Difficulties in family-staff interactions have been described by many authors (Silverstone & Hyman, 1976; Kramer & Kramer 1976; Brody, 1977; Wentzel, 1979). Such difficult interactions have been associated with fewer family visits and lower quality of care for the patient (Tobin & Kulys, 1981) as well as exacerbation of families' feelings of guilt and hostile interactions with institution staffs (Silverstone & Hyman, 1976; Wentzel, 1979; Numerof, 1983).

Several authors have commented on the sources of such difficulties, including confusion over respective roles and responsibilities (Litwak, 1981; Shuttlesworth et al., 1982; Rubin & Shuttlesworth, 1983), family guilt and projected hostility (Kramer & Kramer, 1976; Silverstone & Hyman, 1976; Brody, 1977; Wentzel, 1979) and institutional barriers (Dobrof, 1981; Montgomery, 1983). Numerof (1983) addressed several institutional barriers to positive interactions with families, including one that she labeled the *identified patient syndrome*. This syndrome is typified by an exclusive focus on the problems of the patient and a corresponding lack of attention to the family, except as they can assist the staff to understand the patient. Similarly, Buckholdt (1983), in his study of family conferences in long-term care institutions, concluded that although staffs were sympathetic to family concerns, staff's interests focus primarily on how the family could illuminate the resident's responsiveness to institutional care. Family concerns outside this patient-centered focus were not seen as appropriate issues to which staffs should respond.

Perhaps the identified patient syndrome underlies much of the interest in family involvement in institutions. For although it is often recognized that such involvement may reduce feelings of guilt and feelings of hostility toward the institution, certainly the most commonly cited motive for family involvement is the well-being of the patient. This overall pattern of interaction between families and institutions is one that leads up to describe the family caregivers to institutionalized dementia patients as too often the "forgotten clients." Coupled with indications of the poor physical and emotional health status among many family caregivers to institutionalized patients (Brody, 1977; Tobin & Kulys, 1981) the description "forgotten clients" seems appropriate.

In order for long-term care institutions to respond more fully to family caregivers, information about the needs and resources of these caregivers is critical. Beyond the often-cited feelings of guilt, what strains do family caregivers to institutionalized dementia patients experience, how do they cope with these, and what is their level of physical and mental well-being? This chapter will focus on these issues for family caregivers to institutionalized dementia patients, examining several research questions. These include:

- To what degree do family caregivers to institutionalized dementia patients experience burden associated with this role?
- What are the relationships among caregivers' coping strategies, levels of burden, and well-being?
- What are the relationships among caregiver locus of control, coping strategies, burden, and well-being?

Data from two recent investigations will be presented in examining these questions. This examination will elucidate the characteristics of the "forgotten clients" and provide an empirical basis for designing responsive institutional programs, policies, and practices. In interaction with the institution, family caregivers may then be better supported in meeting their own needs as well as the needs of their institutionalized relative.

### Study 1
### Burden, Coping, and Health Status

In this investigation, family caregivers were defined as the persons who had responsibilities for providing and/or managing the day-to-day care for the patient. The variables investigated were caregiver burden, coping strategies, morale, self-assessed health before and after caregiving began, and selected demographic factors (sex, age, patient residence, and length of caregiving). To gather data, three published documents and one investigator-designed instrument were utilized.

The Caregiver Burden Scale (Zarit et al., 1981) consists of 22 items on feelings about caregiving and has a reported alpha reliability coefficient of .79 (Zarit & Zarit, 1982). Caregiver morale was measured using a 7-item morale scale (Lawton, 1971) that assesses overall happiness and satisfaction with one's life. An investigator-designed instrument was utilized to gather descriptive information about the patient and the caregivers.

The Family Crisis Oriented Personal Evaluation Scales (F-COPES) consists of 30 items that represent 8 coping strategies that individuals may use in response to problems or difficulties (McCubbin et al., 1981). Although these strategies represent "only a small sampling of the expansive repertory of coping responses actually used" (Olson et al., 1983), the F-COPES identifies the frequency of use of 3 internal and 5 external coping strategies. The 3 internal coping strategies are reframing (the ability to redefine stressful experiences in a way that makes them more understandable and manageable); confidence in problem solving; and passivity (avoidance responses to problems) (McCubbin et al., 1981). The 5 external coping strategies reflect the degree to which individuals actually use the social support resources available to them. These social resources include spiritual support, extended families, friends, neighbors, and community services. The F-COPES has an alpha reliability of .86 and test/retest reliability of .81 (Olson et al., 1983).

The participants in the study were family caregivers to dementia patients and were drawn from two sources: support groups for Alzheimer's caregivers and one-time-only educational workshops or lectures on Alzheimer's disease held at hospitals or senior centers throughout the state of Oregon. It is possible that these participants represent a biased sample, that is, caregivers who are seeking advice and support on management of relatives with Alzheimer's disease. A total of 240 caregivers completed questionnaires. Because questionnaires were completed during the meeting times, the response rate was over 90% of those contacted.

Of the respondents, 61% (146 respondents) were members of Alzheimer's support groups and 39% (94 respondents) were not. Initial analysis of all variables indicated no significant differences between respondents who were members of support groups compared to those who were not members. For all future analyses, data from these two sources were combined. The mean age of caregivers was 61.3 years (SD = 14.6) and the mean length of caregiving was 49.1 months (SD = 14.7). Of the respondents, 22% (53 respondents) were male and 78% (187) were female. Of the caregivers, 62% (149) provided care to relatives who resided in the community, either in the caregiver's home (50%) or their own home (12%). Of the caregivers, 28% (91) had relatives who resided in institutions.

There were no significant differences by patient residence in caregiver's or patients' mean ages or length of illness. However, compared to caregivers to community-dwelling patients, caregivers to institutionalized patients were significantly more likely to rate the patient's mental status as poor (31.8% and 52.4%, respectively, $\chi^2 = 13.5$, df = 3).

All findings in Study 1 reported as significant were at probability levels of p < .05.

*Caregiver well-being: burden, morale, and health.* The mean caregiver burden scores were 40.1 (SD = 17.5) for caregivers to community-dwelling patients and 39.6 (SD = 18.7) for caregivers to institutionalized patients. There were no significant differences in burden scores by patient residence (institutionalized versus community dwelling) or by caregiver employment status, income level, caregiver sex or family relationship (spouse, child, child-in-law) to the patient.

Compared to caregivers to community-dwelling patients, caregivers to institutionalized patients gave significantly higher ratings to burden scale items that assessed concerns about not having enough money to provide care, being unable to continue providing care, wishing they could leave the care to someone else, and feeling they should do more.

When the effect of age was controlled using analysis of covariance, caregiver burden scores were significantly higher for caregivers who rated their health as fair or poor, for both caregivers to community-dwelling patients (F[3, 135] = 10.7) and institutionalized patients (F[3, 87] = 17.9). Caregivers' ratings of their health status before caregiving began were not significantly related to the patients' residence, ($\chi^2 = 1.34$, df = 3). However, caregivers' ratings of their current health status were significantly related to patient residence ($\chi^2 = 9.60$, df = 3) with caregivers to institutionalized relatives significantly more likely to rate their current

health status as "fair" or "poor" (community 36.2%, institution 57.1%). Caregivers to institutionalized relatives were also significantly more likely to state that caregiving had had a great negative effect upon their health status (community 28.9%; institution 47.2%; $\chi^2 = 10.50$, df = 2).
Morale scores did not vary significantly by patient residence (community, mean = 3.2, SD = 1.8; institution, mean = 3.00, SD = 1.9; t = .36, df = 238). Burden scores were significantly related to caregivers' morale levels for caregivers to community-dwelling patients (r = -.51) and institutionalized patients (r = -.49).
*Caregiver coping strategies.* Coping strategies used by caregivers did not vary significantly by patient residence. Among the internal coping strategies utilized by family caregivers to institutionalized patients, reframing was rated the highest (mean = 3.86, SD = .72) followed by confidence in problem-solving (mean = 3.59, SD = .84) and passivity (mean = 2.21, SD = .75). For the external coping strategies, community services were rated the highest (mean = 3.72, SD = .93) followed by: friends (3.59, SD = .85); spiritual support (3.53, SD = 1.15); extended family (3.47, SD = .99); and neighbors (2.59, SD = 1.03). For caregivers to institutionalized relatives, burden and morale were significantly positively related to confidence in problem solving (burden r = .39 and morale r = .26). Burden and morale were significantly, negatively related to passivity (burden r = -.28 and morale r = -.25). No other significant relationships were found between coping strategies and burden or morale.
When the effect of age was controlled using analysis of covariance, caregivers to institutionalized patients who reported their own current health status to be poor had significantly higher passivity scores than caregivers who reported their health status to be fair to excellent ($F(3,87) = 6.65$). The use of the other 7 coping strategies did not vary significantly by caregivers' health status levels.

*Study 2:*
*Burden, Locus of Control,*
*and Coping Behavior*

This study (Wright, 1986) investigated in greater depth the psychological characteristics of family caregivers and the relationship of these characteristics to caregiver well-being. Because data collection and analysis are still underway, only preliminary findings can be reported here.

Family caregivers in this study were identified from mailing lists for support groups and education programs for caregivers to dementia patients in eight western states. Questionnaires were mailed directly to 1,000 caregivers by the researchers or by support group leaders; data on the first 442 caregivers who responded are reported here.

The average age of caregivers was 61.2 years (SD = 13.6) and the mean length of caregiving was 36 months. The majority of the respondents were female (73.8%) and most (69%) were members of support groups for caregivers to dementia patients. Of the caregivers, 65% (287) cared for community-dwelling patients and 35% (155) of the caregivers had dementia patients who resided in institutions. Dementia patients who resided in institutions were not significantly different in age from community-dwelling patients but were rated at significantly lower functional levels on the Functional Dementia Scale (Moore et al., 1983) than were community-dwelling patients.

Major variables of interest in this study were caregiver burden levels, life satisfaction, locus of control orientation, and coping behavior. Burden was measured by the Caregiver Burden Scale (Zarit et al., 1982) described under Study 1. Life satisfaction was assessed with a 13-item scale with a test/retest reliability of .79 (Wood et al., 1969).

Locus of control orientation was assessed using a 24-item scale developed by Levenson (1981). This scale assesses internal control and 2 external control orientations, powerful others and chance (the belief that the world is unordered and unpredictable). This scale has internal consistency reliability levels of .68 to .78 for the 3 control dimensions.

Coping behavior was assessed with a 41-item scale (Jalowiec et al., 1984). The scale was factor analyzed on the current sample and produced 4 factors each representing a different type of coping behavior. These were problem-oriented (behaviors that act directly on the problem), avoidant-evasive (e.g., worry, get nervous, do nothing), reframing (e.g., reappraisals of the situation, believing things could be worse), and regressive coping (e.g., actions that may reduce tensions but are in the long run unproductive, such as eating, drinking, cursing, and taking out tensions on someone else). Cronbach's alpha for the scale with this sample was .78.

All findings in Study 2 reported as significant were at probability levels of p < .05.

*Caregiver well-being.* Mean caregiver burden scores did not vary significantly by patient residence (community-dwelling, mean = 41.2 and institutionalized, mean = 42.3). Likewise, life satisfaction scores did not vary significantly by patient residence (community, mean = 5.8 and institutionalized, mean = 5.6).

*Locus of control and coping behaviors.* Although there were no significant differences in caregivers' internal or powerful others control orientations by patient residence, caregivers to institutionalized patients had significantly higher mean scores for chance control orientations reflecting beliefs that the world is unpredictable and uncontrollable (community, mean = 11.5 and institution, mean = 13.2, F = 3.8). Compared to caregivers whose impaired family members resided in the community, caregivers to institutionalized patients had significantly higher mean scores for avoidant-evasive coping behaviors (means = 25.1 and 27.6, respectively, F = 5.3). Caregivers to institutionalized patients also had significantly higher mean scores for regressive coping behaviors (e.g., eating, drinking, getting angry; community, mean = 11.0 and institution, mean = 12.8, F = 4.2). There were no significant differences by patient residence in mean scores for reframing and problem-oriented coping behaviors.

Caregiver burden was significantly positively associated with avoidant-evasive coping strategies (r = .48) and regressive coping (r = .37). Burden was also significantly associated with both powerful others (r = .15) and chance (r = .13) control orientations.

Life satisfaction was significantly positively correlated with problem-oriented coping strategies (r = .20). Life satisfaction was significantly negatively associated with avoidant-evasive coping (r = −.44), regressive coping (r = −.27), powerful others control orientation (r = −.33), and chance control orientation (r = −.40).

## Discussion

Both studies reviewed here indicate that the common belief that institutionalization abates the stresses of caregiving may not be well-founded for relatives of dementia patients. The levels of burden reported by caregivers in both studies are similar to levels reported in earlier studies of caregivers to community-dwelling dementia patients (Zarit et al., 1981; Zarit et al., 1982). Caregiver burden scores were not significantly different between caregivers to community-dwelling or institutionalized patients. However, sources of burden did vary as reported in Study 1. Family caregivers to institutionalized dementia patients reflected both guilt and ambivalence about institutionalized care. Compared to caregivers to community-dwelling patients, caregivers to institutionalized patients more frequently wished that they could leave caregiving to someone else and also more frequently reported that they felt they should be doing more.

The poor physical health status of these caregivers very likely contributed to the decision to institutionalize the patient. Further, in both studies, these caregivers perceived the patient to have more severe cognitive impairment than did caregivers to community-dwelling patients. Thus both the caregivers' health status and the patients' level of impairment would indicate that the decision to institutionalize may have been based upon realistic assessments. Nevertheless, Brody (1977) has pointed out that "regardless of the most reality based determinants of that placement," many caregivers experience tremendous guilt and perceive placement as a personal failure coming after months or years of caregiving with the aim of avoiding institutionalization. Some caregivers in Study 1 captured these feelings in their statements about caregiving:

It was easier to bury my first husband than to place my second husband in the nursing home [72-year-old wife].

Now that my husband is in the nursing home, I am lonely, but I just couldn't take it anymore. My back hurt constantly, I was cross with him, and cried a lot [75-year-old wife].

There are no words to express the trauma of finally having to accept the fact that you cannot care for him any longer [76-year-old wife].

When the time comes that you can't continue there is no choice but the nursing home. It does relieve the physical burden but the mental anguish continues. The caregiver may be burned out and not survive as long as the patient. This nearly happened in our case [69-year-old husband].

There are several possible reasons that caregivers continue to feel burdened following placement (George, 1984). First, although placement alleviates 24-hour caregiving the emotional stress of observing the continued deterioration in the family member continues. Second, placement does not necessarily change a caregiver's level of commitment and involvement. The caregiver may spend many hours at the facility and worry about the person and the care when he or she is away. Third, the caregiver is faced with new concerns. As one woman said,

> Placing my husband in the nursing home didn't mean the end to problems . . . new problems had to be faced [70-year-old wife].

Thus, although institutionalization of the patient may ease some problems for caregivers, new problems or concerns are often confronted.

Before discussing programs, policies, or procedures that may address these new problems, it is important to clarify a major assumption underlying such interventions. Long-term care facilities are an important point on the continuum of care for *both* patients and families. Although long-term care facilities may be the end point in the continuum for many patients, especially dementia patients, these same facilities may serve as the entry point of the continuum for many family members. Institutional interactions with families should recognize this by actively assessing families' needs and resources, independent of how these directly benefit patient care. This role may be particularly critical for older spouses or other family caregivers whose physical and emotional health has been negatively affected by caregiving.

As an important, participating member of the continuum of care, long-term care facilities will actively refer family members to appropriate services outside the facility. These might include health screening and treatment, legal assistance, mental heath, and senior centers. Developing cooperative programs with other services may also be appropriate to meet some families' needs. Finally, long-term care institutions should develop policies and programs that function within the institution to recognize family members as clients and to serve them better. Examples of these are orientation, education, and volunteer or support group programs that meet the family needs and that can be directly related to the institutional experience. Although long-term care facilities do not have the total responsibility for supporting family members, they are a critical point on the continuum of care and they do have the responsibility to assist family members to establish a life within and outside the institution.

Given this perspective, it is possible to discuss programs, policies, and procedures that address the problems family caregivers face when a dementia patient enters a long-term care facility. Significant among these problems are concerns about finances. This fact was seen in both the burden scale and the quotes from caregivers. The reality of nursing home care is that it may deplete a family's resources because health insurance and Medicare do not cover the majority of care for a person with dementing illness. The problem can be particularly acute for the community-dwelling spouse. Caregivers in Study 1 wrote:

> The greatest concern that I have is that I have used up the last of the money we received from the sale of our house. Now we will be using up our small store of stocks and bonds. Then who will look after me [71-year-old wife]?

> After providing care as long as possible and placing the victim in a nursing home and expecting to get some peace of mind, one sees all their assets being used up and a very bleak future. One envies the victim who is not aware of the situation [74-year-old husband].

> When children are responsible for financing their parents' care, it can be devastating—especially when they are raising a family. My mother fell through the cracks on governmental assistance in the community and now medical insurance doesn't cover the costs of care [41-year-old daughter].

Early legal-financial planning may substantially reduce the financial burden associated with institutional care. Done early in the disease process, this legal-financial planning can clarify the responsibilities of children and protect the assets that caregiving spouses need for their own support. This planning means that the possibility of institutional care must be presented to the family early in the disease process.

The responsibility for encouraging early planning falls not only upon the institution staffs but also upon community services and medical professionals. This may be a good opportunity for cooperative educational programming. Few legal and financial planners are well-versed in the needs of families facing dementing illness. Thus professionals working with these families should be aware of competent advisors who can assist families in this specialized area. If these advisors do not exist in a particular community, then the opportunity for developing this resource should be pursued. Further, professionals, together with families facing dementia, should advocate for more equitable financial support for long-term care of dementia patients. Given the significance of caregivers' financial concerns, stronger efforts to work with individual families, to develop systems of competent legal-financial planners, and to influence fiscal policy for institutional care are clearly indicated.

Beyond financial concerns, earlier vows or promises to the patient to avoid institutionalization are also potential sources of concern and guilt for family members. For example, one woman stated, "The most difficult part of this [institutionalization] is that I said to my husband that I would take care of him in sickness and in health, and now I am not doing it." Such feelings may interfere with realistic and timely planning by the caregiver and also may result in unrealistic expectations for the staff (Wentzel, 1979). These potential problems can often be alleviated by allowing caregivers to express their feelings and by supporting them in objectively examining the present conditions compared to those that existed when the promises were made. Caregivers' strengths can be reinforced by pointing out what they can and are still doing to support the patient. Continuing to visit, taking the patient out, providing information to the staff, serving on advisory committees, and actively participating in care planning, implementation, and evaluation are some of the ways that caregivers can take positive actions.

To be effective participants in patient care, families need education and support from institution staff about realistic goals, behavior management, and specific guidelines on positive actions they may take in responding to their relative (Ricci, 1983; Numerof, 1983). Thus caregivers can be assisted to view caregiving in a broad perspective that includes emotional, social, and spiritual components as well as physical care. This perspective can enable family caregivers to regard placement as an end of burdensome physical care but not the end of caring. Further, this active involvement may increase the caregivers' sense of confidence and decrease feelings of passivity and powerlessness.

Institutional procedures that encourage family members to stay close during and beyond the period of transition to the institution demonstrate that long-term care is a shared function. Such procedures have been shown to be helpful to both family members and patients (Solomon, 1983). Similarly, Montgomery (1983) advocated for nursing home care policies and practices that ensure the effective and positive contributions of families. Her research indicted that the optimum care policies are those that treat the family as a client, involving them in the institution and making them feel welcome. Solomon (1983) advocated for active involvement of professionals in assisting families during the period of transition to the institution, noting that these early interventions should be directed toward connecting the family with the institution.

Later intervention efforts can then address the personal problems of the caregiver through counseling, education, and social support. Here institutional programs as well as referrals and cooperative programs with other agencies in the continuum of care may be very important. Whatever the structure, interventions with family caregivers should recognize the potentially negative impact of passive, regressive, and avoidant-evasive coping strategies and the potentially positive impact of active problem-solving and reframing. Studies reviewed in this chapter indicate that family caregivers who have low levels of confidence in problem solving and high levels of passive, avoidant-evasive, and regressive coping strategies were particularly vulnerable to high levels of burden. Although these later coping strategies may provide short-term "respite" from difficult situations the prolonged use of these strategies has been associated with negative physical and mental health outcomes (Folkman, 1984).

Educational and other interventions can be designed to provide family caregivers with support in redefining the difficult situations and in identifying problems that they are able to address effectively. Such interventions should explore the caregivers' experiences both as supporters of the patient and as individuals with needs and lives outside the institution. These interventions should serve to rebuild the caregivers' confidence in problem solving and to reduce the sense of failure that often follows institutional placement. These interventions may also effect the caregivers' diminished sense of control, which was apparent in the high level of beliefs in chance on the locus of control measure in Study 2. The ultimate goal of any such intervention would be to support the caregiver in regaining a sense of personal efficacy and control.

Other educational programs conducted by long-term care facilities can be designed to provide information about institutionalization and dementia. Topics might include "Understanding Changes in You and Your Relative," "Coping With Institutionalization: Feelings, Adjustments, and Strategies," and "Making Your Visits Positive." Although few books have been designed specifically for the family of the institutionalized person with a dementing illness, the following have been helpful to many families: *The 36-Hour Day* (Mace & Rabins, 1981), *Alzheimer's Disease: A Guide for Families* (Powell & Courtice, 1983), *Alzheimer's Disease: A Guide for Families, Spouses, and Friends* (Reisberg, 1983), and *Nursing Home Placement: A Guidebook for Families* (Richards et al., 1984).

Other caregivers, particularly those with limited social support and high levels of burden, may benefit from participation in a support group. The value of a support group was expressed by many caregivers in Study 1:

The support group has helped me to feel less alone and that somehow I can survive [68-year-old wife].

The support group has been my lifeline [72-year-old husband].

It helps me to be able to share what I thought were crazy concerns with others who understand. Although my family and friends try to understand what it's like, it's difficult for them to really do so [73-year-old wife].

A support group can assist caregivers to normalize their experience, provide a forum for openly discussing feelings and concerns, put their personal situation in perspective, decrease stress, and exchange information and skills for coping (Schmall, 1984). However, support groups that focus only on the ventilation of feelings and discussing problems may not help to alleviate burden. The most effective support groups may be those that help individuals to problem solve, reframe difficult situations so they are more manageable, and develop concrete strategies for responding to difficult feelings and situations.

The importance of "homogeneity of problems" facing participants has been described as paramount to the success of self-help groups (Lieberman, 1985). Thus designing support groups specifically for family members of nursing home residents may be advantageous. In such groups issues that are unique to their situation may be better addressed than within a community-wide support group. In institution-based support groups, the unique problems faced by family members can be the focus and family members of long-term residents may also serve as role models to relatives of newly admitted residents. Helpful resources for designing and implementing support groups include *Mobilizing Networks of Mutual Support: How to Develop Alzheimer's Caregivers' Support Groups* (Gwyther & Brooks, 1984) and recent articles by Lieberman (1985), Reever and Thomas (1985), and Schmall (1984).

Specific education, counseling, and social support interventions will vary across institutions, related community health and social service networks, and individual caregivers. What should be common across this diversity should be the recognition that family caregivers to institutionalized dementia patients have special concerns that go beyond the often noted feelings of guilt. These may include feelings of continued burden in caregiving and the sense that the world is unordered and unpredictable. These caregivers may also be utilizing coping behaviors that reflect their lack of confidence in their problem-solving skills, which may ultimately contribute to further deterioration of their well-being. Professionals must recognize that resolution of these issues may require active support and intervention.

A final quote from a caregiver in Study 2 reflects the positive impact of sensitive professional support:

> Finally the dreaded conclusion was reached that he had to go to a nursing home. No one can imagine the devastation I reached at this time. But it had to be done so I had to find a way to cope. At the time of transition to the nursing home the most important help I received was from the social service worker. She made phone calls and gathered and gave me information. There was nothing easy about it, but she was a real buffer. She paid attention to *me,* my needs.

> Believe me there were some terrible days. After 10 months there still are terrible days . . . but the support still helps [68-year-old wife].

When the interface between families and long-term care institutions is fully developed, the feelings of support described by this caregiver will be shared by many more family caregivers as they face one of the most difficult experiences of their lives. Family caregivers will then no longer be forgotten clients but rather will be actively supported in meeting their own physical, social, and emotional needs. Further, in concert with the institution, these family caregivers may then be able to fulfill continued positive caregiving functions.

Most of the interventions that are suggested here are not new ideas. What may be different is the emphasis on seeing the family caregiver as the client. Further, the proposed interventions build upon an empirical base that recognizes the needs of many family caregivers for programs and interactions that actively enhance the psychological coping strategies that are associated with greater well-being. Whatever their exact nature, interventions should recognize that long-term care facilities are part of the continuum of care for families as well as patients.

# PART V

# *Hospice and Family Care*

# 13

# The Interface Among Terminally Ill Elderly, Their Families, and Hospice

JANE MARIE KIRSCHLING

The proliferation of hospice programs in the United States, from one program in 1974 (Gotay, 1985) to approximately 1,500 programs in 1985 (Lamers, in press), has provided families experiencing a terminal illness an alternative to traditional health care services—an alternative that, according to Greer (1983), fills a widely perceived void in the health care system.

The majority of recipients of hospice care are over 65 years of age (Butterfield-Picard & Magno, 1982; Greer, 1983; Quinn, 1984) and have been diagnosed with a malignant neoplasm, or cancer. Although heart disease is the leading cause of death in the elderly (47% of all deaths were attributed to heart disease in 1980) cancer was identified as the cause of death at a rate of 14% in 1980 (Fruehling, 1982).

*Hospice* is a term that is applied to a formal program of medically directed care that emphasizes a humanistic philosophy of care for families experiencing terminal illness. Although the programs vary in the range of available services, eligibility criteria, and institutional affiliations (Greer et al., 1983), the underlying ideology remains consistent. This ideology includes the following tenets: Death is a normal and inevitable part of life; the family must prepare for the terminally ill person's death; and the family must be involved in caring for the dying person (Bass, 1985).

The following chapter will explore the interface among older persons with a terminal illness, their families, and hospice. An overview on hospice care will be provided followed by a framework for highlighting the unique qualities of families and of hospice care. Factors influencing the delivery of hospice care will be identified and family members' perceptions of their needs will be discussed. Finally, the interface between the family and hospice will be addressed. Case examples will be used throughout the chapter and are derived from my clinical experience.

## An Overview of Hospice Care

The National Hospice Organization developed standards for hospice care in 1979. These standards provide a common ground from which hospice programs are developed and implemented. A medically supervised interdisciplinary team provides health care and services aimed at the physical, emotional, and spiritual welfare of the terminally ill person and his or her family. The team often includes a medical director, nurses, social workers, a physical therapist, an occupational therapist, clergy, volunteer coordinator, and bereavement counselors.

Services offered by hospice programs include medical care, educational programs, and social services. The educational programs focus on caring for the ill person in the home and on issues around death and dying. In addition, bereavement services are available for the surviving family members.

Care is palliative and supportive in nature, and is available 24 hours a day, 7 days a week. If the terminally ill person requires inpatient care, every effort is made to ensure continuity and coordination of care. The provision of care is enhanced through the availability of volunteers.

The emphasis on the family unit is a key element in hospice care. Although the term *family* traditionally refers to blood relatives, or relatives by marriage, the standards for hospice programs define *family* as including individuals with significant personal ties as potential family members (Greer et al., 1983).

Bohm and Rodin (1985) identified ways that family members normally provide social support for an elderly member: (1) fulfilling emotional needs, reassuring family members of their worth and value; (2) providing an avenue for feedback; (3) transmitting valuable information, such as clarification of expectations; (4) providing a sense of dependability; and (5) allowing for reciprocity among members while exerting responsibility and feeling efficacious as individuals. However, the presence of illness often alters the relationships among family members, especially in emotional responses to interpersonal and problem areas (Leventhal et al., 1985).

## Framework

Leventhal and his colleagues (1985) proposed a systems framework in order to describe a family's reaction to illness. The framework includes the ill person's psychological and biological systems and the social, or family, system. Each of these systems will be reviewed in relation to families with an elderly member (age 65 or older) who is terminally ill.

### Psychological System

According to Leventhal et al. (1985), the literature on the social psychology of illness highlights three components. The first component involves the representation of illness. The elderly person must consider the identity, causes, and consequences of his or her illness as well as the duration. In the case of a terminal illness the identity and causes vary, but the consequence is death and the duration is relatively short, usually six months or less.

The second component of the ill person's psychological system is coping, which includes planning and action. An ill person's appraisal of an action is the third component. The complexity of appraisal is due, in large part, to the need for expert social communication, or the ongoing interface between health care professionals and the ill person. Appraisal is also affected by the ill person's previous exposure to family members, or friends, who have been ill.

### Biological System

A stage model is used by Leventhal et al. (1985) to describe the biological system. The elderly person and his or her family have already faced many of these stages, including the prediagnostic, diagnostic and pretreatment, treatment, and rehabilitation stages. In the case of hospice care it is the stage of resolution that directly applies to the family, and resolution is viewed in terms of death versus cure. When death appears imminent the ill person is often perceived to be in a terminal stage of his or her illness.

## Family System

The impact of terminal illness on the family cannot be ignored. Olsen (1970) stressed that the family, not just the sick member, is ill. The family system is described by Leventhal et al. (1985) in terms of family structure and function, with structure being divided into the generational division and the biological-legal division.

Family function, as it relates specifically to terminal illness, is affected in three ways. First, the biological function of the family includes the need for someone to provide physical care to the ill person. The second effect is on the psychological functions of the family. These functions are focused on maintaining the self-image of the terminally ill person. Finally, the socioeconomic functions of the family include defining how family members interface with others outside the family unit and the attainment of adequate financial resources.

Hospice care is directed toward the family unit and is aimed at facilitating a family's ability to meet their needs. Although families vary in how they meet their needs, an overall picture does emerge from the systems framework (see Figure 13.1). The terminally ill elder can utilize intrapersonal resources to meet his or her physical or psychological needs (labeled A) in the figure. When the terminally ill elder is unable to meet his or her needs and/or wants additional assistance, then the family can mobilize its energy to address these physical and psychological needs (labeled B). The family must also consider their socioeconomic needs. Finally, the hospice care providers can intervene to meet some of the needs of the terminally ill elder and his or her family (labeled C).

It is this process, or the interface between hospice care providers and families with a terminally ill elder, that will be explored further. This will include identifying factors that influence the delivery of hospice services, what families perceive as their needs during this time, and how the hospice team interfaces with families

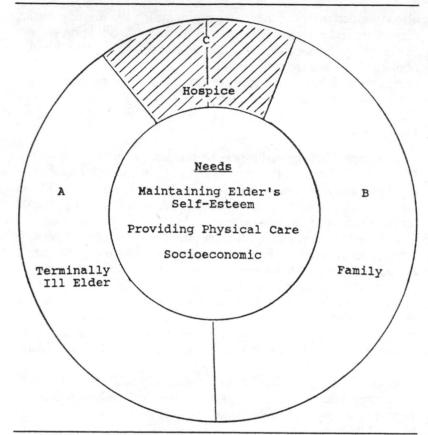

Figure 13.1 The Interface Among Terminally Ill Elderly, Their Families, and Hospice

who have unmet needs or who are requesting intervention by a health care professional.

## Factors Influencing Hospice Care

The interface between families with a terminally ill elderly member and hospice care providers is influenced by a number of factors. Two of the major factors include the timing of the referral for hospice care and the family's receptiveness to hospice care providers.

Terminally ill persons admitted to 25 demonstration hospice programs were studied in a recent national investigation (Greer et al., 1983). The sample included 2,746 terminally ill persons who were admitted to home-care-based programs and 1,143 who were admitted to hospital-based programs. The average length of service provided was 72 days for the home-care programs and 62 days for the hospital-based programs. Of the terminally ill persons, 90% died while receiving hospice services.

Based on the findings of Greer et al. (1983), one gets an understanding of the time period involved with hospice care. Referrals for hospice care, on the average, come two months prior to death. Consequently, intervention strategies must be identified and implemented in an expedient manner. At the same time, the receptiveness of families for hospice care varies considerably.

The receptiveness of families for hospice care is influenced by the following: whether or not the family has unmet needs that they perceive the hospice team can address, and whether or not the family feels that the hospice team can meet their needs in a more thorough or efficient manner. A family's receptiveness for hospice care can be viewed on a continuum. At one extreme a family may openly acknowledge their need for the array of services provided by the hospice interdisciplinary team. On the other extreme the family may feel that they do not have a need for hospice services and therefore refuse to participate in the hospice program. With this in mind, let us consider what families perceive as their needs.

*Families' Perceptions of Their Needs*

A number of research studies have explored the needs of families confronted with a serious illness (Garland et al., 1984; Grobe et al., 1981, 1982; Hampe, 1975; Kane et al., 1985; Neal et al., 1981; Wright & Dyck, 1983, 1984). With the exception of Kane et al. (1985) and Neal et al. (1981), samples were not limited to families with an elderly member or to families receiving hospice services. However, they do provide insight into the needs of families experiencing the terminal illness of an elderly member. It is beyond the scope of this chapter to evaluate these works in greater detail, but the reader is referred to Kirschling (in press) for such a review and to the original works.

The needs of families confronted with a serious illness tend to fall into two categories: the provision of care to the terminally ill person and the interaction between the family and the health care professional. The two categories are not mutually exclusive. Each of these categories will be explored in relation to the unique qualities of the family and of hospice in meeting these needs.

*Provision of care.* The provision of care to the terminally ill person is commonly referred to as *caregiving.* Someone within the family must assume the responsibility for caregiving, or assuring that the ill person's needs are met. Family caregivers are most often elderly women caring for their ill husbands (Shanas, 1979b). An example of this type of situation is provided below:

> *Case 1:* Mr. H was diagnosed with metastatic lung cancer in 1984, at the age of 79. His wife of over 50 years assumed the caregiving role. Mrs. H suffers from chronic back problems. The Hs are Presbyterian, but have not attended church since the onset of his illness. They live in a retirement complex, but their contact with the other residents has steadily declined. Mr. and Mrs. H have one son who expresses a great deal of concern for his mother's health. The son has expressed the need to have his father placed in a nursing home, but Mrs. H refuses.

In the case in which the elderly person is widowed, a middle-aged child will care for his or her terminally ill parent:

> *Case 2:* Mrs. J is a 72-year-old widow who has suffered from congestive heart failure and chronic renal failure since her mid 60s. She was living independently in her own home until her recent physical decline. Mrs. J was moved to her son's home upon the physician's recommendation. The living room was converted into a hospital room because Mrs. J required frequent assistance. A referral for hospice services was made within the week because Mrs. J's family and physician agreed that her illnesses had reached the terminal stage.

Regardless of whether the family member is a spouse or adult child, he or she often assumes the responsibility of providing care without question (Abrams, 1974) and perceives "shouldering the burden" as the only solution (Calkins, 1972).

Archbold (1982b) described two kinds of family caregivers for the frail elderly: family members who provide the actual care, or care providers; and family members who arrange for and supervise someone else in caring for the elderly family member, or care managers. Families receiving hospice service also fall into these two categories. In Case 1, Mrs. H was functioning as a family caregiver. In Case 2, the J family hired a daytime caregiver for Mrs. J and the son functioned as the care manager. The needs of the family members functioning as care providers and care managers may differ in regard to the provision of care. However, the research reviewed does not make the distinction between care providers and care managers. In fact, the research samples tended to be described according to the relationship of the ill person and the family member (i.e., marital partners).

It is my conclusion that the research samples did include some family members who were functioning as care providers and some who functioned as care managers. Consequently, the term *family caregiver* represents family members who are directly responsible for the physical care of the terminally ill elder or who arrange for and supervise someone else in caring for the elderly person.

A number of specific needs have been identified by family caregivers (see Table 13.1). The family caregiver wants to provide for the terminally ill person's needs. In order to do this, the caregiver should have the necessary equipment and be trained in how to care for the ill person. Family caregivers also have expressed a need to communicate with the terminally ill person, as well as other family members. The communication among family members focuses on comforting and supporting each other. Another area of need for family caregivers involves the need to have respite from their responsibilities and assistance with household chores.

An additional need of family caregivers that has not been researched in a systematic way involves securing someone to care for the terminally ill elder when a family member is unable to assume the primary caregiving responsibility. Based on my clinical experiences it appears that the identification of a dependable and knowledgeable caregiver outside of the family unit can be time-consuming and financially draining.

*Interaction with health care professionals.* As family members interact with health care professionals and, in this case, the interdisciplinary hospice team, they need to receive assurance that the terminally ill person is comfortable (see Table 13.1). This involves focusing on the terminally ill person's psychological and biological systems. Families also need to be kept up to date on the ill person's

TABLE 13.1
Needs of Families Experiencing Terminal Illness
of an Elderly Member

*Needs According to Category*

Provision of Care

(1) to be helpful to the terminally ill person
(2) to be with the person when he or she is dying
(3) to communicate with the ill person
(4) to have the necessary equipment
(5) to be trained regarding caring for the terminally ill elderly family member
(6) to have time away from caregiving, or family respite
(7) to have assistance with household upkeep and chores
(8) to receive comfort and support with the family

Interaction with Health Care Professionals

(1) to receive assurance of the terminally ill person's comfort (includes the control of symptoms)
(2) to be informed of the terminally ill person's condition and impending death
(3) to receive acceptance, support, and confort; for example, allowing for the ventilation of emotions, providing spiritual support, and acknowledging the family's preference for location of care
(4) to have help with financial and legal matters

condition; to be informed of impending death; to receive support regarding their preference for the location of care, whether it be in the home or in an institutional setting; and to have help with financial and legal matters. Family members need to feel accepted, supported, and comforted by team members.

## The Interface Between the Family and the Hospice Team

The interface between the family and the hospice team is focused on the following: communication, family education, control of symptoms, provision for respite, pastoral care, and family advocacy. The physical, psychological, and spiritual needs of the terminally ill person and his or her family are considered. The interface between the family and the hospice team is influenced by four factors: the family's perception of their needs, the family's ability to meet their needs successfully within the family unit, the availability of the needed services through a hospice program, and the family's willingness to accept the hospice services.

The needs of families with a terminally ill elder include those that relate to the provision of care and those that relate to the interaction between the family and health care providers. Hospice care is designed to address the 12 needs identified in Table 13.1. However, when comparing hospice care to traditional health care it appears that hospice care is designed to deal specifically with 5 of the needs: the family's need to be trained regarding caring for the terminally ill elder; the need for the family caregiver to have time away from caregiving; the family's need for assurance of the terminally ill person's comfort; the family's need to be informed of the terminally ill person's condition and impending death; and the family's need to receive acceptance, support, and comfort. Although some traditional health care services do attempt to meet these needs, they often fall short when it comes to providing care in a continuous manner. The family receives "bits and pieces" and lacks an overall sense of ongoing involvement on the part of the health care delivery system.

The hospice team strives to communicate accurate information about the elderly person's disease process and eventual death. Chances are that by the time a referral for hospice care is made the family has asked for, or been told, a projected life expectancy for the ill member. This projection will range from days to years. With this projection in mind the family begins to plan for caring for the ill person. When death comes considerably earlier or later than projected the family may experience a wide range of feelings (e.g., relief, anger, or guilt).

Hospice team members encourage families to make the most out of each day. Emphasis is placed on teaching the family about what to expect as the terminally ill person's condition deteriorates. This teaching is undertaken so that the family is not caught off guard when the person dies earlier then expected or lives longer than expected.

According to Blues and Zerwekh (1984), the family also needs information about how to perform basic nursing measures (e.g., medication administration and care of the bedfast person), use of specific techniques (e.g., dressing changes or catheter care) and equipment (e.g., suction machines or oxygen setups), organizing care, and what to do at the time of death. The family may also need basic information on where and how to obtain the necessary equipment and supplies.

The control of symptoms requires ongoing communication among the terminally ill person, family caregiver, hospice nurse, and attending physician. Pain, nausea and vomiting, skin breakdown, constipation, and respiratory distress occur in varying degrees with the terminally ill. Intervention strategies for controlling these symptoms include nonintrusive measures, such as massage and body positioning, and intrusive measures, such as medications and oxygen therapy. Essential to the control of symptoms is the willingness on the part of each person to try different approaches and maintain open lines of communication when symptom management becomes difficult.

The provision of respite from caregiving responsibilities can be accomplished in a variety of ways. The caregiving family member can be relieved of his or her duty by another family member, a friend, a fellow church member, a hired person, or a hospice volunteer. A key component of hospice care is the use of volunteers who have been specially trained in caring for the terminally ill person.

The hospice team also functions as a family advocate. Every effort is made to familiarize the family with the services that are available in the community. A member of the team, often a social worker, will assist the family in obtaining services from community agencies. This can include making arrangements for a lawyer to assist the family with drawing up a will, contacting a social service organization to have a housekeeper come one morning a week, filling out an application for Medicaid, or sorting through unpaid bills.

The spiritual needs of the family experiencing terminal illness of an elderly member are also taken into consideration by the hospice team. A member of the clergy participates in team meetings in order to assist team members with spiritual issues and to identify family members who might benefit from a pastoral care visit. If the family is associated with a church and requests a particular clergy member to visit, a member of the team will contact the individual and ascertain his or her willingness to make a visit. In the case that the clergy is unable to visit, or that the family does not have an established church, the hospice clergy will visit the family.

A final component of hospice care is the availability of bereavement follow-up for surviving family members. Hospice programs vary in the type and quality of bereavement follow-up. A major reason for this variability is the fact that bereavement programs provide a nonreimbursable service. In other words, insurance companies do not cover the cost associated with bereavement follow-up. The types of services offered to family members following the death of the terminally ill person include attendance at the funeral, a sympathy card, reading materials on grief, home visits, phone calls, memorial services, and support groups.

With this description of how the hospice team interfaces with families with a terminally ill elder member, the cases of Mr. H and Mrs. J will be reviewed in order to demonstrate how a hospice team is working with each family to meet their needs.

## Case 1

In 1984 Mr. H, at the age of 79, was diagnosed with metastatic lung cancer. He was referred for hospice care in May of the following year by his physician. At the time of the referral the hospice coordinator talked with Mr. and Mrs. H about the array of services offered by the hospice team and the underlying philosophy of hospice. Mr. and Mrs. H consented to receive hospice care and a nurse made her initial home visit. The nurse assessed Mr. H's physical and psychological well-being and found that his major complaint was that he choked when he ate or drank. Because of this problem, Mr. H's nutritional status was poor. The nurse contacted the attending physician to discuss the case. The physician had discussed with Mr. H the option of inserting a feeding tube into his stomach, however Mr. H had refused.

The nurse visited two to three times a week and focused on alternative ways for enhancing Mr. H's nutritional status. During her visits the nurse provided Mrs. H with information on dietary issues and offered ongoing support to the family. Mr. H became increasingly weaker as the weeks passed and Mrs. H began to show the wear and tear of caring for her ill husband 24 hours a day.

The nurse expressed her concern to the team and the need for respite was identified. A hospice volunteer was assigned and contacted Mrs. H. At first, Mrs. H was reluctant to have the volunteer visit. She consented within a week of the initial contact and the volunteer spent four hours with Mr. and Mrs. H twice a week. Mrs. H would not leave the apartment when the volunteer came because she was unable to drive and did not feel comfortable asking someone to transport her. Mrs. H would rest and do her chores while the volunteer attended to Mr. H's needs. The son worked during the day and assisted his parents in the evening or on the weekend as needed.

When the nurse assessed Mr. and Mrs. H's spiritual needs she discovered that they would like their minister to visit them. The hospice chaplain contacted the minister in order to evaluate his willingness to visit the Hs and offer any assistance he could. The minister did initiate home visits with the family.

As Mr. H's condition deteriorated, the nurse obtained a physician's order to have a home health aide visit three times a week. The home health aide assisted Mr. H with his personal hygiene during her two-hour visit. In addition, the nurse increased her home visits in order to provide support to Mrs. H and instruct her on how to care for Mr. H as he spent increasing time in bed. Safety measures and proper lifting techniques were emphasized because Mrs. H had back problems.

Mrs. H and her son discussed where Mr. H should be cared for as his condition deteriorated. Mrs. H felt strongly that she wanted her husband to die at home. Mr. H did die at home during November. The nurse was in the home at the time of the death and assisted Mrs. H with the necessary arrangements. The hospice team sent a sympathy card to Mrs. H at the time of the death and a letter indicating that a bereavement volunteer would be contacting her within three weeks.

Initially, the bereavement volunteer contacted Mrs. H by phone to introduce herself and to offer to make a home visit. Mrs. H reported that she was doing fine and did not feel the need for someone to visit at that time. The bereavement volunteer then offered to contact her by phone within a week. Mrs. H agreed to a home visit during the second phone contact and the bereavement volunteer went to her apartment for coffee. Mrs. H also received a packet of information from the hospice program describing the various resources available in her community for the recently widowed and some reading material. The bereavement volunteer continued phone contact and periodic home visits for 15 months following Mr. H's death.

\*    \*    \*

The interface between Mr. and Mrs. H and the hospice team developed over time. Fortunately, Mr. H was referred for hospice care six months prior to his death and the team was able to build a trusting relationship with Mr. and Mrs. H before his physical health had significantly deteriorated. The nurse, hospice volunteer, and home health aide assisted Mrs. H in caring for her husband at home. The rest of the team members remained informed of the case through weekly team meetings.

Although Mrs. H might have been able to carry out this responsibility without the involvement of hospice, it appears that the hospice team did make the situation less taxing on Mrs. H. In addition, the bereavement volunteer offered emotional support during the months following the death and provided Mrs. H with information about the types of services available to her as a widow.

Let us consider next the J family. The case of Mrs. J provides the reader with a different perspective on the hospice team.

## Case 2

Mrs. J suffers from congestive heart failure and is 72 years old. Until recently, Mrs. J had cared for herself in the home. Mrs. J moved into her son's living room after her deteriorating physical condition impaired her ability to care for herself. The family consented to hospice care and the hospice nurse made a home visit. During this initial visit the nurse assessed Mrs. J's physical condition as serious. The son and daughter-in-law were aware of the situation and did not want Mrs. J hospitalized. The nurse assessed the family's plans for caring for Mrs. J because both the son and daughter-in-law were employed full time. The family had made arrangements for an adult granddaughter to care for Mrs. J. The family did not feel they needed the assistance of a volunteer or home health aide at this time.

The nurse visited daily in order to evaluate Mrs. J's level of comfort and to assess the family's need for additional support. Mrs. J's congestive heart failure stabilized within three weeks of her admission to hospice care and the nurse decreased her visits to every other day. As Mrs. J's health stabilized she began to confide in the nurse her feelings of loneliness and discomfort with the inconvenience she was causing her family. Mrs. J wanted to return to her own home but realized that she was unable to care for herself. The nurse recommended that the hospice social worker visit in order to explore Mrs. J's feelings further.

The hospice social worker talked with Mrs. J and her son and daughter-in-law individually and then recommended that a family meeting be held in order to get everyone's feelings out into the open. Although apprehensive, the family did agree to the meeting, which the social worker facilitated. Mrs. J shared with her family her feelings of being in the way. The family discussed a variety of alternatives and finally agreed that Mrs. J would be moved out of the living room and into a large bedroom in her son's home.

The hospice social worker explored Mrs. J's feelings of loneliness. Mrs. J expressed that she felt cut off from her friends and church. Mrs. J had been active in her church but was unable to attend Sunday services as her condition deteriorated. In addition, she did not want to bother her family to drive her. The social worker discussed this with the granddaughter, who willingly agreed to attend church with her grandmother. The social worker encouraged Mrs. J to let a hospice volunteer contact her and visit periodically in order that she would have someone closer to her age to talk with. Mrs. J consented to have the volunteer contact her. The volunteer maintains weekly phone contact and visits Mrs. J every two to three weeks.

Mrs. J's physical health has fluctuated during the five months she has been receiving hospice services. The nurse continues her visits in order to assess Mrs. J's health status, as well as the need for additional hospice services. The social worker has discontinued her home visits but is keeping updated on the case through the weekly team meetings.

*    *    *

The J family continue to receive the services of the hospice team. The hospice social worker has served an instrumental role in facilitating communication within the family and the hospice nurse has kept the family abreast of Mrs. J's health status. The J family has been able to make the necessary arrangements to assure that Mrs. J has someone with her in order to see that her needs are met. In addition, the family members have been sensitive to each other's needs for privacy.

## Summary

When an elderly person is diagnosed with a terminal illness, it is essential to take a systems approach, which includes the person's physical and psychological systems and his or her family. Hospice care is designed from a systems perspective for families who are caring for a terminally ill relative. It is the family who assumes the caregiving responsibilities, either as caregivers or as care managers. It is also the family who has to deal with the fact that death is imminent for the elderly person.

Hospice provides a type of care that differs from traditional health care services. Hospice programs utilize a team approach to the delivery of care. The focus is on enhancing the quality of life for the terminally ill elder and his or her family. The emphasis is on palliative care versus cure. Finally, the care is family focused. Although some of the services are focused on the terminally ill person (e.g., symptom control) many are focused on the family (e.g., respite care, assistance with legal and financial concerns, bereavement follow-up).

The fact that families will continue to provide care for their terminally ill elderly members in the future, just as they have in the past, must be acknowledged. Families who have access to hospice care, and who elect to utilize the various services, will receive support in caring for the terminally ill elderly member. This support includes open communication, family education, provision for respite, family advocacy, pastoral care, and bereavement follow-up.

# PART VI

# *Planning for Long-Term Care*

# 14

# Families and
# Supportive Residential Settings
# as Long-Term Care Options

MARY ANNE HILKER

Residential and home-care options for the frail, semi-independent elderly have received increasing attention from researchers, service providers, and policymakers. The desire for long-term care alternatives to nursing homes for those who could receive appropriate care in their own homes or in other nonmedical residential settings has been prompted by economic considerations as well as by consumer preferences for noninstitutional care.

Long-term care services are required by those who have physical or mental impairments that hamper functioning in the activities of daily living. The need for assistance in these activities is particularly evident among those over 85, the age group experiencing the most rapid population growth. National statistics show that nearly one-third of those over age 85 need assistance with personal care (Doty et al., 1985: 70). Although providing help with dressing, bathing, toileting, and other personal care is extremely time-consuming and emotionally demanding, a very large percentage of family caregivers are providing these kinds of assistance (Cantor & Little, 1985: 759).

Although families continue to serve as the major caregivers for the impaired elderly, it is becoming increasingly more difficult for them to do so. Changes in women's participation in the work force, in family size and mobility, in marital stability, and in the growing numbers of the oldest group of elderly all create strains on the caregiving capacities of the family (Shanas & Maddox, 1985: 717; Cantor & Little, 1985: 772). Research has begun to identify the potential emotional, financial, and physical stresses associated with the role of caregiver (Cantor, 1983; Cicirelli, 1983; Noelker & Wallace, 1985).

The growing need for long-term care services, accompanied by serious questions about the family's continued ability to care for impaired older relatives, has led to interest in developing a diversity of long-term care options. These range from the delivery of health, personal, and social services in the home, to a variety of kinds of supportive housing that provide alternatives to nursing home placements for some elderly. A diversity of long-term care services is needed to accommodate the differing preferences, requirements, and resources of the long-term care population.

Increasing numbers of elderly and their families will face the decision of choosing among several types of supportive housing that are part of the continuum of long-term care. These are housing options that provide not only shelter and meals but also assistance with everyday activities and, in some settings, personal care; they are primarily residential, not medical care, facilities. Some of these living arrangements may have social services or health professionals on staff or on call, and others have no professional staff backup. Many of the less formal arrangements try to provide services like those rendered in a family environment by a caregiver to an older relative (Thompson, 1975: 5).

### Supportive Residential Options

The need for supportive housing within the long-term care system is recognized by many professionals in the field (Kahana & Coe, 1975; Thompson, 1976; Huttman, 1977; Kane & Kane, 1980; Brody, 1981; Federal Council on Aging, 1985). Some have pointed out the importance of the structural and technological modifications that would create a supportive environment and allow the elderly to remain in their own homes (Estes & Lee, 1984: 30). Others have focused on group living alternatives—sponsored, organized, and operated in a variety of ways—having the common feature of shared residence in a nonmedical but supportive environment.

Living in a setting in which the individual is not alone and where help with personal care and/or the other activities of daily living are available allows some frail elderly to avoid or delay placement in more intense level of care settings. These "borderline" elderly can avoid costly and inappropriate nursing home care and the equally inappropriate option of living alone (Federal Council on Aging, 1985: 12).

Included here as supportive housing options are those state-licensed residential care facilities for older persons, known by different names in various states, such as board and care home, personal care, adult care, family care, adult congregate living facilities, and domiciliary care. Such facilities are not licensed to provide regular medical or nursing care but can provide oversight and personal care services in addition to room and board. (For the purpose of this discussion the term *board and care* will be used to designate licensed nonmedical care facilities.) Some of these facilities are designed to serve only older individuals, and others serve a mix of ages and target populations.

Some less formal supportive housing arrangements for the frail elderly have developed in recent years. These living arrangements are most appropriate for individuals who cannot or do not wish to live alone because of physical and/or mental impairments, but who do not require extensive personal care or oversight. These informal arrangements involve two or more unrelated individuals who share a single household. These arrangements are not subject (generally speaking, at least) to licensing as caregiving facilities.

The variations of this shared household theme may be divided into two types. First, a private home owner may share his or her home with another person, located either through informal means or through a house-matching agency. Both parties may be elderly, or the match may be between a younger and an older person. The second type is a small-group residence usually sponsored by a religious or community organization (Day-Lower et al., 1982: 7-8). Both of these types of shared households are examined in this chapter.

## Bureaucratic And Legal Issues
## In Supportive Housing

Gordon Streib (1983: 42) has called for additional research on the frail elderly, particularly with reference to their relationship to the bureaucracy and the legal aspects of providing services to them. The families of the frail elderly are often very involved both in the decision for the individual to move to a more supportive care setting and as intermediaries between the older person and care providers. Families may find themselves acting as information gatherers in diverse areas, including the very complex areas of federal entitlements, housing programs, and medical care (Sussman, 1985: 419).

With respect to the supportive housing options discussed in this chapter, what have been the perceptions and responses of bureaucratic structures to the different types of supportive housing for the elderly? What laws and regulations are shaping these long-term care options? What are the linkages between families and bureaucratic structures in supportive housing?

### Defining Supportive Housing

Older people who are impaired and need help with personal care or other tasks of daily living live in many settings. They may receive home-based care from informal (family) supports and/or from formal agencies. Others obtain assistance by moving to some type of supportive living environment. Some supportive environments provide minimal supports, such as apartment complexes that offer housekeeping services and a daily congregate meal. Others, on which this chapter focuses, provide greater support in either licensed group residences or in less formal shared households. Because these latter types serve a frail population, one at risk for nursing home placement, many state governments have a particular interest in defining and regulating them.

Distinguishing among the many types of special living arrangements for older people can be difficult for consumers, their advocates, and for governments. The same type of arrangement may be known by a variety of names depending on the locale. Similarly, very different housing programs or facilities may use the same name. The consumer or his or her advocate may be confused by the array of housing/care services and by the terminology used to distinguish them. State governments may also face difficulties in establishing legal definitions for the purpose of regulating these various supportive housing alternatives.

Among the factors that could be used to differentiate these living arrangements are the types of services provided, the numbers of residents and staff, the characteristics and needs of the residents, the nature of the relationship between the caregiver and the care-receiver, the goals and philosophies of the sponsoring groups or of administration or staff, and the physical design of the dwelling unit. States have paid the most attention to the types of services provided, the size of the facility's population, and the type of specialized population served (such as elderly or developmentally disabled) in defining residential facilities (American Bar Association, 1983: 120-121).

Even for the most formally organized of the supportive housing types, the board and care home, there is a lack of a common definition among the states. In a survey study, Stone et al. (1982) found diverse types and sizes of facilities licensed as board and care programs. At least part of the definitional problem stems from disagreements among state officials as to the nature of board and care facilities: Should they follow the social model or the medical model? Should they continue to be considered as residential facilities or become increasingly institutionlike in structure, size, organization, and services?

Even though much has been done to describe specific models of less formal types of supportive housing, shared living arrangements (Breslow & Van Dyk, 1983; Schreter, 1983; Streib et al., 1984), there are still definitional problems, particularly with small-group residences. How does an unlicensed shared-group residence for older people sponsored by a nonprofit organization actually differ from a licensed board and care home? Major differences may be found in the number of residents and the types of services offered. Group residences with less than a specified number of residents, or those offering no services beyond room and board, do not have to obtain licenses as care facilities. Shared-group living sponsors usually focus on the "familylike" character of the homes—their small size, their noninstitutional atmosphere, the independence of the residents—and may resist being defined in the same category as board and care facilities. At the same time, licensed board and care facilities may emphasize *their* "homelike" atmosphere, too.

Although board and care facilities may tend to serve a relatively more impaired population, there is certainly overlap with the shared housing alternatives in terms of resident characteristics. In fact, where an individual is placed in the overall continuum of long-term care may have less to do with a rational matching of needs and services than on the availability and costs of services and other pragmatic factors (Shanas & Maddox, 1985: 716; Knight, 1985: 43). The distinctions among the resident populations of a nursing home, a board and care home, and a shared living arrangement are not clear-cut.

Obviously, legal definitions are often only approximated in reality. Services or care that are ostensibly offered in a particular residential setting may not be delivered, and help with bathing and dressing may occur in settings that are not licensed to perform personal care duties. Responsibility for ensuring that the appropriate type and quality of services are delivered is ordinarily assumed by the states through their lawmaking and regulatory powers.

### Licensing Requirements and Supportive Housing

The definitional confusion is only part of the larger problem of regulating supportive residential settings. The states' major regulatory mechanism is that of licensure. Licensure is designed to ensure that minimum requirements for health, safety, and quality of services are met in those settings that have at least a certain number of residents and offer particular kinds of services.

Although the content of licensure standards varies from state to state, these requirements tend to focus on the physical plant, food services, administrative procedures, and staffing ratios. Licensing statutes rarely give particular attention to whether or not residents and services are appropriately matched or to the actual delivery of services after placement (American Bar Association, 1983: 211). The focus on the physical plant and other structural aspects of board and care facilities as well as nursing homes is based on the somewhat doubtful assumption that the capacity for good care will result in the provision of good care (Butler, 1979: 1333).

A lack of attention within licensing regulations to the quality of care and services is due in part to the difficulty of measuring these variables. It is obviously easier to define and monitor aspects of the physical plant than to define appropriate services and measures of outcomes (Stone et al., 1982: 7; Eustis et al., 1984: 145).

The majority of the states have enacted residents' or patients' rights statutes for individual nursing homes and, in some states, nonmedical residential facilities subject to licensure and regulation (McDonald, 1984: 585). These statutes have been enacted to preserve the civil and legal rights of the patients/residents, and most contain provisions concerning the right to adequate and appropriate care. Again, defining and measuring quality of care and services is an obstacle to effective oversight and regulation of supportive residential settings.

There are serious problems with the regulatory approach to quality control in long-term care facilities. Eustis and her colleagues (1984: 150) review the evidence that suggests there is widespread noncompliance by nursing homes with both federal and state regulations. With respect to board and care facilities, monitoring and effective oversight are hampered by lack of funding and personnel, the fragmentation and lack of agency coordination, and by weak enforcement authority (Butler, 1979: 1328; Stone et al., 1982: 14-15).

States have a number of enforcement options to bring long-term care facilities into compliance, including delicensing, fines, injunction proceedings, and criminal penalties (American Bar Association, 1983: 160-170). These time-consuming and expensive mechanisms are rarely used by the states. Instead, nonregulatory enforcement actions are more likely to be taken by a regulatory agency when a licensed facility is found to be in noncompliance. The most common nonregulatory mechanism used by the states is the provision of technical assistance by regulatory staff, mostly on an ad hoc basis (Stone et al., 1983: 16).

Some of the supportive housing options discussed in this chapter do not require licensing by the states because of the small numbers of residents and/or the "residential" rather than the care-providing nature of the setting. This lack of formality has been applauded by many who deplore the increased bureaucratization of noninstitutional living arrangements (Donahue et al., 1978: 187; Breslow & Van Dyk, 1978: 66; Murray, 1979: 16; Streib, 1982: 60). Sussman (1985: 425), however, suggests that shared housing experiments starting out as familylike, informal arrangements should anticipate takeover attempts by formal organizations as part of their natural development.

Shared housing involving a private home owner and a tenant is generally outside the states' regulatory interests. This is true even of home sharing that is facilitated or managed by house-matching agencies, although the agency itself may be required to meet certain professional staffing or other standards. Many home owner/ tenant arrangements involve the simple exchange of rent for living quarters, and no services are provided for or expected by the older person, whether he or she is the home owner or the tenant. These types of arrangements could not be characterized as supportive housing.

Small-group residences sponsored by religious or community groups may or may not require licensure, depending on state statutes. Although challenges to the legality of these shared-housing options have more often occurred in the area of zoning, discussed later in this chapter, court cases involving licensure have occurred. As states move increasingly toward locating unlicensed facilities that meet the definition of a licensable unit, more confrontations may take place. Murray (1979: 1) warns, however, that bureaucratic requirements applying to board and care types of facilities may be very inappropriate when transferred to informal shared-housing arrangements.

### Local Land Use Issues and Supportive Housing

The establishment of group living arrangements for the elderly, the disabled, and other individuals with special needs has often been hindered by local zoning restrictions. Both licensed board and care types of facilities and small shared-living arrangements may be affected by ordinances that prohibit or limit their location in all or some residential areas of the municipality and by overly restrictive building codes.

Licensed board and care homes have sometimes been excluded from all residential areas on the grounds they are not residential use, or they are required to obtain special permits for each facility. They have been more typically excluded by strict definitions of *family* in those residential areas limited to single-family homes. Some zoning ordinances define family in the traditional way as those individuals related by blood, marriage, or adoption. Other zoning ordinances treat individuals, related or not, who live as a single housekeeping unit and share kitchen and other facilities, as a family for zoning purposes. The number of unrelated people who are allowed to live together as a household in an area with single-family zoning is typically restricted to a very small number.

Zoning can also be a problem for unlicensed, usually smaller and less conspicuous, shared-living arrangements (Day-Lower et al, 1982: 16). Even home owners who wish to share their homes with one or two others have to be aware of local restrictions on the number of unrelated individuals who may live together. Small shared homes sponsored by nonprofits may also face zoning barriers if they try to locate in single-family areas, the areas most desirable and appropriate for shared-living arrangements.

## Family/Bureaucratic Linkages
## In Supportive Housing

A potential interface between families and bureaucratic structures occurs around quality of services issues in supportive housing. This may occur at the level of the residential setting itself or, less typically, at the level of state and/or local regulatory bodies. Families may also, of course, be involved with other agencies on behalf of the supportive housing resident, including medical, social services, and federal benefit programs.

The extent of a family's involvement with these formal systems depends on a number of factors. These include the interests and resources of the family, prior and present relationships among family members, the opportunities for formal and informal access to bureaucratic structures, and the needs and preferences of the older individual.

Families are often involved in the decision-making process that precedes the move to more supportive living environments. They may initiate contacts with potential facilities or private home owners, visit them, assess their suitability, and provide advice and information to the older individual. They may also help negotiate contracts or other agreements pertaining to fees, services, the use of space and facilities, and conditions of termination.

It may be particularly important for families to maintain or assume roles as linking agents between the older person and bureaucratic structures in supportive housing settings. Unlike an increasing number of nursing homes, personal care homes and shared housing arrangements usually have neither staff nor volunteers to perform these linking functions; exceptions to this occur in some small-group residences sponsored by religious organizations. The role of family caregivers in matching the individual to services and other formal support systems, as suggested by Springer and Brubaker (1984: 125), may be as necessary after, as well as prior to, a move to supportive housing.

Supportive living arrangements differ on the extent of information sharing with families and on how information is shared. Some have built-in opportunities for families to interact with other residents and their families and with staff and administration. Regularly scheduled meetings between staff/administration and residents and their families, and family support-group meetings held in or sponsored by the facility more typically occur in nursing homes than in personal-care homes or shared living arrangements.

Families' interactions with the supportive housing "facility" may be limited to one other home sharer or, in the cases of small shared-group residences or small personal-care homes, with one or two paid staff and the small number of other residents. Presumably, in small and less formal settings, families could more easily monitor the situation, but complacency with their "just-like-home" nature could be unwarranted. When does "individual attention" become unnecessary supervision, and "respect for privacy and autonomy" become benign neglect? These are questions we must ask of all long-term care settings, including informal types of supportive living arrangements.

**Ensuring Quality of Services**

The existence of licensure requirements, residents' bills of rights, and inspections by state monitoring agencies obviously does not ensure quality of services. Conversely, the absence of formal bureaucratic oversight does not signal a poor quality supportive living arrangement. Where the states do regulate, there are problems with adequate enforcement as well as with conceptualizing and measuring the qualitative aspects of a residential setting. Residents, their families, and communities have both formal and informal alternatives in dealing with quality of services issues in licensed supportive housing.

Residents of board and care types of settings may face some of the same problems as nursing home patients. Violation of residents' rights, involuntary transfers out of the facility, lack of access to the facilities by outsiders, and inappropriate care are problems common to both (National Senior Citizens Law Center, 1985: 1). Residents of nursing homes and board and care homes and their families may take private legal action in response to these issues or for abuse or neglect. Private litigation on behalf of long-term care residents is becoming more frequent, but the difficulty of establishing monetary damages when the plaintiff is elderly and has little earning potential, and the residents' fear of retaliation by the facility have made private civil litigation infrequent and difficult (Butler, 1979: 1369-1370).

Families of board and care facilities also have recourse to long-term care ombudsman programs in an increasing number of states. These programs provide a mechanism for external monitoring of all long-term care facilities by investigating the complaints of residents, families, or anyone who contacts them. However, the extent to which an ombudsman should act as an advocate on behalf of the resident instead of a mediator between the facility and the resident is in question (Butler, 1980: 695).

The elderly and their families face quality of services and/or care issues in less formal shared-housing options just as they do in licensed facilities. Situations involving a private home owner and a tenant are often handled very casually, with just verbal agreements about the rights and responsibilities of the two parties. Pritchard (1983) found a major cause of breakups of matches between home owners and tenants to be related to noncompliance with specific expectations that had been based only on verbal agreements. For example, if an older home owner expects a tenant to perform household tasks and to remain in the home every night to provide security in exchange for his or her rent, these expectations should be expressed in formal agreements. Although individuals may prefer informal agreements, written leases are usually recommended by house-match agencies.

Similarly, in small group residences sponsored by nonprofit groups, there is often no lease, contract, or other formal agreement. Setting out the expectations, rights, and obligations of all parties—the resident, his or her family, and the sponsors and/or staff of the home—may lessen future conflicts and misunderstandings. For example, the terms under which a resident must seek other living arrangements should be understood. If the resident becomes too ill or impaired to function in the shared household what steps will be taken, by whom?

It is generally recognized that ensuring quality of services for all long-term care residents demands the participation of outsiders—families, friends, and church and community groups. Informal groups can provide needed outside contacts for more isolated residents, and can monitor services. Butler (1980: 620) points out that advocacy groups composed of church or civic group members in addition to family and friends of residents, are more stable and, consequently, more likely to be effective.

Some states have enacted laws to ensure community presence in nursing homes by requiring citizen care-review committees (Butler, 1980: 620). Citizens also serve as volunteers on long-term care ombudsman committees. Butler (1980: 620) found that many long-term care facilities have felt threatened by the presence of community organizations and have denied them access. Where states have not enacted laws or regulations authorizing such access, community groups have had to sue to obtain right of access.

The family's potential role in assuring quality of services in supportive housing extends beyond the bounds of the residence itself. Johnson (1985: 181) suggests that quality of care in nursing homes requires outside citizen monitoring of the performance of both facilities and state enforcement agencies; this is most effectively accomplished through organized advocacy groups that families may initiate or join. Where the state regulates supportive housing, similar groups could advocate active enforcement by state agencies.

Families may become increasingly involved, through churches, synagogues, and occupational and fraternal groups in the planning and development of supportive housing arrangements. Religious organizations have been in the forefront of the development of small-group residences for older people (Streib et al., 1984: 110). Local congregations, motivated by the needs of their own families as well as by those of the larger community, have successfully started and operated small-group housing and house-matching services.

Attempts to establish supportive housing for older people have sometimes been abandoned because of legal liability concerns and because of problems with local zoning and housing codes, discussed earlier in this chapter. Active involvement of older people, their families, and advocacy groups are needed to ensure that communities create opportunities for the inclusion of these long-term care options in appropriate neighborhood settings.


## Conclusions

If present trends continue, the need for a variety of supportive housing options for older people will increase. Although not providing regular medical care, these housing options can provide a supportive environment that is appropriate for many semi-independent older people. Assistance with personal care and/or other needs can be provided in many types of settings, ranging from board and care homes regulated and monitored by the states to informal shared living arrangements often sponsored by non-profit groups.

Bureaucratic structures in our society are charged with ensuring quality of long-term care services. Although some supportive housing falls under the aegis of state and/or local regulatory bodies, other less formal arrangements are not required to meet licensure or regulatory standards. In all types of supportive living arrangements residents and their families have both informal and formal means of dealing with quality of services issues.

The ability of the supportive housing arrangement to respond to changing needs and preferences of residents is one critical quality of services issue, as it is in all long-term care settings and programs. If the amount or intensity of care must be increased, decisions about relocation or about alterations in the services and/or facilities of the present housing arrangement are required. When care levels increase, the issue of increasing formal regulations as well as family oversight and involvement arise.

If informal shared housing becomes more like a caregiving than a residential setting, regulatory agencies of the state may require it to conform to licensing and other standards. Bureaucratic structures may move to formalize these living arrangements in order to fulfill the obligations they share with families to protect dependent individuals in our society.

# 15

## Family Structure and Proximity of Family Members

*Implications for Long-Term Care of the Elderly*

DONALD E. STULL
EDGAR F. BORGATTA

Providing long-term care for our elderly is one of the most important social issues facing policymakers (Meltzer, 1982; Montgomery, 1981). In particular, the dollar cost to the public for long-term care is a critical concern (Eustis et al., 1984). Government expenditures for nursing home care increased from \$11.5 billion in 1980 to \$15 billion in 1982 (U.S. Bureau of the Census, 1983). The situation is becoming more compelling as a larger number of older adults are living longer and reaching ages where health care needs are greater or where conditions occur that reduce or end the ability to take care of one's self and maintain effective autonomy in daily activities. It is likely that this situation will become more important in the decades ahead as the large post-World War II Baby Boom cohort moves into postretirement ages in the second and third decades of the twenty-first century. This large group, which appears

AUTHORS' NOTE: The authors wish to thank Rhonda Montgomery for her valuable discussions in the earlier stages of preparing this manuscript, and for her useful comments on an earlier draft.

to be experiencing lower fertility rates relative to previous generations, may require a greater amount of formally provided care.

Historically, most legislation associated with long-term care focused on nursing homes and neglected other aspects of long-term care (Eustis et al., 1984). More recently, though, policymakers, health care providers, and researchers have begun to acknowledge the multifaceted nature of the long-term care system (for example, nursing homes, home helper and chore services, as well as care provided by the family), with these different aspects of this system responding to the different needs of the clients.

Recognizing that families and care receivers have different needs and that not all elderly need similar levels of care, providers of formal long-term care services have sought to meet these different needs through such services as home helper and chore services, home-delivered meals, transportation services, and nursing homes (Eustis et al., 1984). Yet, the extent to which each of these services will be needed in the future depends on a number of factors, including the number of frail elderly, the availability and willingness of family members to care for their elderly relatives, and the availability of public and private resources to pay for long-term care.

Policymakers are aware that the level of public resources necessary for long-term care of the elderly is related to the extent of family resources devoted to their care (Callahan et al., 1980; Montgomery et al., in press; Soldo, 1982; Stoller, 1985). Thus one of the central data needs in this area is to determine the current levels and patterns of family caregiving, and the levels and patterns that are likely in the future. An important aspect of this is information on family structure and proximity of family members. Such information will give some indication of the possible availability of family members to provide care for those who are currently in need of care and, by extension, those who will need care in the future.

The purpose of the present chapter is to identify and discuss the current level of knowledge about family structure and the geographical distribution of family members. Associated with this knowledge, and of critical importance for long-term care policy, is the amount of care given by family members. The amount of care available and the amount of care potentially available in the future will be determined in a limiting way by the presence of relatives who can provide care.

## The Current State of Knowledge

It is generally acknowledged that there is substantial intergenerational social interaction (e.g., Harris & Associates, 1975; Leigh, 1982; Shanas et al., 1968; Shanas, 1977, 1979a, 1979b; Sussman, 1965). A number of studies have found that most elderly live within a short traveling time of at least one child (e.g., Adams, 1968; Kivett, 1985; Montgomery & Borgatta, 1985b; Shanas et al., 1968; Shanas, 1979a, 1979b). Although these rates of social interaction are fairly high, it is, however, unclear to what extent these family members would be available for providing long-term care for their elderly relatives. That is, talking on the phone with one's relatives once a week may not necessarily be indicative of the availability or the willingness of that family member to provide care for the elderly relative. Nor would the fact that at least one child lives in close proximity to the older parent be a certainty that the child would provide care for the parent. Consequently, in order to develop long-term care policy, it is necessary to know the *availability* of family members who can provide long-term care and the *willingness* of potential caregivers to provide care.

Currently, little is known about the supply of informal caregivers (Montgomery et al., in press). This stems, in part, from problems of conceptualizing and measuring the availability of potential caregivers (Soldo, 1982). Additional problems arise when we take into account sociodemographic changes. Some researchers have argued that such things as increases in life expectancy, smaller families, increases in the number of women in the work force, and the high divorce rates of the last two decades may have an impact on the availability of caregivers in the future (Chiswick, 1976; Sheppard, 1978; Treas, 1977). Others, however, point out that even with the increase of women's participation in the labor force, they continue to provide care for older relatives, suggesting that some demographic changes may not lessen the availability of caregivers (Brubaker, 1985). Instead, as Brubaker (1985) points out, there may be a need to develop ways to reduce the stress these women may experience as a result of having several major responsibilities.

The number of older persons receiving informal long-term care is unknown. However, some estimates have been made. For example, the Congressional Budget Office (1977) estimated that between

3 and 6.7 million functionally disabled adults (many of whom were over the age of 65) were receiving some informal care in 1976. However, in terms of developing a rational policy of long-term care, a range of nearly 4 million people means the difference in allocation of billions of dollars.

It has been reported by a number of authors that social factors such as marital status, living arrangement, and the magnitude of the informal support network may be as important in determining the risk for long-term care as are health and disability (Butler & Newacheck, 1981; Davis & Gibbon, 1971; Eustis et al., 1984; Palmore, 1976; Townsend, 1965; Vincente et al., 1979). Butler and Newacheck (1981) state that persons who are widowed are as much as 5 times more likely to be institutionalized when compared to married persons. Persons who are divorced or separated or never married are up to 10 times more likely to be institutionalized. Palmore (1976) indicates that persons who live alone, those who have never married or are separated, and those with no children or 1 or 2 children have higher rates of institutionalization. Townsend (1965) reports that many functionally disabled older persons with children are able to remain at home and are placed in an institution only when their disability becomes extreme. Vincente et al. (1979) found that those who were older, unmarried, and living alone were more likely to be placed in a nursing home.

It seems clear that the availability of potential caregivers is important in determining the demand for formal long-term care services. Thus it becomes critical to determine the availability of informal care providers. This can be done, in part, by looking at the structures of families and households to determine the number of elderly living alone or with relatives, and by looking at the proximity of these family members—family members who live close to an elderly relative are more likely to provide care than those who live farther away. Two data sets will be used for this chapter: (1) 1980 census public use microdata, and (2) a sample of households from a small area in the state of Washington.

## Data

*Census data.* Census public use microdata for 1980 for the whole United States (1 in 1,000 sample) contain household- and individual-level information from the census "long form" and are not aggregate data as is the case of reports available through the Bureau of the Census. For the present chapter data were extracted so that a "case" was composed of selected household information followed by selected individual information for each of the related persons in the household. In this way, a tally of households containing various combinations of relatives could be made. A 10% sample (yielding a 1 in 10,000 sample) of households in which the householder was 40 or older is used for the present chapter (N = 4,854).

*Small area sample.* Because the census data provide information only on family structure within a given household, a second data set is used to look at both family structure *and* the geographical distribution of family members for households in a small area sample in the state of Washington. These data were collected as part of a survey of households to determine the use of health care and community services by families with elderly relatives. There were two parts to this survey. The first part was a random telephone screen interview that asked questions about household composition and the location of family members not living in the respondent's household (in the county or outside of the county; that is, within one hour's drive or greater than one hour's drive). Information was obtained for a total of 677 households. An extensive questionnaire was mailed to households that contained at least one person 60 years of age or older. These people were asked questions about the number of various relatives in the household and outside of the household, and whether or not the respondent provided any care for an adult relative.

These two data sets will provide the information on family structure and geographical distribution of family members for the present chapter. It will be shown, however, that even if we make a number of assumptions about the data, we are still left with many questions about the availability of caregivers.

### Results

*Census microdata.* The designation of householder was made by the individual(s) filling out the census form (U.S. Bureau of the Census, 1983). In 1980, the term *householder* was used in place of the previous designation, *head of household*. The householder is the first adult household member listed on the census questionnaire. Prior to 1980, the husband was always considered the head of the household. However, beginning in 1980, respondents were told to list the person (or one of the persons) in whose name the home was owned or rented. If a married couple owns the house jointly, either the husband or wife may be listed first.

Table 15.1 presents a summary of information from the 1980 census public use microdata. This table indicates the number and frequency of various kinds of household and family structures for certain householder characteristics. All frequencies in the tables can be multiplied by 10,000 to obtain the estimated values in the population. For example, the totals for the table can be multiplied by 10,000, indicating that in 1980 there were approximately 48.5 million single-family households with a householder 40 years of age or older and approximately 22.6 million single-family households with a householder 60 and older. This table is broken down by the sex of the householder, age of the householder (40 and older, 60 and older), and whether or not the householder has a spouse. The numbers in the cells indicate the frequency and proportion of householders with one or more children, one or more siblings, or one or more parents living in the household.

In Table 15.1 it can be seen that most (approximately 90%) male householders without spouses have no other close relatives living in the household with them (row 1 of Table 15.1). This is particularly true of the males 60 and over without spouses—nearly 95% of them live alone. Compared with the other 3 groups (rows), it can be seen that male householders without spouses, 40 years of age and older, are the least likely to have children living with them, yet are the most likely to have siblings and/or parents living with them.

Row 2 of Table 15.1 presents information on married couple households (male householder) 40 and older and 60 and older. Very few of these households have a sibling or parent of the householder in the household. They are, however, the most likely to have children living in the household, regardless of the age of the householder.

In row 3 of Table 15.1 information on family structure of households headed by females without spouses is presented. As with the male householders without spouses, this group is much less likely to have children living at home than those households with a male householder and spouse. However, nearly twice the proportion of

TABLE 15.1
Selected Summary Information from the 1980 Census Public Use Microdata

| | % 40+ with 1 or More Children in Home | % 60+ with 1 or More Children in Home | % 40+ with 1 or More Siblings in Home | % 60+ with 1 or More Siblings in Home | % 40+ with 1 or More Parents in Home | % 60+ with 1 or More Parents in Home |
|---|---|---|---|---|---|---|
| Male householder | | | | | | |
| without spouse | 12.8 (490)[a] | 7.2 (249) | 4.3 (490) | 6.0 (249) | 3.3 (490) | 1.6 (249) |
| with spouse | 49.6 (2846) | 18.4 (1041) | 0.6 (2846) | 0.6 (1041) | 1.2 (2846) | 0.7 (1041) |
| Female householder | | | | | | |
| without spouse | 24.7 (1429) | 11.1 (925) | 3.8 (1429) | 3.8 (925) | 2.5 (1429) | 0.8 (925) |
| with spouse | 29.2 (89) | 12.8 (47) | 0 (89) | 0 (47) | 2.2 (89) | 0 (47) |
| Totals | (4854) | (2262) | (4854) | (2262) | (4854) | (2262) |

NOTE: Numbers in parentheses are the total numbers of householders for the given marital status and age. Percentages within each cell represent proportions of those frequencies.
a. In 10,000s.

253

female householders without spouses than male householders without spouses have children living at home. This is probably a reflection of patterns of marriage, divorce, and mortality. For example, male householders without spouses are likely never to have been married or are likely to be divorced without residential custody of the children. Given patterns of mortality, it is less likely that these men are widowed than their female counterparts. For the female householders without spouses, on the other hand, they are likely to be either divorced and with custody of the children or widowed (for the 60 and older group).

Row 4 shows family structures for female-headed households with spouses. Although one might be tempted to combine this group with the male householders with spouses (row 2), the family structure of female householders with spouses have characteristics of both the male-headed households with spouses (row 2) and female-headed households without spouses (row 3). For example, a smaller proportion of female householders with spouses have any children at home compared to male householders with spouses. In other words, they are similar to female householders without spouses in this regard. However, like male householders with spouses, female householders with spouses are not at all likely to have any siblings at home, compared to female householders without spouses. Finally, female householders, 40 or older, with or without spouses are more likely to have any parents at home compared to male householders, 40 or older, with spouses.

The information presented in this table raises some interesting questions with regard to availability of caregivers, and we could speculate on the availability of caregivers. For example, householders (male or female) with spouses are more likely to have children living at home than are householders without spouses (male or female). On the other hand, householders (male or female) without spouses are more likely to have siblings and/or parents living with them than are householders with spouses. In terms of available caregivers, those with spouses are more likely to have children immediately available (in addition to spouses) than are those without spouses. However, those without spouses are more likely to have siblings immediately available.

Another interesting finding is that male householders without spouses and female householders (with or without spouses) are the most likely groups to have parents in the household. For these parents, this represents their immediately available source of care-givers. Unfortunately, we do not know if these householders are providing care for their elderly parents. If, however, these living arrangements reflect caregiving patterns, then the fact that male householders without spouses (40+ and 60+) have parents living with them, may prove to be an interesting finding about the extent to which some older males care for elderly relatives.

There is an interesting implication of some of these findings. It was mentioned above that householders (male or female) without spouses are less likely to have children living with them but more likely to have siblings or parents living with them than are house-holders with spouses. Given that living with others can effectively delay institutionalization (Butler & Newacheck, 1981), this group may, by living with others, be postponing their own movement or the movement of their relatives into an institution.

These data indicate that the vast majority (80% or more) of those 60 and older are either living with spouses only or are living alone. Although these data give us some sense of family structure within a household, they do not indicate the geographical distribu-tion of family members nor the amount of care needed, given, or received by various family members. In particular, for those peo-ple 60 and older who are living with spouses only or are living alone, we have no indication of the number of relatives who live in close proximity to the older adult, and thus represent a pool of avail-able caregivers.

The census data are important in that they can show for various age groups and householder characteristics what proportion of households contain only one person or have at least one relative living with the householder. Because we know that people 65 and older have a need for care more frequently and are at a greater risk of institutionalization (Eustis et al., 1984), we can make estimates from these data as to the number of people in this high-risk group who are currently living alone or with another relative. However, we do not know the reasons for sharing a household, nor do we know how many of those who do not share a household are in need of care. Additionally, we do not know how close other relatives are geographically or the care they require or give. The second data set discussed in this chapter moves us a little closer to this goal.

*Small area sample.* In the random sample of households in a small area in the state of Washington, 677 respondents completed the initial telephone interview. Of these, 250 (37%) were 60 years of age or older. Each of these respondents was sent a longer questionnaire asking additional questions about family structure, use of health care and community services, whether or not they provided care for an adult relative, and other background information. Of these 250 respondents, 170 (68%) completed the longer questionnaire. These data are used for the present discussion.

Although these data are limited by the number of respondents, they provide much more detailed information on family structure than do census data by asking about relatives in the household and the geographical distribution of family members outside of the household. In addition, there is a question asking about the care the respondent provides. Responses to this latter question provide some basic information on the number of individuals 60 and older who are currently providing care for an adult relative. Information from this sample is presented in Table 15.2 for respondents 60 and older.

According to this information, 80% of the male respondents and 56% of the female respondents currently live with their spouse. These proportions correspond closely to those in the population (U.S. Bureau of the Census, 1983: 83% of males 55 and older are married; 54% of females 55 and older are married). Very few of these persons have other relatives living in their households. However, approximately half of the respondents have at least one child or one sibling living within one hour's drive.

Table 15.3 presents summary information for mutually exclusive groups on the basis of marital status, household structure, and geographical distribution of family members. It can be seen that few of the men live alone (approximately 8%); however, most of those men who do live alone have no other relatives nearby (within one hour). Of the women in the sample, one-third live alone, and nearly half of these women have no other relatives living within an hour's drive. These proportions of unmarried older adults likely reflect the differences in mortality of males and females. However, more of these unmarried men are without a local family support network than are the women (80% of these men compared to 46% of these women). If these proportions are at all representative of those in the general population and we apply them at the national level, that means that approximately 2.5 million males and 5 million females 60 and older are without a local family support network.

TABLE 15.2
Family Structure and Proximity of Family Members
for Respondents Who Completed the Small Area Sample
Telephone Interview and Questionnaire

|  | Males, 60+ (n = 61) % | Females, 60+ (n = 109) % |
|---|---|---|
| Living with spouse | 80.3 | 56.0 |
| 1+ parents/in-laws in home | 3.3 | 2.8 |
| 1+ children in home | 4.9 | 2.8 |
| 1+ brothers in home | 1.6 | 0.9 |
| 1+ sisters in home | 1.6 | 0 |
| 1+ grandchildren in home | 3.3 | 0 |
| 1+ other relatives in home | 4.9 | 0.9 |
| 1+ other people in home | 4.9 | 5.5 |
| 1+ children within 1 hour | 21.3 | 26.6 |
| 1+ children greater than 1 hour | 75.4 | 75.2 |
| 1+ siblings within 1 hour | 18.0 | 29.4 |
| 1+ siblings greater than 1 hour | 67.2 | 66.1 |
| 1+ other close relatives greater than 1 hour | 68.9 | 56.9 |
| Care for other adult relative(s) | 16.4 | 8.3 |

There is one piece of information from this sample that has not been discussed. In looking back at Table 15.2, what is particularly interesting is the proportion of respondents who are caring for another adult relative. A total of 16% of the males and 8% of the females report caring for another adult relative. Although it is uncertain from these data who the respondent is caring for, we can make some speculative estimates. Of the men who are caring for someone, all are living with a spouse, and half of these have another relative (child or grandchild) living with them. Of the women who are caring for someone, one-half live alone, one-third are living with their spouse, and the remaining women are living with either one or two parents, a child, or an unrelated person. Over one-half of these women have a child or sibling living within one hour's drive.

TABLE 15.3
Summary Information from Small Area Sample

| | Males, 60+ (n = 61) % | Females, 60+ (n = 109) % |
|---|---|---|
| Living alone, no relatives within one hour* | 6.6 | 16.5 |
| Living alone, 1+ relatives within one hour* | 1.6 | 19.3 |
| Married, no relatives at home, no relatives within one hour* | 49.2 | 29.4 |
| Married, no relatives at home, 1+ relatives within one hour | 21.3 | 15.6 |
| Married, 1+ relatives at home, no relatives within one hour | 4.9 | 4.6 |
| Married, 1+ relatives at home, 1+ relatives within one hour | 4.9 | 6.4 |
| Not married, living with other relatives | 6.5 | 6.4 |
| Other living arrangements | 5.0 | 1.8 |
| Total | 100.0 | 100.0 |

*Significant difference of proportions, $p < .05$.

It is likely that the men who are caring for someone are primarily providing for their spouses. The women appear to be caring for spouses, if present. Otherwise, they may be caring for a parent who lives with them or a sibling who lives nearby. These findings are in line with past research that has shown that caregivers are most likely to be a spouse, if one is available (Brody, 1981). However, it is usually the wife who cares for the husband, due to longer life expectancy of women and the age difference between husband and wife; older women are usually cared for by children, generally daughters (Brody, 1981). This is the basis of what is called the "principle of substitution" (Shanas, 1979a), and may be in operation with some of the women who are caregivers in this sample. That is, some of them may be caring for a parent or sibling who may not have a spouse to care for them.

The reason why a larger proportion of the men than the women report that they are caring for someone is unclear. In terms of raw numbers for this sample, the *number* of men and women caring for someone is roughly the same. It may be the case that given the difference in proportions of men and women 60 and older in the population, and the difference in proportions of these men and women who are married, the respective proportions of men and women who are caring for someone are indeed meaningful. It is, however, interesting to note that if these men are "caring" for their spouses, is it truly help with activities of daily living that they are providing, or is it a reflection of the male role of "provider" that is entering into the assessment of the man as caring for someone? Or could it be some combination of these two? That is, do men consider "caring for someone" and the "provider role" as synonymous independent of actually "providing care"? If some men are defining themselves as "caregivers" based upon their role as provider, then this is a definitional concern, albeit an interesting one. If, however, these men are truly caring for their spouses, then there may be a large segment of the older male population that is providing care, but is unknown to researchers or policymakers. These questions need to be addressed in future research.

### Summary and Conclusions

The present chapter has used census data and a survey of a small area to give a sense of the family structure of American households containing adults 60 years of age or older. The sample for the small area provides additional population-based information on the geographical distribution of family members, as well as the proportion of males and females 60 and older who are caring for adult relatives. Unfortunately, these data do not indicate *who* is being cared for by the respondent or whether or not the respondent is being cared for by a relative.

Several existing national data sets have been reviewed in another paper (Montgomery et al., in press) regarding the information they contain on family structure, proximity of family members, exchange of aid, functional ability of older relatives, and availability of caregivers. It was determined that none of these data sets is adequate for use in assessing the current need for long-term care, nor as baseline data for making projections of those who will need care and those who can provide care.

The present chapter has shown that the vast majority of those who are 60 and older and married have no other relatives in the household. However, according to the small area study, a substantial proportion of these people appear to have at least one close relative nearby (within one hour's drive). Although we are also able to get a sense of the proportion of those 60 and older who are caring for an adult relative, it is still unclear who the recipients of this care are and whether or not the respondent is in need of care or is receiving care.

At the time of this book's publication, the census data will be 6 years old. The country's population will have increased by over 12 million people since those data were collected (U.S. Bureau of the Census, 1985). The age group of 65 and older is expected to increase from 17 million in 1985 to over 21 million in the year 2000 (U.S. Bureau of the Census, 1983). It is clear that researchers and policymakers need to keep in mind these and other sociodemographic changes and the possible impacts of these changes. For example, how will patterns of caregiving be affected with more women in the labor force and more women having fewer children? Clearly, these factors will change the limits of caregivers available, but other changes that may result are less clear.

The data presented in this chapter move us closer to the goal of rational policymaking. Yet, information on household structure and proximity of family members provides us with only part of what is needed for policymaking. This information indicates the maximum *limit* of caregivers available for certain groups of people, but indicates nothing about the *willingness* of those potential caregivers to provide care. This is a problem that is common to research that has looked at the living arrangements of, and the degree of interaction among, family members. However, one could ask whether willingness even becomes a consideration or an option for relatives of older adults in need of care.

An additional concern is that of matching services with the needs of the willing family and the elderly client (Brubaker, 1983). As mentioned above, caregivers and their elderly care receivers often have different needs, and different families have different needs. Locating where the greatest needs are likely to be and providing resources for services to fill those needs is of particular importance. Yet, as Brubaker (1983) points out, providing aid to family caregivers should be a supplement to, not a replacement for, the care provided by those family members. Thus one important area of future research is to determine the potential needs for family supports that maintain the caregiving tasks within the family setting, thereby reducing the public burden, while keeping willing family members from becoming overly burdened. Research that focuses on the extent of family caregiving in terms of the availability of caregivers is one aspect of this perspective that is now being considered. Data from this research will give a better sense of where to allocate resources to match services with the needs of the family members willing to care for their elderly relatives.

It is clear that the information required for policymaking is something that is not easily obtained. Yet, in order to develop rational long-term care policy, we need more systematic population-based data collection that will provide information not only on the structure of households and the proximity of kin, but also on the extent of care needed by elderly relatives, the extent of care provided by family members, and the willingness of family members to provide care.

# REFERENCES

ABRAMS, R. D. (1974). *Not Alone with Cancer*. Springfield, IL: Charles C Thomas.
ACHENBAUM, W. (1978). *Old Age in the New Land*. Baltimore: John Hopkins University Press.
ADAMS, B. N. (1968). *Kinship in an Urban Setting*. Chicago: Markam.
ALLINSON, M. (1982). Voluntary help. *Nursing Mirror, 10*, 55-56.
ALTSCHULER, J., JACOBS, S., & SHIODE, D. (1985). Psychodynamic time-limited groups for adult children of aging parents. *American Journal of Orthopsychiatry, 55*, 397-404.
AMERICAN BAR ASSOCIATION. (1983). *Board and Care Report: An Analysis of State Laws and Programs Serving Elderly Persons and Disabled Adults* (Report to the Department of Health and Human Services Grant 90 DJ 001/01).
APPLEBAUM, R., SEIDL, F. W., & AUSTIN, C. D. (1980). The Wisconsin community care organization: Preliminary findings from the Milwaukee Experiment. *Gerontologist, 20*, 350-351.
ARCHBOLD, P. G. (1982a). All-consuming activity: The family as caregiver. *Generations, 7*, 12-13, 40.
ARCHBOLD, P. G. (1982b). An analysis of parent caring by women. *Home Health Care Services Quarterly, 3*(2), 5-26.
ARLING, G., HARKINS, E., & ROMANIUK, M. (1984). Adult day care and the nursing home. *Research on Aging, 6*, 225-241.
BARNEY, J. L. (1977). The prerogative of choice in long-term care. *The Gerontologist, 17*, 309-314.
BARRETT, M. (1980). *Women's Oppression Today: Problems in Marxist Feminist Analysis*. London: Verso.
BASS, D. M. (1985). The hospice ideology and success of hospice care. *Research on Aging, 7*(3), 307-327.
BASS, D. M. & NOELKER, L. S. (1985). *The influence of family caregivers on elder's use of in-home services: An expanded conceptual framework*. Presented at the annual meeting of the Gerontological Society of America, New Orleans.
BERNARDOS, J. (1985). Family ideology: Identification and exploration. *The Sociological Review, 33*, 275-297.

BLAU, D. & BEREZIN, M. A. (1982). Neuroses and character disorders. *Journal of Geriatric Psychiatry,* 15(1):55-97.

BLAZER, D. (1978). Working with the elderly patient's family. *Geriatrics,* 33, 117-123.

BLENKNER, M. (1965). Social work and family relationships in family life. In E. Shanas & G. F. Streib (eds.), *Social Structure and the Family: Generational Relations.* Englewood Cliffs, NJ: Prentice-Hall.

BLENKNER, M. (1969). The normal dependencies of aging. In R. Kalish (ed.), *The Dependencies of Old People.* Detroit, MI: University of Michigan— Wayne State University, Institute of Gerontology.

BLUES, A. G. & ZERWEKH, J. V. (1984). *Hospice and Palliative Nursing Care.* Orlando, FL: Grune & Stratton.

BOHM, L. C. & RODIN, J. (1985). Aging and the family. In D. C. Turk & R. D. Kerns (eds.), *Health Issues and Families: A Life-Span Perspective* (279-310). NY: John Wiley.

BOOTS, S., & HOGAN, C. (1981). Creative movement and health. *Topics in Clinical Nursing,* 3(2), 23-31.

BRADBURN, N. M. (1969). *The Structure of Psychological Well-Being.* Chicago: Aldine.

BRADSHAW, B. R., BRANDENBURG, C., BASHAM, J., & FERGUSON, E. A. (1980). Barriers to community-based long-term care. *Journal of Gerontological Social Work,* 2, 185-198.

BARRESI, C. M., & BRUBAKER, T. H. (1979). Clinical social workers' knowledge about aging: Responses to the 'facts on aging' quiz. *Journal of Gerontological Social Work,* 2, 137-146.

BRENNAN, P. L. & STEINBERG, L. D. (1983-4). Is reminiscence adaptive? Relations among social activity level, reminiscence, and morale. *International Journal of Aging and Human Development,* 18(2), 99-110.

BRESLAU, L. (1984). Ties to family and the need for geriatric care. *Journal of Geriatric Psychiatry,* 17, 189-201.

BRESLIN, L. (1978). Aging: A family dilemma. *Psychiatric Quarterly,* 50(1), 55-58.

BRESLOW, R. W., VAN DYK, M. W. (1978). *Developing Group Homes for Older People: A Handbook for Community Groups.* Rockville, MD: Jewish Council for the Aging of Greater Washington, Inc.

BRODY, E. M. (1977). *Long-Term Care of Older People.* NY: Human Sciences Press.

BRODY, E. M. (1978). The aging of the family. *Annals of the American Academy of Political and Social Science,* 438, 13-27.

BRODY, E. M. (1981). 'Women in the middle' and family help to older people. *The Gerontologist,* 21(5), 471-480.

BRODY, E. M. (1985). Parent care as a normative family stress. *The Gerontologist,* 25, 19-29.

BRODY, E. M. & LANG, A. (1982). They can't do it all: Aging daughters with aged mothers. *Generations,* 7, 18-20, 37.

BRODY, S. J., POULSHOCK, S. W., & MASCIOCHI, C. F. (1978). The family care unit: A major consideration in the long-term support system. *The Gerontologist,* 18, 556-561.

BROTMAN, H. B. (1980). Every ninth American. In U.S. Senate Committee on Aging, *Developments in Aging: 1979 Part 1.* Washington DC: GPO.

BRUBAKER, E. (1986). Caregiving for a dependent spouse: Three case studies. *American Behavioral Scientist, 29,* 485-496.

BRUBAKER, E. (1983). Providing services to older persons and their families. In T. H. Brubaker (ed.), *Family Relationships in Later Life.* Beverly Hills, CA: Sage.

BRUBAKER, T. H. (1985). *Later Life Families.* Beverly Hills, CA: Sage.

BRUBAKER, T. H., & BARRESI, C. M. (1979). Social workers' levels of knowledge about old age and perceptions of service delivery to the elderly. *Research on Aging, 1,* 213-232.

BUCKHOLDT, D. R. (1983). The family conference: The social control of human development. *Journal of Family Issues,* 4(4), 613-632.

BUCKHOLDT, D. R., & GUBRIUM, J. F. (1983). Therapeutic pretense in reality orientation. *International Journal of Aging and Human Development,* 16, 167-181.

BURNSIDE, I. (1984). *Working With the Elderly: Group Process and Techniques.* Monterey, CA: Wadsworth Health Sciences Division.

BUTLER, L. H. & NEWACHECK, P. W. (1981). Health and social factors relevant to long-term care policy. In J. Meltzer, F. Farrow, & H. Richman (eds.), *Policy Options in Long-Term Care.* Chicago: University of Chicago Press.

BUTLER, P. A. (1979). Assuring the quality of care and life in nursing homes: The dilemma of enforcement. *North Carolina Law Review,* 57, 1317-1382.

BUTLER, P. A. (1980). A long-term health care strategy for legal services. *Clearinghouse Review.* October, 613-622.

BUTLER, R. N. (1963). The life review: An interpretation of reminiscence in the aged. *Psychiatry,* 26, 65-76.

BUTTERFIELD-PICARD, H. & MAGNO, J. (1982). Hospice the adjective, not the noun. *American Psychologist,* 37, 1254-1259.

CALKINS, K. (1972). Shouldering the burden. *Omega,* 3, 23-36.

CALLAHAN, J., DIAMOND, L. D., GIELE, J. Z., & MORRIS, R. (1980). Responsibility of families for their severely disabled elders. *Health Care Financing Review,* 1, 29-48.

CANTOR, M. H. (1979). Neighbors and friends: An overlooked resource in the informal support system. *Research on Aging,* 1, 434-463.

CANTOR, M. H. (1980). The informal support system: Its relevance to the lives of the elderly. In E. F. Borgatta & N. G. McCluskey (eds.), *Aging and Society: Current Research and Policy Perspectives* (pp. 133-144). Beverly Hills, CA: Sage.

CANTOR, M. H. (1983). Strain among caregivers: A study of experience in the United States. *The Gerontologist,* 23(6), 597-604.

CANTOR, M. H. & LITTLE, V. (1985). Aging and social care. In R. H. Binstock & E. Shanas (eds.), *Handbook of Aging and the Social Sciences, 2nd Edition.* NY: Van Nostrand Reinhold.

CARRILIO, T. & EISENBERG, D. (1983). Informal resources for the elderly: Panacea or empty promises. *Journal of Gerontological Social Work,* 6(1), 39-48.

CATH, S. (1972). The geriatric patient and his family: The institutionalization of a parent—a nadir of life. *Journal of Geriatric Psychiatry, 5*, 25-26.

CHAPPELL, N. L. (1985). Social support and the receipt of home care services. *The Gerontologist, 25*, 47-54.

CHISWICK, B. R. (1976). The demand for nursing home care: An analysis of the substitution between institutional and noninstitutional care. *Journal of Human Resources, 11*, 295-316.

CICIRELLI, V. G. (1981). *Helping Elderly Parents—The Role of Adult Children.* Boston, MA: Auburn House.

CICIRELLI, V. G. (1983). Adult children and their elderly parents. In T. Brubaker (ed.), *Family Relationships in Later Life.* Beverly Hills, CA: Sage.

CLIFFORD, A. (1985). Your mother is ours now. *Journal of Gerontological Nursing, 10*(9), 44.

COE, R. M. (1976). Professional perspectives on aging. *The Gerontologist, 15*, 136-137.

COHEN, P. M. (1983). A group approach for working with families of the elderly. *The Gerontologist, 23*(3), 248-250.

COMPTROLLER GENERAL OF THE UNITED STATES (1977). *The Well-Being of Older People in Cleveland, Ohio: A Report to Congress.* Washington, DC: General Accounting Office.

COULTON, C. & FROST, A. K. (1982). Use of social and health services by the elderly. *Journal of Health and Social Behavior, 23*, 330-339.

COWARD, R. T. (1979). Planning community services for the rural elderly: Implications from research. *The Gerontologist, 19*, 275-282.

COWARD, R. T. & LEE, G. R. (eds.). (1985). *The Elderly in Rural Society.* NY: Springer.

CROSSMAN, L. & KALJIAN, D. (1984). The family: Cornerstone of care. *Generations, 8*, 44-46.

DAVIS, B. & CHALLIS, D. (1980). Experimenting with new roles in domiciliary service: The Kent Community Care Project. *The Gerontologist, 20*, 288-299.

DAVIS, S. M. & GIBBIN, M. J. (1971). An area-wide examination of nursing home use, mis-use, and non-use. *American Journal of Public Health, 16*, 1146-1153.

DAY-LOWER, D., DRAYTON, B., & MULLANEY, J. W. (1982). *National Policy Workshop on Shared Housing: Findings and Recommendations.* Philadelphia: Shared House Resource Center, Inc.

DEIMLING, G. T. & BASS, D. M. (Under editorial review). Mental status among the aged: Effects on spouse and adult-child caregivers. *Journal of Gerontology.*

DEMOS, J. (1970). (T3)The Little Commonwealth: Family Life in Plymouth Colony. NY: Oxford.

DINGWALL, R., EEKELAAR, J., & MURRAY, T. (1983). *The Protection of Children: State Intervention and Family Life.* Oxford: Blackwell.

DOBROF, R. (1976). *The care of the aged: A shared function.* Unpublished doctoral dissertation, Columbia University School of Social Work.

DOBROF, R. (1981). Guide to practice. In R. Dobrof & E. Litwak (eds.), *Maintenance of Family Ties of Long-Term Care Patients: Theory and Practice.* Washington, DC: Government Printing Office, DHHS Publication No. (ADM) 81-400.

DOBROF, R. & LITWAK, E. (1981). *Maintenance of Family Ties of Long-Term Care Patients, Theory and Guide to Practice.* Rockville, MD: National Institute of Mental Health.

DONAHUE, W.T., PEPE, P., & MURRAY, P. (1978). *Assisted Independent Living in Residential Congregate Housing: A Report on the Situation in the United States.* Washington, DC: International Center for Social Gerontology.

DOTY, P., LIU, K., & WIENER, J. (1985). An overview of long-term care. *Health Care Financing Review,* 6(3), 69-78.

DUKE UNIVERSITY CENTER FOR THE STUDY OF AGING AND HUMAN DEVELOPMENT (1978). *Multidimensional Functional Assessment: The OARS Methodology* (2nd ed.). Durham, NC: Author.

EGGERT, G. M., BOWLYOW, J. E., & NICHOLS, C. W. (1980). Gaining control of the long-term care system: First returns from the Access Experiment. *The Gerontologist,* 20, 356-363.

EISENDORFER, C. & COHEN, D. (1981). Management of the patient and family coping with dementing illness. *Journal of Family Practice,* 12 (5), 831-837.

ESTES, C. L. & PHILIP, R. L. (1984). Social, political and economic background of long-term care policy. In C. Harrington, R. J. Newcomer, C. L. Estes, & Associates (eds.), *Long-Term Care of the Elderly: Public Policy Issues.* Beverly Hills, CA: Sage.

EUSTIS, N. N., GREENBERG, J. N., & PATTEN, S. K. (1984). *Long-Term Care for Older Persons: A Policy Perspective.* Monterey, CA: Brooks/Cole.

EYDE, D. R. and RICH, J. A. (1983). *Psychological Distress in Aging.* Rockville, MD: Aspen Systems.

FABRY, J. B. (1968). *The Pursuit of Meaning: Logotherapy Applied to Life.* Boston, MA: Beacon Press.

FEDERAL COUNCIL ON AGING (1985). *Annual Report to the President 1984.* Washington, DC: U.S. Department of Health and Human Services.

FEDERAL REGISTER (1984). Department of Health and Human Services, Office of Development Services. FY 1985 Coordinated Discretionary Funds Program; Availability of Funds and Request for Preapplications; Notice (Aug. 23).

FENGLER, A. P. & GOODRICH, N. (1979). Wives of elderly disabled men: The hidden patients. *The Gerontologist,* 19, 175-183.

FERREIRA, A. J. (1963). Decision-making in normal and pathological families. *Archives of General Psychiatry,* 8:68-73.

FILLENBAUM, G. G. & SMYER, M. A. (1981). The development, validity, and reliability of the OARS multidimensional functional assessment questionnaire. *Journal of Gerontology,* 36, 428-434.

FISCHER, L. R. & HOFFMAN, C. (1984). Who cares for the elderly: The dilemma of family support. *Research in Social Problems and Public Policy,* 3, 169-215.

FOLKMAN, S. (1984). Personal control and stress and coping processes: A theoretical analysis. *Journal of Personality and Social Psychology, 46,* 839-852.

FRANKFATHER, D. L., SMITH, M. J., & CARO, F. G. (1981). *Family Care of the Elderly.* Lexington, MA: D. C. Heath.

FRIEDMAN, S. R. & KAYE, L. W. (1980). Homecare for the frail elderly: Implications for an interactional relationship. *Journal of Gerontological Social Work, 2,* 109-123.

FRUEHLING, J. A. (ed.). (1982). *Sourcebook on Death and Dying* (1st ed.). Chicago: Marquis Professional Publications.

FURSTENBERG, F. (1981). Remarriage and intergenerational relations. In R. W. Fogel et al., (eds.), *Aging Stability and Change in the Family.* NY: Academic Press.

GARLAND, T. N., BASS, D. M., & OTTO, M. E. (1984). The needs of patients and primary caregivers a comparison of primary caregivers' and hospice nurses' perception. *The American Journal of Hospice Care,* 1(3), 40-45.

GELFAND, D. E., OLSON, J. K., & BLOCK, M. R. (1978). Two generations of elderly in the changing American family: Implications for family services. *The Family Coordinator, 27,* 395-403.

GENDEL, M. H. & REISER, D. E. (1981). Institutional counter transference. *American Journal of Psychiatry, 138,* 508-511.

GEORGE, L. K. (1984). The burden of caring. *Duke University Center Reports on Advances in Research,* 8(2), 1-6.

GETZEL, G. S. (1982). Helping elderly couples in crisis. *Social Casework, 63,* 515-521.

GIDRON, B. (1978). Volunteer work and its rewards. *Volunteer Administration,* 11(3), 18-27.

GLOSSER, G. & WEXLER, D. (1985). Participants' evaluation of educational/support groups for families of patients with Alzheimer's disease and other dementias. *The Gerontologist, 25,* 232-236.

GOFFMAN, E. (1961). *Asylums.* NY: Anchor Books.

GOLDSTEIN, R. (1983). Adult day care: Expanding options for service. In G. Getzel & M. J. Mellor (eds.), *Gerontological Social Work Practice in Long-Term Care.* NY: Haworth Press.

GOLDSTEIN, R. (1983). Psychotherapy of the elderly, Case #1: Institutionalizing a spouse—who is a client? *Journal of Geriatric Psychiatry,* 16(1), 41-49.

GOODMAN, J. G. (1980). *Aging Parents: Whose Responsibility?* NY: Family Service Association of America.

GOTAY, C. C. (1985). Research issues in palliative care. *Journal of Palliative Care,* 1(1), 24-31.

GREER, D. S. (1983). Hospice: Lessons for geriatricians. *Journal of the American Geriatrics Society,* 31(2), 67-70.

GREER, D. S., VINCENT, M., BIRNBAUM, H., SHERWOOD, S., & MORRIS, J. N. (1983). *National Hospice Study Preliminary Final Report Extended Executive Summary.* Providence, RI: Brown University.

GROBE, M. E., AHMANN, D. L., & ILSTRUP, D. M. (1982). Needs assessment for advanced cancer patients and their families. *Oncology Nursing Forum,* 9(4), 26-30.

268    AGING, HEALTH, AND FAMILY

GROBE, M. E., ILSTRUP, D. M., & AHMANN, D. L. (1981). Skills needed by family members to maintain the care of an advanced cancer patient. *Cancer Nursing*, 4(5), 371-375.

GUBRIUM, J. F. (1975). *Living and Dying at Murray Manor.* NY: St. Martin's.

GUBRIUM, J. F. (1980a). Patient exclusion in geriatric staffings. *Sociological Quarterly,* 21, 335-348.

GUBRIUM, J. F. (1980b). Doing care plans in patient conferences. *Social Science and Medicine,* 14A, 659-667.

GUBRIUM, J. F. (ed.). (1983). Institutionalization and the family. Special issue of *Journal of Family Issues,* 4(4).

GUBRIUM, J. F. (1986a). *Oldtimers and Alzheimer's: The Descriptive Organization of Senility.* Greenwich, CT: JAI Press.

GUBRIUM, J. F. (1986b). The social preservation of mind: The Alzheimer's disease experience. *Symbolic Interaction.*

GUBRIUM, J. F. (frthcg.). Structuring and destructuring the course of illness: The Alzheimer's disease experience. *Sociology of Health and Illness.*

GUBRIUM, J. F. & BUCKHOLDT, D. R. (1977). *Toward Maturity: The Social Processing of Human Development.* San Francisco: Jossey-Bass.

GUBRIUM, J. F. & BUCKHOLDT, D. R. (1982a). *Describing Care: Image and Practice in Rehabilitation.* Boston, MA: Oelgeschlager, Gunn & Hain.

GUBRIUM, J. F. & BUCKHOLDT, D. R. (1982b). Fictive family: Everyday usage, analytic and human service considerations. *American Anthropologist,* 84, 878-885.

GUBRIUM, J. F. & KSANDER, M. (1975). On multiple realities and reality orientation. *The Gerontologist,* 15, 142-145.

GUBRIUM, J. F. & LYNOTT, R. J. (1985a) Alzheimer's disease as biographical work. In W. A. Peterson & J. Quadagno (eds.), *Social Bonds in Later Life* (349-367). Beverly Hills, CA: Sage.

GUBRIUM, J. F. & LYNOTT, R. J. (1985b). Family rhetoric as social order. *Journal of Family Issues,* 6, 129-152.

GWYTHER, L. P. & BLAZER, D. G. (1984). Family therapy and the dementia patient. *American Family Physician,* 29(5), 149-156.

GWYTHER, L. P. & BROOKS, B. (1984). *Mobilizing Networks of Mutual Support: How to Develop Alzheimer's Caregivers' Support Groups.* Durham, NC: Duke University.

GWYTHER, L. P. & MATTESON, M. A. (1983). Care for the caregivers. *Journal of Gerontological Social Work,* 6(1), 39-48.

HAMNER, M. L. (1984). Insight, reminiscence, denial, projection: Coping mechanisms of the aged. *Journal of Gerontological Nursing,* 10(2), 66-68.

HAMPE, S. D. (1975). Needs of the grieving spouse in a hospital setting. *Nursing Research,* 24(2), 113-119.

HAREVEN, T. (1971). The history of the family as an interdisciplinary field. *Journal of Interdisciplinary History,* 2, 399-414.

HARRIS, LOUIS & Associates. (1975) *The Myth and Reality of Aging in America.* Washington, DC: National Council on Aging.

HARTFORD, M. E. & PARSONS, R. (1982). Groups with relatives of dependent older adults. *The Gerontologist,* 22, 394-398.

HARTMAN, A. (1981). The family: A central focus for practice. *Social Work,* 26, 7-13.

HAYSLIP, B., RITTER, M. L., OLLMAN, R. M., & McDONNELL, C. (1980). Home care services and the rural elderly. *The Gerontologist,* 20, 192-199.

HAYTER, J. (1982). Helping families of patients with Alzheimer's disease. *Journal of Gerontological Nursing,* 8(2), 81-86.

HESS, B. & SOLDO, B. (1985). Husband and wife networks. In W. J. Saur & R. T. Coward (eds.), *Social Support Networks and the Care of the Elderly: Theory, Research and Practice.* NY: Springer.

HIRSHFIELD, I. & DENNIS, H. (1979). Perspectives. In P. Ragan (ed.), *Aging Parents.* Los Angeles: University of California Press.

HODGSON, J. H. & QUINN, J. L. (1980). The impact of the triage health care delivery system on client morale, independent living and the cost of care. *The Gerontologist,* 20, 364-371.

HOREJSI, C. R. (1983). Social and psychological factors in family care. In R. Perlman (ed.), *Family Home Care.* NY: Haworth Press.

HOROWITZ, A. & SHINDELMAN, L. (1983). Reciprocity and affection: Past influences on current caregiving. *Journal of Gerontological Social Work,* 5, 5-19.

HUGHSTON, G. A. & MERRIUM, S. D. (1982). Reminiscence: A nonformal technique for improving cognitive functioning in the aged. *International Journal of Aging and Human Development,* 15(2), 130-149.

HUSSIAN, R. A. (1981). *Geriatric Psychology: A Behavioral Perspective.* NY: Van Nostrand Reinhold.

HUTTMAN, E. D. (1977). *Housing and Social Services for the Elderly: Social Policy Trends.* NY: Praeger.

IKELS, C. (1983). The process of caretaker selection. *Research on Aging,* 5, 491-509.

JACKSON, B. N. (1984). Home health care and the elderly in the 1980s. *The American Journal of Occupational Therapy,* 38, 717-720.

JACKSON, D. D. (1957). The question of family homeostasis. *Psychiatric Quarterly,* 31, 79-90.

JACKSON, D. D. (1965). Family rules. *Archives of General Psychiatry,* 12, 589-594.

JALOWEIC, A., MURPHY, S., & POWERS, M. (1984). Psychometric assessment of Jaloweic Coping Scale. *Nursing Research,* 33, 157-161.

JARRETT, W. H. (1985). Caregiving within kinship systems: Is affection really necessary? *The Gerontologist,* 25, 5-10.

JOHNSON, C. L. (1983). Dyadic family relations and social support. *The Gerontologist,* 23, 377-383.

JOHNSON, C. L. & CATALANO, D. S. (1983). A longitudinal study of family supports to impaired elderly. *The Gerontologist,* 23(6), 612-618.

JOHNSON, E. S. & BURSK, B. J. (1977). Relationships between the elderly and their adult children. *The Gerontologist,* 17, 90-96.

JOHNSON, S. H. (1985). State regulation of long-term care: A decade of experience with intermediate sanctions. *Law Medicine and Health Care,* 13(4), 173-188.

KAHANA, E. & COE, R.M. (1975). Alternatives in long-term care. In *Long-Term Care: A Handbook for Researchers, Planners and Providers*. NY: Spectrum.

KANE, R. L. & KANE, R. A. (1980). Alternatives to institutional care of the elderly: Beyond the dichotomy. *The Gerontologist*, 20(3), 249-259.

KANE, R. L., KLEIN, S. J., BERNSTEIN, L., ROTHENBERG, R., & WALES, J. (1985). Hospice role in alleviating the emotional stress of terminal patients and their families. *Medical Care*, 23(3), 189-197.

KAYE, L. W. (1985). Home care for the aged: A fragile partnership. *Social Work*, 30, 312-317.

KELLY, J. T., HANSON, R. G., GARETZ, F. K., SPENCER, D., & PATTEE, J. (1977). What the family physician should know about treating elderly patients, Part I. *Geriatrics*, 32, 97-100.

KEYS, B. & SZPAK, G. (1983). Day care for Alzheimer's disease: Profile of one program. *Postgraduate Medicine*, 71, 245-248.

KING, K. S. (1982). Reminiscing psychotherapy with aging people. *Journal of Psychosocial Nursing and Mental Health Services*, 20(2), 21-25.

KIRSCHLING, J. M. (in press). The experience of terminal illness on adult family members. *The Hospice Journal*.

KIRSCHNER, C. (1985). Social work practice with the aged and their families: A systems approach. *Journal of Gerontological Social Work*, 8, 55-69.

KIVETT, V. R. (1985). Consanguinity and kin level: Their relative importance to the helping network of older adults. *Journal of Gerontology*, 40, 228-234.

KLEIN, D. M. & HILL, R. (1979). Determinants of family problem-solving effectiveness. In W. R. Burr et al., (eds.), *Contemporary Theories about the Family* (vol. 1). NY: Free Press.

KNIGHT, B. G. (1985). The decision to institutionalize. *Generations*, Fall, 42-44.

KNIGHT, S., MARKSON, E., CRESCENZI, C., HOFFMAN, S., & BISSONNETTE, A. (1982). An analysis of types and costs of health care services provided to an elderly inner-city population. *Medical Care*, 20, 1090-1100.

KOSBERG, J. I., CAIRL, R., & KELLER, D. M. (in press). The cost of care index: A case management tool for screening informal care providers. *The Gerontologist*.

KRAMER, C. & KRAMER, J. (1976). *Basic Principles of Long-Term Care*. Springfield, Ill: Charles C Thomas.

KREPS, J. M. (1977). Intergenerational transfers and the bureaucracy. In E. Shanas & M. Sussman (eds.), *Family, Bureaucracy and the Elderly*. Durham, NC: Duke University Press.

KROUT, J. (1983). Knowledge and use of services by the elderly: A critical review of the literature. *International Journal of Aging and Human Development*, 17, 153-167.

KULYS, R. & TOBIN, S. S. (1980). Older people and their responsible others. *Social Work*, 25, 138-145.

KULYS, R. & TOBIN, S. S. (1980-1981). Interpreting the lack of future concerns among the elderly. *International Journal of Aging and Human Development*, 11, 31-46.

KUYPERS, J. (1969). *Elderly persons en route to institutions: A study of chang-ing perceptions of self and interpersonal relations.* Unpublished doctoral dis-sertation, University of Chicago, Chicago, IL.

KUYPERS, J. A. & BENGTSTON, V. L. (1983). Toward competence in the older family. In T. Brubaker (ed.), *Family Relationships in Later Life.* Beverly Hills, CA: Sage.

LAMERS, W. M. (in press). Hospice care in North America. In S. B. Day (ed.), *Cancer, Stress and Death.* NY: Plenum.

LANDSBERGER, B. H. (1985). *Long-Term Care of the Elderly, A Comparative View of Layers of Care.* NY: St. Martin's.

LASCH, C. (1977). *Haven in a Heartless World.* NY: Basic Books.

LAWTON, M.P. (1971). The functional assessment of elderly people. *Journal of the American Geriatrics Society,* 19(6), 465-481.

LAWTON, M. P. & BRODY, E. (1969). Assessment of older people: self-maintaining and instrumental activities of daily living. *The Gerontologist,* 9, 179-186.

LAWTON, M. P., MOSS, M., & GRIMES, M. (1985). The changing service needs of older tenants in planned housing. *The Gerontologist,* 25, 258-264.

LAZARUS, L. W. & WEINBERG, J. (1980). Treatment in the ambulatory care setting. In E. W. Busse & D. G. Blazer (eds.), *Handbook of Geriatric Psychi-atry* (chapter 20). NY: Van Nostrand Reinhold.

LAZARUS, R. & FOLKMAN, S. (1984). *Stress, Appraisal, and Coping.* NY: Springer.

LEBOWITZ, B. O. (1979). Old age and family functioning. *Journal of Geronto-logical Social Work,* 1, 111-118.

LEE, G. R., & LASSEY, M. L. (1982). The elderly. In D. A. Dillman & D. J. Hobbs (eds.), *Rural Society in the U.S.: Issues for the 1980s.* Boulder, CO: Westview Press.

LEIGH, G. K. (1982). Kinship interaction over the family life span. *Journal of Marriage and the Family,* 44, 197-206.

LEONARD, L. E. & KELLY, A. M. (1975). The development of a community-based program for evaluating the impaired older adult. *The Gerontologist,* 15, 114-118.

LEVENSON, H. (1981). Differentiating among internality, powerful others and chance. In H. M. Lefcourt (ed.), *Research with the Locus of Control Con-struct.* NY: Academic Press.

LEVENTHAL, H., LEVENTHAL, E. A., & VAN NGUYEN, T. (1985). Reactions of families to illness: Theoretical models and perspectives. In D. C. Turk & R. D. Kerns (eds.), *Health Issues and Families: A Life-Span Perspec-tive* (108-145). NY: John Wiley.

LIEBERMAN, M. (1985). Self-help groups. *Generations,* 10(1), 45-49.

LIEBERMAN, M. A. & TOBIN, S. S. (1983). *The Experience of Old Age: Stress, Coping and Survival.* NY: Basic Books.

LITWAK, E. (1965). Extended kin relations in an industrial democratic society. In E. Shanas & G. Streib (eds.), *Social Structure and the Family.* Englewood Cliffs, NJ: Prentice-Hall.

LITWAK, E. (1981). Theoretical basis for practice. In R. Dobrof & E. Litwak
(eds.), *Maintenance of Family Ties of Long-Term Care Patients: Theory and
Practice*. Washington, DC: Government Printing Office, DHHS Publication
No. (ADM) 81-400.
LITWAK, E. (1985). *Helping the Elderly: The Complementary Roles of Infor-
mal Networks and Formal Systems*. NY: Guilford.
LITWAK, E. & MEYER, H. J. (1966). A balance theory of coordination
between bureaucratic organizations and community primary groups. *Admin-
istrative Science Quarterly*, 11, 31-58.
LONGINO, C. F., WISEMAN, R. F., BIGGAR, J. C. & FLYNN, C. B. (1984).
Aged metropolitan-nonmetropolitan migration streams over three census
decades. *Journal of Gerontology*, 39, 721-729.
LOSSING, G. (1979). Volunteers also have needs. *Hospitals*, (July), 231-233.
LOWENTHAL, M. & ROBINSON, B. (1977). Social networks and isolation.
In R. Binstock & E. Shanas (eds.), *Handbook of Aging and the Social Sci-
ences*. NY: Van Nostrand Reinhold.
LOWY, L. (1985). *Social Work with the Aging: The Challenge and Promise of the
Later Years* (2nd ed.). NY: Longman.
LYNOTT, R.J. (1983). Alzheimer's disease and institutionalization: The ongo-
ing construction of a decision. *Journal of Family Issues*, 4, 559-574.
LYONS, W. (1982). Coping with cognitive impairment: Some family dynamics
and helping roles. *Journal of Gerontological Social Work*, 4, 3-20.
MAAS, M. & BUCKWALTER, K. C. (1985). Evaluation of a special Alz-
heimer's unit. ANF Grant Proposal.
MACE, N. L. & RABINS, P. V. (1981). *The 36-Hour Day*. Baltimore, MD:
John Hopkins University Press.
MACE, N. L. & RABINS, P. V. (1984). *A Survey of Day Care for the Demented
Adult in the United States*. Washington, DC: National Council on The Aging.
MACKAY, A. (1983). Organic brain syndrome and nursing care. *Journal of
Gerontological Nursing*, 9(2), 74-85.
MADDOX, G. L. (1975). Families as context and resource in chronic illness. In
S. Sherwood (ed.), *Long-Term Care: A Handbook for Researchers, Planners
and Providers*. NY: Spectrum.
MANCINI, J. A. & SIMON, J. (1984). Older adults' expectations of support
from family and friends. *Journal of Applied Gerontology*, 3, 150-160.
MARKHAM, E. (1979). Ethnicity as a factor in the institutionalization of the
ethnic elderly. In D. Gelfand & A. Kutzik (eds.), *Ethnicity and Aging*. NY:
Springer.
MASCIOCCHI, C., THOMAS, A., & MOELLER, T. (1984). Support for the
impaired elderly: A challenge for family caregivers. In W. H. Quinn & G. A.
Hughston (eds.), *Independent Aging* (113-131). Rockville, NY: Aspen.
McAULEY, W. & ARLING, G. (1984). Use of in-home care by very old people.
*Journal of Health and Social Behavior*, 25, 54-64.
McAULEY, W. J., ARLING, G., NUTTY, C., & BOWLING, C. (1980). *Final
Report of the Statewide Survey of Older Virginians* (Research Series No. 3.).
Richmond: Virginia Commonwealth University, Virginia Center on Aging.

McAULEY, W. J. & BLIESZNER, R. (1985). Selection of long-term care arrangements by older community residents. *The Gerontologist*, 25. 188-193.

McCORMACK, D. & WHITEHEAD, A. (1981). The effect of providing recreational activities on the engagement level of long stay geriatric patients. *Age and Aging*, 10, 287-291.

McCUBBIN, H., OLSON, D., & LARSEN, A. (1981). Family crisis oriented personal evaluation scales (F-COPES). St. Paul: University of Minnesota, Family Social Science.

McDONALD, K. M. (1984). Residents in a life care retirement community: The need for improved legislation. *Journal of Family Law*, 23, 583-615.

McMORDIE, W. R. & BLOM, S. (1979). Life review therapy: Psychotherapy for the elderly. *Perspectives in Psychiatric Care*, 17(4), 162-166.

MELTZER, J. W. (1982). *Respite Care: An Emerging Family Support Service.* Washington, DC: The Center for the Study of Social Policy.

MILLER, M. B. & HARRIS, A. P. (1967). The chronically ill aged: Paradoxical patient-family behavior. *Journal of the American Geriatric Society*, 15: 480-495.

MOEN, E. (1978). The reluctance of the elderly to accept help. *Social Problems*, 25, 293-303.

MONK, A. (1983). Family supports in old age. *Home Health Care Services Quarterly*, 3, 101-111.

MONTGOMERY, R. J. V. (1981). *Toward a Rational Policy for Family Involvement in Long-Term Care.* Washington: University of Washington, Long-Term Care Gerontology Center.

MONTGOMERY, R. J. V. (1983). Staff-family relations and institutional care policies. *Journal of Gerontological Social Work*, 6(1), 25-38.

MONTGOMERY, R. J. V. & E.F. BORGATTA, (1985a). *Creation of burden scales.* Paper presented at the 38th annual meeting of the Gerontological Society of America, November 22-26, New Orleans, Louisiana.

MONTGOMERY, R. J. V. & E. F. BORGATTA (1985b). *Family Support Project.* Final report to the Administration on Aging. University of Washington: Institute on Aging/Long Term Care Center.

MONTGOMERY, R. J. V., GONYEA, J. G., & HOOYMAN, N. R. (1985). Caregiving and the experience of subjective and objective burden. *Family Relations*, 34, 19-26.

MONTGOMERY, R. J. V., HATCH, L. R., STULL, D. E., BORGATTA, E. F., & PULLUM, T. (in press). Family extension and dependency. In E. F. Borgatta & R. J. V. MONTGOMERY (eds.), *Critical Issues in Aging.* Beverly Hills, CA: Sage.

MONTGOMERY, R. J. V., STULL, E. E., & BORGATTA, E. F. (1985). Measurement and the analysis of burden. *Research on Aging*, 7, 137-152.

MOORE, J., BOBULA, J., SHOET, T., & MISCHEL, M. (1983). A functional dementia scale. *Journal of Family Practice*, 16, 499-503.

MORONEY, R. (1976). *The Family and the State: Considerations for Social Policy.* New York: Longman.

MORONEY, R. M. (1983). Families, care of the handicapped and public policy. *Home Health Care Services Quarterly.* 3, 188-213.

MORRIS, J. & SHERWOOD, S. (1983-1984). Informal support resources for vulnerable elderly persons: can they be counted on, why do they work? *International Journal of Aging and Human Development*, 18, 81-98.

MORYCZ, R. (1985). Caregiving strain and the desire to institutionalize family members with Alzheimer's disease. *Research on Aging*, 7, 329-361.

MUNNICHS, J. (1977). Linkages of old people with their families and bureaucracy in a welfare state, the Netherlands. In E. Shanas & M. B. Sussman (eds.), *Family, Bureaucracy and the Elderly*. (92-119) Durham, NC: Duke University Press.

MURRAY, P. (1979). *Shared Homes: A Housing Option for Older People*. Washington, DC: International Center for Social Gerontology.

NATIONAL INSTITUTE OF HEALTH (NIH)(1981). NIH studies causes of Alzheimer's disease. *Special Report on Aging*. Washington, DC: NIH Publication No. 80-2135, pp. 16-18.

NATIONAL INSTITUTE ON ADULT DAY CARE (1984). *Standards for Adult Day Care*. Washington, DC: National Council On The Aging, Inc.

NATIONAL SENIOR CITIZENS LAW CENTER WASHINGTON WEEKLY, (1985). 11(46), 22-44.

NAVA, M. (1983). From utopian to scientific feminism: Early feminist critique of the family. In L. Segal (ed.), *What is to be Done About the Family?* (65-105). Harmondsworth, England: Penguin.

NEAL, M. B., WHITE, D. L., & BUELL, J. S. (1981). *Conceptualizing Quality Terminal Care for the Elderly* (tech. rep.). Portland, OR: Portland State University, Institute on Aging, School of Urban Affairs.

NELSON, G. M. (1983). A comparison of Title XX services to the urban and rural elderly. *Journal of Gerontological Social Work*, 6, 3-23.

NOELKER, L. S. & HAREL, Z. (1978). Aged excluded from home health care: An interorganizational solution. *The Gerontologist*, 18, 37-41.

NOELKER, L. S. & SHAFFER, G. (in press). How care networks form and change. *Generations*.

NOELKER, L. S. & TOWNSEND, A. L. (1985). The quality of the older parent-child relationship and the caregiving process. Paper presented at the XIIIth International Congress of Gerontology, New York.

NOELKER, L. S., TOWNSEND, A. L., & DEIMLING, G. (1984). *Caring For Elders and the Mental Health of Family Members: A Report on the Study's First Three Years (1980-1983)*. Cleveland, OH: Benjamin Rose Institute.

NOELKER, L. S. & WALLACE, R. W. (1985). The organization of family care for impaired elderly. *Journal of Family Issues*, 6, 23-44.

NUMEROF, R. (1983). Building and maintaining bridges: Meeting the psychological needs of nursing home residents and their families. *Clinical Gerontologist*, 1(4), 53-67.

O'BRIEN, C. (1982). *Adult Day Care*. Monterey, CA: Wadsworth Health Sciences Division.

O'BRIEN, J. E. & WAGNER, E. L. (1980). Help seeking by the frail elderly: Problems in network analysis. *The Gerontologist*, 20, 73-83.

O'CONNOR, P. (1981). Long-term care facilities and organization theory: Some research suggestions. In R. Fogel, E. Hatfield, S. Kiesler, & E. Shanans (eds.), *Aging: Stability and Change in the Family*. NY: Academic Press.

OLIVER, R. & BOCK, F. A. (1985). Alleviating the distress of caregivers of Alzheimer's disease patients: A rational-emotive therapy model. *Clinical Gerontologist*, 3, 17-34.

OLSEN, E. H. (1970). The impact of serious illness on the family system. *Postgraduate Medicine*, 47(2):169-174.

OLSON, D. H., McCUBBIN, H. I., BARNES, H., LARSEN, A., MUXEN, M. & WILSON, M. (1983). *Families: What Makes Them Work*. Beverly Hills, CA: Sage.

ORY, M., WILLIAMS, T., EMR, M., LEBOWITZ, B., RABINS, P., SALLO-WAY, J., SLUSS-RADBAUGH, T., WOLFF, E., & ZARIT, S. (1985). Families, informal supports, and Alzheimer's disease: Current research and future agendas. *Research on Aging*, 7(4), 623-644.

PALMORE, E. (1976). Total chances of institutionalization among the aged. *The Gerontologist*, 16, 504-507.

PALMORE, E. (1983). Health care needs of the rural elderly. *International Journal of Aging and Human Development*, 18, 39-45.

PEPPARD, N. (1985). Alzheimer special care nursing home units. *Nursing Homes*, 8(1), 25-28.

PERLMAN, R. & GIELE, J. Z. (1982). An unstable triad: Dependents' demands, family resources, community supports. *Home Health Care Services Quarterly*, 3, 12-44.

PINKSTON, E. & LINSK, N. (1984). *Care of the Elderly: A Family Approach*. NY: Pergamon.

POULSHOCK, S. W. & DEIMLING, G. T. (1984). Families caring for elders in residence: Issues in the measurement of burden. *Journal of Gerontology*, 39, 230-239.

POWELL, L. S. & COURTICE, K. (1983). *Alzheimer's Disease: A Guide for Families*. Reading, MA: Addison & Wesley.

PRATT, C., SCHMALL, V., WRIGHT, S., & CLELAND, M. (1985). Burden and coping strategies of caregivers of Alzheimer's patients. *Family Relations*, 34, 27-34.

PRATT, C., WRIGHT, S., & SCHMALL, V. (in press). Burden, coping, and health status: A comparison of family caregivers to community-dwelling and institutionalized dementia patients. *Journal of Gerontological Social Work*.

PRITCHARD, D. C. (1983). The art of matchmaking: A case study in shared housing. *The Gerontologist*, 23(2), 174-179.

QUADAGNO, J. (1982). *Aging in Early Industrial Society*. NY: Academic.

QUINN, S. J. (1984). Elderly in hospice. *The American Journal of Hospice Care*, 1(1), 27-30.

QUINN, W. N. & KELLER, J. F. (1983). Older generations of the family: Relational dimensions and quality. *American Journal of Family Therapy*, 11, 23-34.

RANSOM, B. (1985). *An overview of adult day care—part of a symposium on perspectives on adult day care: Intergenerational and disease specific problems*. Presented at the 38th annual meeting of the Gerontological Society, New Orleans, Louisiana.

RATHBONE-McCUAN, E. (1976). Geriatric day care—a family perspective. *The Gerontologist*, 16, 517-521.

REECE, D., WALZ, T., & HAGEBOECK, H. (1983). Intergenerational care providers of non-institutionalized frail elderly: Characteristics and consequences. *Journal of Gerontological Social Work,* 5, 21-34.

REEVER, K. & THOMAS, E. (1985). Training facilitators of self-help groups for caregivers to the elderly. *Generations,* 10(1), 50-52.

REIDER, N. (1953). A type of transference to institutions. *Journal of the Hillside Hospital,* 2, 23-29.

REISBERG, B. (1983). *A Guide to Alzheimer's Disease: for Families, Spouses and Friends.* NY: Free Press.

REVERE, V. & TOBIN, S. S. (1980-1981). Myth and reality: The older person's relationship to his past. *International Journal of Aging and Human Development,* 12, 15-26.

RICCI, M. (1983). All-out support for an Alzheimer's patient. *Geriatric Nursing,* 4(60), 369-371.

RICHARDS, M., HOOYMAN, N., HANSEN, M., BRANDTS, W., SMITH-DIJULIO, & DAHM, L. (1984). *Nursing Home Placement: A Guidebook for Families.* Seattle: University of Washington.

RILEY, M. (1983). The family in an aging society: A matrix of latent relationships. *Journal of Family Issues,* 4, 439-454.

ROBINSON, G. & THURNHER, M. (1979). Taking care of aged parents: A family cycle transition. *The Gerontologist,* 19, 586-593.

ROMANIUK, J. G., ROMANIUK, M. J., FINLEY, R. B., & WOOD, J. B. (1984). *Mental Health and Aging: Concepts and Connections: A Training Manual.* Richmond: Virginia Commonwealth University, Virginia Center on Aging.

ROOK, K. & DOOLEY, D. (1985). Applying social support research: Theoretical problems and future directions. *Journal of Social Issues,* 41, 5-28.

ROOZMAN-WEIGNESBERG, C. & FOX, M. (1980). A groupwork approach with adult children of institutionalized elderly: An investment in the future. *Journal of Gerontological Social Work,* 2, 355-362.

ROSEN, A. J. (1975). Group discussions: A therapeutic tool in crisis. *Journal of Gerontological Social Work,* 2, 355-362.

ROSENMAYR, L. (1977). The family—a source of hope for the elderly? In E. Shanas and M.B. Sussman (eds.), *Family, Bureaucracy and the Elderly* (132-157). Durham, NC: Duke University Press.

ROSOW, I. (1967). *Social Integration of the Aged.* NY: Free Press.

RUBIN, A. & SHUTTLESWORTH, G. (1983). Engaging families as support resources in nursing home care: Ambiguity in the subdivision of tasks. *The Gerontologist,* 23(6), 632-636.

SAFFORD, F. (1980). A program for families of the mentally impaired elderly. *The Gerontologist,* 20, 656-660.

SAFIRSTEIN, S. (1967). Institutional transference. *Psychiatric Quarterly,* 41, 557-566.

SAINSBURY, P. & GRAD DE ALARCON, J. (1970). The effects of community care on the family of the geriatric patient. *Journal of Geriatric Psychiatry,* 4, 23-41.

SCHLESINGER, M. R., TOBIN, S. S., & KULYS, R. (1981). The responsible child and parental well-being. *Journal of Gerontological Social Work,* 3, 3-16.

SCHMALL, V. (1984). What makes a support group good? *Generations*, 9(2), 64-67.

SCHMIDT, M. G. (1980). Failing parents, aging children. *Journal of Gerontological Social work*, 2, 259-268.

SCHNASE, R. C. (1982). Therapeutic reminiscence in elderly patients. *Journal of Nursing Care*, 15(2), 62-64.

SCHRETER, C. (1983). *Room for rent: Shared housing with non-related older Americans*. Doctoral Dissertation, Bryn Mawr College.

SCHWIRIAN, P. (1982). Life satisfaction among nursing home residents. *Geriatric Nursing*, 3(2), 111-114.

SCOTT, J. P. (1983). Siblings and other kin. In T. H. Brubaker (ed.). *Family Relations in Later Life*. Beverly Hills, CA: Sage.

SCOTT, J. P. & ROBERTO, K. (1985). Use of informal and formal support networks by rural elderly poor. *The Gerontologist*, 25, 624-630.

SEELBACH, W. C. (1978). Correlates of aged parents' filial responsibility, expectations and relations. *The Family Coordinator*, 27, 341-350.

SEELBACH, W. C. & SAUER, W. J. (1977). Filial responsibility expectations and morale among aged parents. *The Gerontologist*, 19, 3-9.

SHANAS, E. (1977). *National Survey of the Aged*. Chicago: University of Illinois, Chicago Circle.

SHANAS, E. (1979a). Social myth as hypothesis: The case of the family relations of older people. *The Gerontologist*, 19, 3-9.

SHANAS, E. (1979b). The family as a social support system in old age. *The Gerontologist*, 19, 169-174.

SHANAS, E. (1980). Older people and their families: new pioneers. *Journal of Marriage and the Family*, 42, 9-15.

SHANAS, E. & MADDOX, G. L. (1985). Health, health resources, and the utilization of care. In R. H. Binstock & E. Shanas (eds.), *Handbook of Aging and the Social Sciences (2nd Edition)*. NY: Van Nostrand Reinhold.

SHANAS, E. & SUSSMAN, M. (1977). Family bureaucracy: Comparative analyses and problematics. In E. Shanas & M. Sussman (eds.), *Family, Bureaucracy, and the Elderly*. Durham, NC: Duke University Press.

SHANAS, E., TOWNSEND, P., WEDDERBURN, D., FRIIS, H., MILJOJ, P., & STEHOUWER, J. (1968). *Old People in Three Industrial Societies*. NY: Atherton Press.

SHEPPARD, H. L. (1978). The economics of population, mortality, and retirement. In *Economics of Aging: The Economic, Political, and Social Implications of Growing Old in America*. Washington, DC: *National Journal*.

SHUTTLESWORTH, G., RUBIN, A., & DUFFY, M. (1982). Families versus institutions: Incongruent role expectations in the nursing home. *The Gerontologist*, 22(3), 200-208.

SILVERMAN, A. G. & BRACHE, C. I. (1979). 'As parents grow older': An intervention model. *Journal of Gerontological Social Work*, 2, 77-85.

SILVERSTONE, B. & HYMAN, H. (1976). *You and Your Aging Parent*. Springfield, IL: Charles C Thomas.

SMITH, K. F. & BENGTSTON, V. L. (1979). Positive consequences of institutionalization: Solidarity between elderly parents and their middle-aged children. *The Gerontologist*, 19, 438-447.

SMOLIC-KRKOVIC, N. (1977). Aging, bureaucracy, and the family. In E. Shanas and M.B. Sussman (eds.), *Family, Bureaucracy and the Elderly* (75-89). Durham, NC: Duke University Press.

SNOW, D. L. & GORDON, J. B. (1980). Social network analysis and intervention with the elderly. *The Gerontologist,* 20, 463-467.

SOLDO, B. J. (1982). *Supply of Informal Care Services: Variations and Effects on Service Utilization Patterns.* Working paper, the Urban Institute, Washington, DC.

SOLDO, B. J. & MYLLYLUOMA, J. (1983). Caregivers who live with dependent elderly. *The Gerontologist,* 23, 605-611.

SOLOMON, R. (1983). Serving families of the institutionalized aged: The four crises. In S. Getzel & M. J. Mellor (eds.), *Gerontological Social Work Practice in Long-Term Care* (83-96). New York: Haworth Press.

SPRINGER, D. & BRUBAKER, T. H. (1984). *Family Caregivers and Dependent Elderly: Minimizing Stress and Maximizing Independence.* Beverly Hills, CA: Sage.

SQUIER, D. A. (1984). *The Effects of Decentralization on In-Home, Long-Term Care Services.* Unpublished M.A. Thesis, University of Kansas, Lawrence, Kansas.

STAFFORD, F. (1980). A program for families of the mentally impaired elderly. *The Gerontologist,* 20, 656-660.

STATE OF KANSAS, DEPARTMENT OF SOCIAL AND REHABILITATIVE SERVICES (1982). *Waiver request to the Secretary of the U.S. Dept. of Health and Human Services.* Topeka, KS.

STEINITZ, L. (1981). *Informal supports in long-term care: Implications and policy options.* Presented to the National Conference on Social Welfare.

STEINMETZ, S. K. & AMSDEN, D. J. (1983). Dependent elders, family stress, and abuse. In T. Brubaker (ed.), *Family Relationships in Later Life.* Beverly Hills, CA: Sage.

STEPHENS, R. C., BLAU, Z. S., OSER, G. T., & MILLER, M. D. (1978). Aging, social support systems, and social policy. *Journal of Gerontological Social Work,* 1, 33-45.

STOLLER, E. P. (1982). Sources of support for the elderly during illness. *Health and Social Work,* 7, 111-122.

STOLLER, E. P. (1985). Exchange patterns in the informal support networks of the elderly: The impact of reciprocity on morale. *Journal of Marriage and the Family,* 42, 335-342.

STONE, R., NEWCOMER, R. J., & SAUNDERS, M. (1982). *Descriptive Analysis of Board and Care Policy Trends in the 50 States.* San Francisco: University of California, Aging Health Policy Center.

STREIB, G. F. (1972). Older families and their troubles: familial and social responses. *The Family Coordinator,* 21, 5-19.

STREIB, G. F. (1977). Bureaucracies and families: Common themes and directions for further study. In E. Shanas and M. B. Sussman (eds.), *Family, Bureaucracy and the Elderly* (204-214). Durham, NC: Duke University Press.

STREIB, G. F. (1982). The continuum of living arrangements. In G. Lesnoff-Caravaglia (ed.), *Aging and the Human Condition.* NY: Human Science Press.

STREIB, G. F. (1983). The frail elderly: Research dilemmas and research opportunities. *The Gerontologist,* 23(1), 40-44.

STREIB, G. F. & BECK, R. W. (1980). Older families: A decade review. *Journal of Marriage and the Family,* 42, 937-959.

STREIB, G. F., FOLTS, W. E., & HILKER, M. A. (1984). *Old Homes New Families: Shared Living for the Elderly.* NY: Columbia University Press.

STREIB, G. F. & SHANAS, E. (1965). An introduction. In E. Shanas & G. F. Streib (eds.), *Social Structure and the Family: Generational Relations.* Englewood Cliffs, NJ: Prentice-Hall.

SUSSMAN, M.B. (1965). Relationships of adult children with their parents in the United States. In E. Shanas & G. F. Streib (eds.), *Social Structure and Family: Generational Relations.* Englewood Cliffs, NJ: Prentice-Hall.

SUSSMAN, M.B. (1977). Family, bureaucracy and the elderly individual: An organizational/linkage perspective. In E. Shanas & M. B. Sussman (eds.), *Family, Bureaucracy and the Elderly.* Durham, NC: Duke University Press.

SUSSMAN, M.B. (1979). *Social and economic supports and family environments for the elderly.* Final Report to Administration on Aging.

SUSSMAN, M.B. (1985). The family life of old people. In R. Binstock & E. Shanas (eds.), *Handbook of Aging and the Social Sciences.* NY: Van Nostrand Reinhold.

TABER, M. A., ANDERSON, S., & ROGERS, C. J. (1980). Implementing community care in Illinois: Issues of cost and targeting in a statewide program. *The Gerontologist,* 20, 380-388.

TAIETZ, P. (1975). Community complexity and knowledge of facilities. *Journal of Gerontology,* 30, 357-362.

THOMPSON, M. M. (1975). *Congregate housing for older adults: Assisted residential living combining shelter and services.* A working paper prepared for use by the Special Committee on Aging, U.S. Senate 94th Congress, 1st Session. Washington, DC: Government Printing Offices.

THOMPSON, M. M. (1976). *Training Guide on Sheltered Housing for the Elderly.* Baltimore: State of Maryland Office on Aging.

THORNE, B. (1982). Feminist rethinking of the family: An overview. In B. Thorne & M. Yalom (eds.), *Rethinking the Family: Some Feminist Questions* (1-24). NY: Longmans.

THORNE, B. & YALOM, M. (eds.). (1982). *Rethinking the Family: Some Feminist Questions.* NY: Longmans.

TIEJEN, A. (1980). Integrating formal and informal support systems: the Swedish experience. In J. Garbarino, S. H. Stocking, & Associates (eds.), *Protecting Children From Abuse and Neglect.* San Francisco: Jossey-Bass.

TOBIN, S.S. (1972). The earliest memory as data for research in aging. In R. Kastenbaum & S. Sherwood (eds.), *Research, Planning and Action for the Elderly: Power and Potential of Social Sciences.* NY: Behavioral Publications.

TOBIN, S. (1980). Institutionalization of the aged. In N. Dalton & N. Lohman (eds.), *Transitions of Aging.* NY: Academic Press.

TOBIN, S. S. (in press). Psychodynamic treatment of the family and the institutionalized individual. In N. Miller & G. Cohen (eds.), *Psychodynamic*

*Research Perspective on Development, Psychopathy, and Treatment in Later Life.* NY: International Universities Press.

TOBIN, S. S. & ETIGSON, E. C. (1968). Effects of stress on earliest memory. *Archives of General Psychiatry,* 19, 435-444.

TOBIN, S. S. & KULYS, R. (1980). Family and services. In C. Eisdorfer (ed.), *Annual Review of Gerontology and Geriatrics* (vol. 1). NY: Springer.

TOBIN, S. S. & KULYS, R. (1981). The family in the institutionalization of the elderly. *Journal of Gerontological Social Work,* 3, 3-16.

TOBIN, S. S. & LIEBERMAN, M. A. (1976). *A Last Home for the Aged: Critical Implications of Institutionalization.* San Francisco: Jossey-Bass.

TOBIN, S. S. & TOSELAND, R. (1985). Models of services for the elderly. In A. Monk (ed.), *Handbook of Gerontological Services.* NY: Van Nostrand Reinhold.

TOWNSEND, A. L. & POULSHOCK, S. W. (1986). Intergenerational perspectives on impaired elders' support networks. *Journal of Gerontology,* 41, 101-109.

TOWNSEND, P. (1965). The effects of family structure on the likelihood of admission to an institution in old age. In E. Shanas & G. F. Streib (eds.), *Social Structure and Family: Generational Relations.* Englewood Cliffs, NJ: Prentice-Hall.

TRAGER, B. (1980a). *Home Health Care and National Policy.* NY: Haworth.

TRAGER, B. (1980b). *Adult day health care—a conference report.* Hearing before the subcommittee on health and long-term care. Washington, DC: Government Printing Office.

TREAS, J. (1977). Family support systems for the aged: Some social and demographic considerations. *The Gerontologist,* 17, 486-491.

UNGER, D. G. & POWELL, D. R. (1980). Supporting families under stress: The role of social networks. *Family Relations,* 29, 566-574.

U.S. BUREAU OF THE CENSUS (1980). Census of population supplementary reports: Washington, D.C.: U.S. Government Printing Office.

U.S. BUREAU OF THE CENSUS (1982). General population characteristics. Virginia. *1980 Census of Population* (PC80-1-B48). Washington, DC: U.S. Government Printing Office.

U.S. BUREAU OF THE CENSUS (1983a). Detailed population characterstics, Virginia. *1980 Census of Population* (PC80-1-D45). Washington, DC: U.S. Government Printing Office.

U.S. BUREAU OF THE CENSUS (1983b). *Statistical Abstracts of the United States: 1984* (104th ed.). Washington, DC.

U.S. BUREAU OF THE CENSUS (1985). *Current Population Reports,* Series P-25, No. 978.

U.S. CONGRESSIONAL BUDGET OFFICE (1977). Long-Term Care for the Elderly and Disabled. Washington, DC: Government Printing Office.

VAN ECK, L. A. (1972). Transference to the hospital. *Psychotherapy and Psychosomatics,* 20, 135-138.

VINCENTE, L., WILEY, J. A., & CARRINGTON, R. A. (1979). The risk of institutionalization before death. *The Gerontologist,* 19, 361-367.

WEEKS, J. R. & CUELLAR, J. B. (1981). The role of family members in the helpline networks of older people. *The Gerontologist,* 21, 388-394.

WEIHL, H. (1977). The household, intergenerational relations and social policy. In E. Shanas & M. B. Sussman (eds.), *Family, Bureaucracy and the Elderly* (117-131). Durham, NC: Duke University Press.

WEINER, M. B., BROK, A. J., & SNADOWSKY, A. M. (1978). *Working with the Aged: Practical Approaches in the Institution and Community.* Englewood Cliffs, NJ: Prentice-Hall.

WEISSERT, W. G. (1976). Two models of geriatric day care: Findings from a comparative study. *The Gerontologist, 5,* 420-427.

WENTZEL, M. (1979). *The Emotional Effects of Institutionalization upon the Family.* Denton: North Texas State University, Center for Studies in Aging.

WIDMER, G., BRILL, R., & SCHLOSSER, A. (1978). Home health care: Services and cost. *Nursing Outlook, 35,* 488-493.

WILMER, H. A. (1962). Transference to the medical center. *California Medicine, 96,* 173-180.

WOOD, V., WYLIE, M., & SHEAFOR, B. (1969). Analysis of a short self-report measure of life satisfaction. *Journal of Gerontology, 24,* 465-469.

WRIGHT, K. & DYCK, S. (1983). *Family needs of hospitalized adult cancer patients.* (Available from Stella Dyck, College of Nursing, University of Saskatchewan, Saskatoon, Saskatchewan.)

WRIGHT, K. & DYCK, S. (1984). Expressed concerns of adult cancer patients' family members. *Cancer Nursing, 7*(5), 371-374.

WRIGHT, S. (1986). *The relationship of personal and social resources on coping and well-being in caregivers to dementia patients.* Doctoral Dissertation, Oregon State University, Department of Human Development of Family Studies.

YORDI, C. L. & WALDMAN, J. (1985). A consolidated model of long-term care: Service utilization and cost impacts. *The Gerontologist, 25,* 389-397.

YORK, J. & CALSYN, R. (1977). Family involvement in nursing homes. *The Gerontologist, 17*(5), 500-505.

ZARETSKY, E. (1976). *Capitalism, the Family and Personal Life.* NY: Harper & Row.

ZARIT, J. M., GATZ, M., & ZARIT, S. H. (1981). *Family relationships and burden in long-term care.* Paper presented at the meetings of the Gerontological Society, Toronto, Ontario.

ZARIT, S. H., REEVER, K. E., & BACH-PETERSON, J. (1980). Relatives of the impaired elderly: Correlates of feelings of burden. *The Gerontologist, 20*(6), 649-655.

ZARIT, S. H. & ZARIT, J. M. (1982). Families under stress: Interventions for caregivers of senile dementia patients. *Psychotherapy: Theory, Research, and Practice, 19,* 461-471.

ZAWADSKI, R. T. & ANSAK, M. L. (1983). Consolidating community-based long-term care: Early returns from the On Lok Demonstration. *The Gerontologist, 23,* 364-369.

ZIMMERMAN, S. (1976). The family and its relevance for social policy. *Social Casework, 57,* 547-553.

ZIMMERMAN, S. (1985). *Families of elderly disabled persons: The role of adult day care.* Paper presented at the National Association of Social Workers.

ZUNG, W. W. K. (1965). A self-rating depression scale. *Archives of General Psychiatry, 12,* 63.

ZUSMAN, J. (1967). Some explanations of the changing appearance of psychiatric patients. *International Journal of Psychiatry, 3*(4), 216-237.

# About The Authors

**Rosemary Blieszner** is Assistant Professor of Family and Child Development at Virginia Polytechnic Institute and State University, and Associate Director for Research of its Center for Gerontology. Her research interests include developmental processes of adult social relationships, the connection between social relationships and life satisfaction, and the impact on social relationships of family stressors such as long-term care and Alzheimer's disease.

**Edgar F. Borgatta** is Director of the Institute on Aging, University of Washington, and is currently working on studies of the relationship of life expectancy and population change, and the relationship of these to periods of dependency in the population.

**Ellie Brubaker** is an Assistant Professor in the Department of Sociology and Anthropology at Miami University, Oxford, Ohio. Her research has been published in the *Journal of Gerontological Social Work, American Behavioral Scientist,* and *Gerontology and Geriatrics Education.* Also, she has authored or coauthored chapters in several books related to gerontology. Her research interests are concentrated on practice and policy issues related to service delivery to older persons and their families.

**Timothy H. Brubaker** is a Professor in the Department of Home Economics and Consumer Sciences and is affiliated with the Family and Child Studies Center at Miami University, Oxford, Ohio. His books include *Family Relationships in Later Life* (edited, 1983), *Family Caregivers and Dependent Elderly* (coauthored, 1984), and *Later Life Families* (1985). His research has been published in a number of scholarly journals and he has contributed chapters to many books. Currently, he is the editor of *Family Relations,* published by the National Council on Family Relations.

**Kathleen Coen Buckwalter** is an Associate Professor at the University of Iowa College of Nursing. Her clinical and research interests focus on geriatric mental health.

**Peggye Dilworth-Anderson** is currently Associate Professor of Psychology and Coordinator of the Adulthood and Aging Studies Program at Northeastern Illinois University. Her professional and research interests are in the areas of intergenerational relations in the family, support systems in families, and the impact of chronic illness on family relations. Some of her previous publications have focused on family support systems and aged blacks, adult day care for the elderly, older minority women, and intergenerational relations in the black family. She is currently Chair of the Ethnic-Minority Section of the National Council on Family Relations and a former fellow in applied gerontology for the Gerontological Society of America.

**Jaber F. Gubrium** is Professor of Sociology at the University of Florida and is the founding editor of a new interdisciplinary quarterly, the *Journal of Aging Studies*. Formerly he was a Professor of Sociology at Marquette University. Gubrium continues to develop a long-term research project on the social organization of care in human service institutions, which resulted in a number of publications, among them: *Living and Dying at Murray Manor; Caretakers; Describing Care: Image and Practice in Rehabilitation.* Current research concerns the descriptive organization of senility, reported in part in the forthcoming book, *Oldtimers and Alzheimer's.*

**Geri Richards Hall** is a gerontological Clinical Specialist II at the University of Iowa Hospitals and Clinics. She maintains an independent practice, consulting to hospital corporations and long-term care agencies on the development of gerontological programs. She is also a graduate student at the University of Iowa.

**Jan Hare** is a doctoral candidate in Family Studies in the Department of Human Development and Family Studies, Oregon State University. Her research interests include adaptation to chronic and terminal illnesses throughout the life span and the impact of such illnesses upon patients, families, and professional caregivers. In addition to her academic work she is actively involved in community education and support programs for families facing terminal illness and bereavement.

**Laurie Russell Hatch** is Assistant Professor of Sociology at the University of Kentucky. Her research interests focus on relationships between individuals and the social structure. Her most recent work examines the effects of occupational structures and family roles and men's and women's retirement outcomes.

**Mary Anne Hilker** is Assistant Director of the Center for Governmental Responsibility, College of Law, University of Florida, Gainesville. She earned her Ph.D. in sociology from the University of Florida in 1983. She is coauthor of *Old Homes, New Families: Shared Living for the Elderly* (with G. Streib and W. E. Folts). Her research interests are in living arrangements for older people, long-term care, and legal rights of the elderly.

**Jane Marie Kirschling** is an Assistant Professor in the Department of Family Nursing at the Oregon Health Sciences University in Portland. She received her doctorate in psychiatric/community mental health nursing from Indiana University in 1984. Her clinical and research activities are focused on families receiving hospice care prior to and after death of the terminally ill family member.

**Jay A. Mancini** is Associate Professor of Family and Child Development at Virginia Polytechnic Institute and State University, and also an Associate Director of its Center for Gerontology. He received the M.S. at Kansas State University and the Ph.D. at the University of North Carolina at Greensboro, both in family and child development. He is the author of *Aged Parents: Perspectives on Close Relationships with Adult Children* (in press). Since 1979 he has been an associate editor of the *Journal of Marriage and the Family*.

**William J. McAuley** is Director of the Center for Gerontology at Virginia Polytechnic Institute and State University, and Associate Professor of Family and Child Development. He has published his research on demography, long-term care, and aging policy issues in journals such as *The Gerontologist, Journal of Marriage and the Family,* and *Journal of Health and Social Behavior.*

**Rhonda J.V. Montgomery** is Director of the Institute of Gerontology at Wayne State University, Detroit, Michigan. Until recently, she was the Deputy Director of the Institute on Aging at the University of Washington. Her recent work has focused on factors associated with caregiving and the causes and consequences of caregiver burden. She is also interested in health service utilization among the elderly and social policy for the elderly.

**Janette K. Newhouse** is Assistant Professor of Family and Child Development at Virginia Polytechnic Institute and State University. She serves as Extension Specialist in Adult Development and Aging for the Virginia Cooperative Extension Service. Her research interests focus on service utilization patterns among rural elders and the caregiving network of older people.

**Linda S. Noelker** is Acting Associate Director for Research at the Margaret Blenkner Research Center of the Benjamin Rose Institute. She received her M.A. and Ph.D. in sociology from Case Western Reserve University. She has published articles on institutional, community, and family care of the aged. Her current research interests are the quality of intergenerational relations and the relationship of the informal and formal support systems.

**Clara Pratt** is Associate Professor of Human Development and Family Studies, and Director of the Program on Gerontology at Oregon State University. Her research interests include the psychosocial aspects of chronic disease and the family, and professional caregivers to the chronically ill elderly. She is an active member of several community boards and organizations concerned with community long-term care services for the elderly and their families.

**Jill Quadagno** is Professor of Sociology at the University of Kansas. She is the author of *Aging in Early Industrial Society: Work, Family and Social Policy in Nineteenth Century England* (Academic Press, 1982) and coeditor with Warren Peterson of *Social Bonds in Later Life: Aging and Interdependence* (Sage, 1985). She is currently writing a historical monograph on the origins and development of social security in the United States.

**Vicki Schmall** is Associate Professor of Human Development and Family Studies and Gerontology Specialist for the Extension Service at Oregon State University. Her research interests include family caregiving and family education. Nationally recognized as an outstanding educator, she has developed gerontology education programs and resources for lay and professional audiences throughout the country.

**Cebra Sims** is a graduate student in the Department of Psychology at the University of Kansas. She is writing her dissertation on stress among family caregivers.

**D. Ann Squier** is a graduate student in the Department of Sociology at the University of Kansas. Her master's thesis examined the effects of decentralization on in-home, long-term care services. A paper from that project won the Graduate Student Award from the Social Research, Planning and Practice Section of the Gerontological Society in 1985.

**Donald E. Stull** is a research analyst at the Institute on Aging, University of Washington. His research interests include family relationships in later life and the impact of demographic factors on long-term care. He is currently working on a longitudinal study of married couples in retirement.

**Sheldon S. Tobin** is Director of the Ringel Institute of Gerontology and Professor in the School of Social Welfare, the State University of New York at Albany. After receiving his doctorate in 1963 from the Committee on Human Development of the University of Chicago, he remained at the University as a faculty member until coming to SUNY at Albany in 1982. In 1985 he was appointed Editor-in-Chief of *The Gerontologist*. Among his major publications are 5 books and over 75 chapters and scholarly papers that have focused primarily on psychosocial aspects of aging and on services for the elderly.

**Aloen L. Townsend** is a Senior Research Assistant at the Margaret Blenkner Research Center of the Benjamin Rose Institute, Cleveland, Ohio. She received her Ph.D. in social psychology from the University of Michigan, Ann Arbor. Her research interests include family and adult development, social support, and social psychological well-being.

**Georgia Walker** is a graduate student in the Department of Sociology at the University of Kansas. In her dissertation she is analyzing the impact of policy changes on hospitals under the Medicare system. In 1984 she was awarded first place in the Caroline Rose Graduate Paper Competition by the Midwest Sociological Society.

**Scott Wright** is Assistant Professor of Family and Consumer Studies at the University of Utah. Working in collaboration with researchers at the university's Rocky Mountain Gerontology Center and Oregon State University, he is currently involved in research focusing on the psychological coping strategies utilized by family caregivers to dementia patients.